BERSERK!

Throughout the cafeteria, screaming terrified customers found what cover they could under scattered chairs. Then they held their breath, afraid that the slightest movement might attract the gunman's attention. No one on the glass-littered, blood-splashed floor knew who would be the next victim of the killer with the "cold, blank look, like the evil robot in *The Terminator*."

Dear Reader:

The book you are about to read is the latest bestseller from St. Martin's True Crime Library, the imprint *The New York Times* calls "the leader in true crime!" Each month, we offer you a fascinating account of the latest, most sensational crime that has captured the national attention. *The Milwaukee Murders* delves into the twisted world of Jeffrey Dahmer, one of the most savage serial killers of our time; *Lethal Lolita* gives you the *real* scoop on the deadly love affair between Amy Fisher and Joey Buttafuoco; *Whoever Fights Monsters* takes you inside the special FBI team that tracks serial killers; *Garden of Graves* reveals how police uncovered the bloody human harvest of mass murderer Joel Rifkin; *Unanswered Cries* is the story of a detective who tracked a killer for a year, only to discover it was someone he knew and trusted; *Bad Blood* is the story of the notorious Menendez brothers and their sensational trials; *Fallen Hero* details the riveting tragedy of O.J. Simpson and the case that stunned a nation.

St. Martin's True Crime Library gives you the stories *behind* the headlines. Our authors take you right to the scene of the crime and into the minds of the most notorious murderers to show you what really makes them tick. St. Martin's True Crime Library paperbacks are better than the most terrifying thriller, because it's all true! The next time you want a crackling good read, make sure it's got the St. Martin's True Crime Library logo on the spine—you'll be up all night!

Charles E. Spicer, Jr.
Senior Editor, St. Martin's True Crime Library

BERSERK!

Motiveless Random Massacres

GRAHAM CHESTER

ST. MARTIN'S PAPERBACKS

First published in Great Britain in 1993;
Michael O'Mara Books edition 1993.

Published by arrangement with Michael O'Mara Books

BERSERK!

ISBN: 0-312-95442-5

Printed in the United States of America

St. Martin's Paperbacks edition/January 1995

10 9 8 7 6 5 4 3 2 1

For Mary and Pearl

Acknowledgments

I am grateful to the many people who were generous enough to offer me their assistance, insights and encouragement during the preparation and writing of this book.

I owe a special debt to my research assistant, Mary Costello; also to Dr. Brigid Greenup, for her help on medical matters, and to my parents, Ray and Julie Chester, for their unwavering faith and support.

My sincere thanks to David Roberts at Michael O'Mara Books, and to my editor, Yvonne Holland, and my agent, Ann Reynolds.

CONTENTS

INTRODUCTION

"Time to pay."

That was the announcement made by George Hennard, on Wednesday 16 October 1991, moments before he opened fire in a Texas restaurant, cold-bloodedly shooting dead twenty-two people. Lunchtime patrons were packed into Luby's Cafeteria in Killeen, Bell County, a town lying in the sizeable shadow of the Fort Hood army base, sixty miles north of the Texas capital, Austin.

At 12:40 P.M. Hennard crashed his pick-up truck through Luby's front window. He climbed out, produced two 9-mm Glock-17 semiautomatic pistols, for which he had a total of eight magazines, and started shooting. As horrified customers cowered in terror, he roamed the 296-seat cafeteria, calmly picking off his victims one by one. He appeared to kill without rhyme or reason, on one hand sparing a young mother and her daughter, on the other pitilessly blowing away a man on his knees. He reloaded his weapons several times during the slaughter. It only ended when, low on ammunition and wounded by police bullets, he shot himself dead.

Eddie Sanchez witnessed the start of the carnage. He had just dropped off his girlfriend, Angela Wilson, a Luby's employee, when he noticed a blue pick-up approaching, make a sudden left turn, jump the kerb and smash straight through the window into the restaurant. Angela had already entered the building. She would later tell reporters, "As soon as the truck stopped, people started getting up to help people pinned under the truck or under tables sent flying. People were even heading for the cab of the truck— to make sure the driver was all right!" They watched in disbelief as he jumped out of the truck and said, "This is what Bell County has done to me!" Then he started shooting. A man who was stuck under the pick-up tried to wriggle free. Hennard turned and blasted him in the head, killing him instantly. He then strode towards the long line of customers queuing at the service counter. He went along the line, systematically aiming and firing, asking his victims, "Was it all worth it?"

Throughout the cafeteria, screaming terrified customers found what cover they could under the scattered chairs and tables. Then, they held their breath, afraid that the slightest sound might attract the gunman's attention. No one on the glass-littered, blood-splashed floor knew who would be the next victim of the killer with the "cold, blank look, like the evil robot in *Terminator*." One employee shut herself in the freezer to escape him. She would be there for two hours and would need hospital treatment for hypothermia. Another employee would be found an incredible nineteen hours after the massacre, hiding in the industrial dishwasher, afraid to come out.

Anica McNeil and her 4-year-old daughter, Lakeshia, survived not because of the ingenuity of their hiding place but because of one inexplicable moment of mercy on the part of the gunman. Hennard took aim at Anica, her mother, Olga Taylor, and little Lakeshia as they huddled together under a table—but did not fire. He told Anica, "You! Get the baby and get out and tell everybody Bell County was bad today." Anica grabbed her daughter and raced out through the shattered window to the safety of the car park—

while Hennard mercilessly gunned down her mother. Olga Taylor had joined the ever-growing list of innocent people who were paying with their lives for some unspecified crime of which George Hennard had found them guilty.

He moved deeper into the restaurant, killing as he went. Under a table towards the rear, Tommy Vaughn, a motor mechanic, decided somebody had to do something. Choosing his moment, he leapt to his feet and hurled his 330-pound body through one of the plate-glass windows. His charitable act allowed many people at the back of the restaurant to escape to safety. Many more, though, remained trapped and at the mercy of the cold-blooded gunman. The bodies of the dead and dying littered the floor.

Aden McElveen, who had taken cover beneath Hennard's truck, heard the wail of police sirens: "I picked my head up to see where the killer was and he began walking toward me. I kept asking myself, 'Am I going to be next?' But out of nowhere the police barged in. I heard one of the officers shout: 'Drop your gun!'" The gunman screamed back an obscenity and suddenly there were bullets flying everywhere.

Hennard was hit twice. He crawled towards the cloakrooms at the rear of the cafeteria and, lying on his back, fired a single shot through his right temple. At 12:51 P.M., police officer Charles Longwell radioed to his colleagues outside: "The suspect is down. Send in the ambulances—as many as you've got!"

Twenty-three people lay dead. Another twenty-five were wounded, two in a critical condition. Coroner Robert Stubblefield would declare, "I haven't seen anything like this—not since Korea."

The autopsy found Hennard had no drugs or alcohol in his blood. A note at his house gave no clues to his motive. Police Chief Francis Giacomozzi concluded, "The whos, whats, whens and whys, we may never be able to figure them out."

• • •

The Luby's Cafeteria massacre is a typical example of a form of murder that has become all too familiar in recent years.

The violence erupts suddenly, without warning. For no readily discernible reason, a man will arm himself with a gun, or guns, and take himself to some public place. He will begin shooting people, picking off his victims apparently at random. He will display little, if any, sign of emotion. In a brief but devastating assault his bullets will scar and shatter the lives of individuals, families and whole communities, and the seemingly meaningless slaughter will frequently end with a bullet in his own brain—from either his gun or that of a police marksman. In the terrible silence that follows, there is often little to be done but help the wounded—and count the dead.

While more and more men are going publicly berserk with guns, and while the growing death roll of victims stretches from North America to Europe to Australasia, the motives of these most antisocial and apparently indiscriminate killers remain elusive. The fundamental questions remain unanswered. Why did George Hennard run amok in that Texas restaurant in 1991? And why did Marc Lépine walk into the Université de Montréal in 1989 and massacre fourteen? Why did Michael Ryan rampage through Hungerford, slaughtering sixteen in 1987? Why did Julian Knight shoot dead seven in a suburb of Melbourne, earlier the same year?

Although mass murderers claim far fewer lives than do road accidents, for example, or war, or industrial malpractice, they make a disproportionately large contribution to a prevailing climate of fear of violence—and to the mistrust and suspicion it engenders. As criminologists Jack Levin and James Alan Fox have noted in their study, *Mass Murder: America's Growing Menace*, "The logic seems to be: 'If it can happen here, it can happen anywhere, at any time, to anyone . . . even me.'" For this reason, if for no other, the study of these killers is important.

This book examines many of the major cases from around the world, explores what Police Chief Giacomozzi called "the whos, whats, whens and whys," and attempts to discover whether there is any pattern to the killings or whether they are truly meaningless, motiveless and random.

1

Deeds to Astound the World

The man known as Wagner von Degerloch was born in Eglosheim, near Ludwigsburg, in southwest Germany in 1874, to a big-drinking, big-talking peasant father and an allegedly promiscuous mother. The father died when Wagner was two years old. The mother remarried, but her second marriage ended in divorce when Wagner was seven. At school, it was recognized that he was unusually intelligent. He applied himself well and on leaving school received a public stipend to study to become a teacher. Literature was his great passion and in his spare time he wrote poetry.

By 1902, he was living and working in a village called Muehlhausen. He began an affair with the innkeeper's daughter, but it became publicly known and as a result he was transferred to a poor, isolated community, Radelstetten, nearby. The innkeeper's daughter gave birth to a girl in the summer of 1903 and Wagner married her in December. Four more children followed, although the last died in infancy.

The family lived in Radelstetten for ten years. Wagner was considered by his neighbours to be "an admirable citizen, dignified, somewhat quiet," and the best teacher the village had ever had. During this period he began penning dramas with grand biblical and historical themes. He never succeeded in finding a producer or publisher for his plays but had some of them printed at his own expense.

In 1912, he was transferred to Degerloch, a suburb of Stuttgart. He maintained his excellent record as a schoolteacher and apparently enjoyed the stimulation and culture of the large city. According to friends and colleagues, his only failing was a tendency towards grandiosity and loquaciousness when under the influence of alcohol. After three or four glasses of beer he was given to boasting about his literary talent. "He compared himself to Shakespeare, Schiller and Goethe. Occasionally he would comment that one day he would become a famous man and do deeds that would astound the world. Nothing was made of this bragging, since the next day he would perform his work in the accustomed quiet and conscientious way." All who knew him considered him to be a well-balanced and intelligent individual, leading an exemplary middle-class life.

The Muehlhausen Massacre and Wagner's Secrets

Dr. Hilde Bruch gives a full account of Wagner's crime.

During the night of September 4, 1913, the citizens of Muehlhausen ... were awakened by several large fires. As they ran into the street, they were met by a man, his face covered by a black veil, who was armed with two pistols. He shot with great accuracy and killed eight men and one girl immediately; twelve more were severely injured. Then his two pistols ran out of ammunition, and he was overpowered and beaten down with such violence that he was left for dead; however, he was only unconscious. He had 198 more bullets in his possession. The innkeeper identified the murderer as his 39-year-old brother-in-law, who had been a schoolteacher in this village more than ten years earlier.

Wagner confessed that during the preceding night he had quietly killed his wife and four children . . . He also confessed that he had come to Muehlhausen to take revenge on the male inhabitants for their scorn and disdain for him. However, even while lying severely wounded and exposed to the hatred of the attacked people, he noticed that no one employed the term of abuse that would refer to his sexual sins, which he felt had been the cause of all the persecution, ridicule, and condemnation.

There was a general outcry of horror about his deed, and public opinion demanded his execution. A violent newspaper debate raged because Wagner's life was spared when it was recognized, during the pretrial examination, that he was mentally ill. He was committed to an insane asylum, where he spent the rest of his life, twenty-five years.

[The] fateful chain of events had its beginning, according to his self-accusation, with one or more sodomistic acts in the late summer of 1901 [in Muehlhausen], when he was 27 years old . . . Before this he had felt persistently and excessively guilty about masturbation, in which he had indulged since the age of 18 . . . Of decisive importance was the fact that his sexual urges and acts stood in irreconcilable contrast to his high moral standards and ethical concepts. His deep sense of guilt never diminished . . . he soon began to make certain "observations" and to "hear" certain slanderous remarks, which led to the unshakeable conviction that his crime was known. He felt himself continuously observed, mocked, and ridiculed, and lived in constant dread of arrest. He was determined not to suffer this public shame and humiliation, and therefore he always carried a loaded pistol.

Possibly to defend himself against further sexual deviations, he began an affair with the innkeeper's

daughter . . . he married her (with many inner mis-
givings) . . . He felt that he no longer loved her and
that she was intellectually not his equal; he considered
her more a servant than a wife.

The first years in his new position [in Radelstetten]
were relatively free of tension as long as he did not
believe that they "knew" about his sexual crime. But he
never forgot what he had done. His pessimistic mood
led to a recurrence of hypochondriacal complaints. In
1904 his whole existence became so intolerable that he
decided . . . to end his own life. He wanted to drown
himself in a lake . . . [but] he was too cowardly . . .
Then he planned to throw himself before an oncoming
train; here, too, his courage failed him . . . Gradually
he began also to make "observations" in Radelstetten
and felt convinced that the people of Muehlhausen had
communicated their "knowledge" to the people at his
new location. He could notice it because of certain
insinuations and the occasional arrogance which some
allegedly showed against him. He felt caught in the old
dilemma: there was never a direct statement, but he
"heard" pointed remarks containing hints. He knew if
he reacted he would be publicly humiliated.

Gradually the conviction ripened that there was only
one way out. He must kill himself and his children, *out
of pity* to save them from a future of being the target of
contempt and evil slander and *to take revenge* on the
people of Muehlhausen who had forced him to this
horrible deed . . . Since the men of Muehlhausen had
started and spread the slander, they had to die. In a
life that as a whole had been a series of depressing
and frustrating disappointments, he was grateful that
it had been given to him to avenge his terrible torture
and suffering.

Beginning in 1906 or at the latest in 1907, he
developed a plan for destruction and murder . . . He
collected and carefully hid weapons and all other

objects needed for his plan, practised sharpshooting in remote parts of the woods, and worked out his strategy, much like a commander planning a military action. He kept detailed diaries on all his plans. But over and over again he shrank away from their execution . . . he felt that he was "too weak." So he tried to retrain himself and wrote homicidal dramas . . . to a large extent with the intent of putting himself in the role of murderer and arsonist . . . Finally he had indoctrinated himself to such an extent that the execution [of the murders] went "like clockwork, quite mechanically." He acted as though under a compulsion, like "having been pushed into it," and described his mental state as "apathetic and excited at the same time."

Wagner died an embittered man, not because he had committed mass murder and had been declared insane but because he had failed to find acclaim as a literary figure . . . At autopsy his brain showed no gross pathology; it was sent for microscopic study . . . and no abnormal findings were reported . . . Professor Gaupp, who spent a lifetime trying to understand the psychological forces of this man's background, character, and experiences, concluded his series of papers with the statement that in spite of all the efforts to follow his mental processes, there remains a part that is beyond human comprehension.

Professor Gaupp meticulously recorded his study of Wagner, and Dr. Hilde Bruch's succinct condensation of Gaupp's work is quoted here at some length in order to give a glimpse of the contemporary response to what was, in 1913, a new kind of murder. With a modern perspective, however, and with Gaupp's comprehensive documentation, a reassessment of the Wagner case is possible.

Wagner with Hindsight

Wagner turned to mass murder after failing to realize his career ambitions and after failing to achieve the level of social status he believed he deserved. It is a theme this book encounters time and again as the twentieth century unfolds, but it has its roots in the industrial revolution, when old community allegiances and bonds were broken, and the traditional social matrix was shattered. If kin and neighbours became competitors and rivals, they did so in the scramble to realize the hitherto undreamt of freedom of upward social mobility promised by the new economic order. The new system fostered this yearning by penalizing those who could not or would not participate (the unemployed, the unemployable and the under-achievers), as much as it rewarded those who could and did.

In the twentieth century this ideology has been beautifully refined and polished. The introduction of universal education, and a vast range of agencies and institutions, policies and programmes, with the aim of helping people better themselves, have made striving for social advancement the duty of all. The idea that making it to the top is both possible for anyone and enormously rewarding, has been propagated by Hollywood rags-to-riches stories and by the creation of vast galaxies of "stars" (actors, astronauts, fashion models, pop musicians, sports players and those who are famous for nothing other than being famous), which serve as guiding lights, and ever-present reminders that being a "somebody" in our societies constitutes the pinnacle of human achievement.

If the myths of the industrial and post-industrial nations have succeeded in mobilizing the required amount of enterprise, effort and wealth-creation for the system to be self-perpetuating, then they have also created a subtle dissatisfaction among many people who feel they are not being rewarded quite as handsomely as their endeavours deserve. Mass killers are just such people, except their dissatisfaction is particularly profound, for they are both the greatest believers in the ideology and the least well equipped to cope with the stresses and demands imposed by the reality. Wagner von Degerloch is an excellent example.

He was shaped to a large extent, as all of us are, by the nature of his family. The son of a braggart father and an apparently promiscuous mother, he doubtless suffered taunts and insults from his more fortunate fellows. Bruch records: "He was known in the village as the 'widow's boy' and suffered from depressions, suicidal thoughts and nightmares." Whatever the precise nature of his family, then, he was mocked and derided because of it, and it fostered in him an acute degree of morbid sensitivity.

In contrast, the other important institution responsible for a child's development, the school, recognized that he was unusually intelligent, encouraged him to hold his intellect in high esteem and rendered him susceptible to overestimating, to a more serious extent than many of his fellows, his importance in the world. If he had been born a century earlier, he would never have found himself in such a position. As it was, he was spawned in a brave new age and, even as a boy, was a devoted disciple of its principal tenets. He had social ambition in abundance, he appreciated that his intellect was a marketable asset and he distrusted and was wary of his fellows. (Not only were they potential rivals, but they had also helped orchestrate, with their taunts and insults, his miserable childhood.)

With his brain and a public stipend, Wagner effected an escape from his humble peasant origins. His flight up the social ladder to the professional classes was not, however, the end of his problems. On the one hand, as Bruch says, "His profession of schoolteacher was not satisfactory to him. He considered himself in all seriousness as one of the greatest dramatists of his time." On the other hand, as a morbidly sensitive individual of peasant stock, he was extremely insecure in the alien world of middle-class manners and etiquette. He did not know quite how to behave or what exactly was expected of him and he adopted the kind of straight-jacketed conservatism common to nervous newcomers from the lower orders. He invariably dressed overformally, some of his associates noticed a certain amount of affectation, and he spoke High German, even at home, rather than the local dialect used by everyone else of whatever background. Later, after being committed to the mental asylum, he embraced the appropriate body for his arch-conservatism, the Nazi Party, and was tremendously proud to have been the first inmate of his hospital to do so.

Often killers' accounts of their lives vary depending on whom they are addressing—detectives, psychiatrists, priests, lawyers—and whether they like or loathe or want to please or antagonize their questioners. As we know from Bruch, "a confidential, even friendly relationship developed between [Wagner] and Professor Gaupp." So it is not surprising that Wagner was inclined to discuss the root causes of his murderous deed with a Freudian overemphasis on sex and guilt that doubtless warmed the heart of his psychiatrist.

His brief, pre-marital, homosexual affair was not, however, at the heart of his murderous rage. That grew from his lack of literary and social success. His act of sodomy was important because it provided him with a mechanism with which to explain this lack of success. If his sexual crime was known and there was a conspiracy to punish him for it, then his failure was accounted for—and, importantly, in a manner that did not call into question the great literary talent he believed he possessed. It was a highly convenient explanation.

Doubtless at this juncture the psychiatrists cried "Eureka!" Here were the first signs of paranoia and persecution mania, of a man losing his grip on reality and sinking into the realm of the insane. Ironically, though, just a few decades later, every right-minded German was thinking like Wagner.

Where the men of Muehlhausen were his scapegoat, Jews were the scapegoat of his compatriots.

Wagner's rationale for murderous revenge was only genuinely viable because he had the complicity of his society. Germany, at the turn of the century, was violently hostile to homosexuality. Dr. Magnus Hirschfeld, author of *Sappho and Socrates*, and other humanitarians of the time were desperately trying to obtain the revocation of the notorious Paragraph 175 of the Criminal Code, but were fighting a losing battle. The reactionary mood of the nation was so strong, in fact, that it would precipitate, after the defeat of German Imperialism in the First World War, the resurrection of the hideous *Fehme* organization, whose agenda was the cleansing and regulation of German social, political and religious life through systematic murder.

Wagner's fear of being unmasked as a sodomist, in a deeply puritanical culture, where the *Fehme* was about to be reborn, is understandable enough. Nevertheless, he was able to keep his fears in check so long as he maintained the belief that he would one day be recognized as a literary genius. As his life progressed, though, the prospect of his realizing these dreams gradually faded.

His affair with the innkeeper's daughter turned into a débâcle when she fell pregnant and it became publicly known. He did the honourable thing and married her. For the slavishly conservative Wagner, deserting the girl, if not actually unthinkable (it does seem to have crossed his mind), was, nevertheless, wholly unacceptable, on account of the social condemnation he would inevitably have suffered. Marrying her was nearly as bad. Almost certainly, he suspected she would be a hindrance to his career and social ambitions. If he did, he was right. Bruch tells us: "She objected to his spending money and time on his literary interests." She bore more children and "he was unhappy about the birth of each child and felt confined by the financial hardship of a large family subsisting on the meagre income of a village schoolteacher." His poems and dramas had generated no commercial interest and he was footing the cost of publishing them himself.

By 1906 or 1907, a turning point had been reached where reality stood in incontrovertible opposition to his dreams, and he finally embraced the tempting explanation for his failure that had been threatening to seduce him for the past five years. The dedication and energy with which he had previously, and so fruitlessly, pursued literary success was transferred to realizing a new goal; revenge.

The great appeal of a mass murderous odyssey, for a man like Wagner, is that, in so many ways, the journey resembles the one he has already undertaken as a regular citizen. Both expeditions begin with grand ambitions: to be a great writer, to kill a great number of people. In both cases, the goal is the same: to become—either through fame or infamy—a somebody. Both courses demand a high level of commitment, single-minded determination, the ability to exploit one's fellows for the benefit of oneself, planning, training and long hours of hard work. But fame is difficult to achieve and depends very much on factors beyond the seeker's control. Infamy, though, is far easier, and is almost entirely within his own hands. Moreover, the pay-off for the mass murderer is a profoundly satisfying triptychal reward (his satisfaction is often so complete that he terminates his life there and then): first, he gains revenge on those he holds responsible for his failure to realize his original ambitions; second, he thumbs his nose at the whole social system that had promised him so much but delivered so little; and third, in spite of everything, he becomes a somebody. Wagner was, without doubt, seeking the joys of this unholy trinity.

His first victims were his wife and children. Bruch noted that "In his biography he spoke of himself as 'the angel of pity,' " and that he considered the murder of his family an act of mercy. This is possible. Family massacres committed out of love are not unknown. It seems equally possible, though, that Wagner held his family responsible, in part at least, for his failure to realize his literary and social ambitions. If he did, then their deaths were as much a part of his desire for revenge as were the murders in Muehlhausen.

When he was beaten unconscious in Muehlhausen, he was nowhere near the end of his mission. He had 198 more bullets in his possession and had evidently planned to use them. In 1938, when he knew that death from tuberculosis was imminent, he still felt, according to Bruch, "that even if he had killed all of [the citizens of Muehlhausen] it would not have balanced the suffering that had been inflicted on him."

After wiping out the village's populace, Bruch tells us, "Wagner had planned to return to his brother's house the following night with the intent of killing him and his family and of burning down his house as well as the house in which he had been born. As a final step he had planned to proceed to the royal castle in Ludwigsburg, overpower the guards, set fire to the castle, and die in the flames or jump off its walls, thereby terminating his own life." This constitutes the second element of his campaign: a spectacular, incendiary demonstration of his contempt for the whole of society, burning and obliterating all trace of his humble peasant origins and destroying the social order's most potent and visible symbol, the royal castle.

As a final measure, just to be certain that he would secure his place in the Hall of Infamy, he made a public announcement, in the form of a letter, confessing his crimes, intended as an editorial in Stuttgart's main newspaper. He could thus die happy in the knowledge that the success of his mission was guaranteed and that his deeds would astound the world.

The Asylum Years

Wagner pleaded sanity, remarking sarcastically: "If I am insane, then a madman has been teaching all these years."

The diagnosis of the psychiatrists, of course, invalidated his campaign as the mindless convulsions of a lunatic and during the first few years of his confinement, he pleaded for the reopening of his case so that he might be condemned and executed, a sane man. His requests fell on deaf ears. Less than a year after the murders, Germany, as a nation, was pursuing its own grand ambitions to a bloody climax in the First World War and Wagner begged to be allowed to fight at the front and die for his country. This wish was also denied him.

Finally, when he realized that his destiny was to be confined for life, he turned again to his first love, literature. It was a bizarre irony that he was now in the perfect position for devoting himself to writing: his every basic need was taken care of; his place in the institution's social system—the status of patient—was fixed and uncomplicated; there were no wife and children to drain his energies; he had an extensive library at his disposal and the state had given him more time than he knew what to do with. Hardly surprising, then, that, as Bruch relates, there followed "several years in which it seemed that the paranoic affect had diminished."

During this period, he began writing a drama, which he called *Wahn (Delusion)*, based on the life of King Ludwig II of Bavaria. He worked on the project tirelessly. When it was complete, he considered it the best work he had ever done. "He was bitterly disappointed when this drama . . . was not accepted for stage production and he felt deeply hurt that his work aroused only the interest of psychiatrists, as the product of a sick mind, and not that of literary persons," Bruch reports. When a drama by Franz Werfel, with similar themes, was produced in Stuttgart, Wagner was convinced that Werfel had stolen the idea from him. Thereafter, he became increasingly preoccupied with the idea that other successful writers had plagiarized his work. He believed, for example, that the movie *Ben Hur* (1907) had been based on another of his dramas. He suspected a Jewish conspiracy.

Ironically, in the latter years of his life, Wagner, who had joined the Nazi Party in 1929, who wrote long, patriotic documents for the High Command, and who agreed with all the Party's racial excesses, was, in the context of the prevailing culture, as sane a man as many of those who had been involved in the process of declaring him mad. When he died in 1938 at the age of 64, Germany was again on the point of pursuing grand national ambitions to annihilate all its enemies—in the orgy of slaughter that was the Second World War.

2

A Day of Judgment

On the morning of Tuesday 6 September 1949, in a modest, stuccoed house, jammed between a cobbler's shop and a pharmacy in East Camden, New Jersey, 50-year-old Freda Unruh worked her way through a pile of ironing. It was too early yet for there to be any warmth in the sun and Freda, a frail woman, wore a thick jumper over her housecoat to stave off the morning chill. At eight o'clock, she abandoned the ironing to give her son, 28-year-old Howard, the morning call he had asked for in a note he'd left on the kitchen table the night before. She then set about making him breakfast. Howard, meanwhile, washed, shaved and dressed. Today was a big day for him and he chose his best dark suit, a white shirt and bow tie, which gave him an air of sombre formality befitting the gravity of the occasion.

During the next hour, he ate a hearty breakfast, spent some time downstairs in the cellar, and finally returned to the living room where he switched on the radio. At quarter past nine, Freda entered the room. Her boy suddenly wheeled around, a heavy wrench in his raised hand. Freda drew away, pleading, "Howard, you can't do this to me." Then, as he stared at her expressionlessly, she turned and raced to the house of a neighbour, Mrs. Caroline Pinner. A few minutes later, gunshots echoed and re-echoed around the small Delaware River community and Freda cried, "Howard, oh, Howard, they're to blame for this," before fainting in the Pinners' front room.

Accounts differ as to the precise sequence of events during Unruh's thirteen-minute rampage through the neighbourhood, but we know how his victims died—"I shot them in the chest first and then I aimed for the head"—and that a 27-year-old cobbler John Pilarchik was the first. Pilarchik was busy in his shop, at 3206 River Avenue. Shortly before 9:20 A.M. he glanced up as a shadow slid towards him across the shop floor, in advance of the tall, lean figure of his neighbour, Howard Unruh. Pilarchik was a veteran of the Second World War, but had long ago discarded any soldierly vigilance he might once have possessed. He simply stared in dumb bewilderment as Unruh, with the morning sunlight filtering past his silhouetted figure, raised his right arm to a horizontal position. The muzzle flash that preceded the roar of a 9-mm Luger pistol discharging in his face was John Pilarchik's last mortal vision. Unruh about-turned and walked calmly back out into the street.

Other local shopkeepers met the same fate as the cobbler. Clark Hoover's barbershop was two doors away. There was a white-painted carousel horse in the centre of the shop, which Hoover used while cutting children's hair, and a blond boy, 6-year-old Orris Smith, was seated on it, submitting to a shearing, when Unruh entered. "I've got something for you, Clarkie," Unruh said to the barber. Orris Smith's mother watched incredulously as the well-dressed young man coolly shot both Clark Hoover and little "Brux" (her pet name for her son) and then walked out of the shop as nonchalantly as he had entered. Orris toppled slowly from the carousel horse, landing on the floor with a thud. Mrs. Smith, still scarcely able to believe her eyes, rushed to his side, gathered him up in her arms and staggered out into the soft September sun. "My boy is dead. I know he's dead," she cried, staring about her, dazed and confused.

Next, Unruh visited the tailor's shop, at 3214 River Avenue. The tailor, Thomas Zegrino, was out at the time, but his wife of a month, Helga, was working at the back of the shop. "She looked at me and started to say 'Oh no, no' and I shot her more than once," Unruh later recalled.

Three members of the Cohen family were killed in the pharmacy farther down the road. Maurice Cohen was climbing out of an upstairs window when he was shot in the back. He keeled over, bounced off a roof and plummeted headlong into the street. Maurice's wife, Rose, and his elderly mother, Minnie, were also shot. Unruh fired three times into a cupboard where Rose was hiding, then opened the door and shot her in the head. In another room, Minnie was telephoning the police. Unruh walked in, pushed the pistol in her face and pulled the trigger. Then he went back downstairs. Hidden in another closet, 12-year-old Charles Cohen was the only member of the household to survive.

James Hutton, an insurance agent, lived in nearby Westmont, but was a familiar figure in the River Avenue neighbourhood. Like the shopkeepers, he had known Howard for many years; in fact, he was the Unruh family's own agent. Hutton was in the doorway of the pharmacy when the killer sidled up to him. "Excuse me, sir," Unruh said, then shot him dead. He would later tell detectives, "That man didn't act fast enough. He didn't get out of my way."

Unruh also knew, at least by sight, his youngest victim, 2-year-old Thomas Hamilton. Tommy lived at 3208 River Avenue and was peeping out of a window when a bullet hit him between the eyes.

Not all Unruh's victims, though, were known to him. Alvin Day, a visiting TV repairman, had driven into River Avenue unaware that it had become the arena for one man's private war. Like John Pilarchik, Day was a Second World War veteran. One of his favourite remarks was that the Germans had never been able to find a bullet with his name on it. Unfortunately for Day, a fellow American citizen, Howard Unruh, had.

Helen Wilson, her 9-year-old son, John, and her mother, Emma Matlack, were also strangers to Unruh. They were in their car, waiting at traffic lights at the junction of River Avenue and Thirty-second Street, when Unruh spotted them. He walked up to the car and fired through the window. Mrs. Wilson, the driver, and Mrs. Matlack, the front-seat passenger, were killed outright. Little Johnny clung to life for eighteen hours in hospital before succumbing to the bullet lodged at the base of his brain.

The occupants of another vehicle, two women and their daughters, were more fortunate. They heard shooting but thought it was a car backfiring and they continued steadily on their way down the street. For some reason, Unruh completely ignored them. A bakery van driver had a narrow escape, ducking as a bullet whizzed by his ear, and a teenager, who was crossing the road a block away, was hit twice in the leg, but survived.

At some point during the rampage, Unruh himself was wounded. Frank Engel, who ran a tavern across the road from Unruh's house, had bolted his front door at the start of the shooting and ushered his customers to the back of the room. Unruh had shot up Engel's door but had not managed to get in, and had moved on down the street to Dominick Latela's restaurant where he fired more shots, kicked in a glass pane, but also failed to gain entry. Frank Engel, meanwhile, rushed upstairs to his apartment. He opened a window and took aim at Unruh with a .38-calibre pistol. He fired and hit, but Unruh simply walked on without even acknowledging he had been shot. Engel did not fire again. "I wish I had," he would later tell reporters. "I could have killed him then. I could have put a half-dozen shots into him. I don't know why I didn't do it."

After ten minutes of shooting, River Avenue was all but deserted. Shopkeepers—those not already lying dead— had locked and barred their doors; screaming parents had shepherded their children to safety. The emergency services were being flooded with telephone calls from frantic residents.

Unruh tried the door of the American Stores Company, a grocery opposite Cohen's pharmacy, but it was locked. Earl Horner, the clerk, was crouched nervously behind the counter with his customers. Unruh fired several shots into the shop, but failed to hit anyone. He turned away, and headed off down Thirty-second Street where he entered a house that backed onto his mother's. In the kitchen, he found Madeline Harrie and her 16-year-old son, Armand. Unruh fired twice at Mrs. Harrie but missed both times. She began to shout and he fired again, wounding her in the shoulder. Armand tried to shield his mother and got a bullet in each arm for his pains. Unruh then struck him over the head with the butt of the Luger, knocking him to the floor.

Several neighbours saw Unruh leave the Harrie's place and pause to spit on the doorstep. It had just turned half past nine. The sound of police sirens could now be heard and the killer, his gun empty, headed back to his mother's house. He was inside by the time police cars and motorcycles screeched into the neighbourhood. Only thirteen minutes had passed since he fired his first shot: thirteen people now lay dead or dying; three more lay wounded. Young Charlie Cohen had come out onto the pharmacy porch and was screaming hysterically, "He's going to kill me. He's killing everybody."

As police officers surrounded 3202 River Avenue, they were fired upon from an upper-storey window. They returned the fire, pouring round after round into Unruh's room, shattering the windows and riddling the walls. Unruh, by some miracle, was not killed in the dense mesh of lead, and a gun battle raged for some time. Meanwhile, a local newsman, Philip Buxton, of the *Courier-Post*, keen to check out what seemed like wild reports coming into his office, got hold of a telephone number: The phone was finally answered and Buxton spoke with a man.

"Is this Howard?"

"Yes, this is Howard. What's the last name of the party you want?"

"Unruh."

"Who are you and what do you want?"

"I'm a friend and I want to know what they're doing to you."

"Well, they haven't done anything to me yet, but I'm doing plenty to them."

"How many have you killed?"

"I don't know yet—I haven't counted 'em, but it looks like a pretty good score."

"Why are you killing people?"

"I don't know. I can't answer that yet—I'm too busy."[1]

Unruh was indeed busy. Tear gas canisters had just been hurled into his room and he staggered to the window, eyes streaming and gasping for air. "Okay," he choked. "I give up. I'm coming down."

A minute later, with fifty police guns trained on him, he stepped out into the yard with his arms raised. Cops swarmed across the flowerbeds of morning-glory. "What's the matter with you?" one of them demanded. "You a psycho?" Unruh gave the officer a level stare. "I'm no psycho," he said. "I have a good mind."

The Killer's Life

Howard Barton Unruh was born on 21 January 1921, the first son of Samuel Unruh, a dredge boat worker, and his wife, Freda. He was raised in the Delaware River neighbourhood of small businessmen, shopkeepers, traders and their families, which he would later decimate. His early childhood was unremarkable, except he was a little slow in learning to walk and talk. In school, he was considered an average student, polite and reserved, who seemed to prefer reading his Bible to the company of his fellows. He inspired no great emotional response from his peers, one way or the other; in fact, people barely had reason to notice him, far less become a friend or enemy. When his parents separated, in about 1930, he was already rather introverted. He had a lot more affection for his mother than for his father and it was with his mother that he lived, along with his younger brother, James, when his parents went their separate ways.

By early adolescence, Unruh was a somewhat withdrawn and reclusive boy. He favoured hobbies that he could pursue on his own; he started a stamp collection and built elaborate train sets. He never tired of playing with his trains, even as an adult. He was mesmerized by the precision mechanics and engineering, by the critical track intersections and complex loco interaction—ultimately, by the supreme order and efficiency of the systems he constructed. He developed his brain along the same lines. He went to considerable lengths to train his memory, and doctors examining him after the rampage were amazed by his powers of recall and by his obsessive attention to, and retention of, detail. "His mind is more in the nature of a systematized card file than a dynamic force acting on its environment," Dr. Harold Magee wrote in his notes. "Its chief intellectual function is the storage and reproduction of factual material."

The extreme efficiency and orderliness of the rational, logical part of Unruh's brain was in marked contrast to the great turmoil he was experiencing on an emotional level. There, his mind was a short-circuiting confusion of conflicting feelings and urges, involving his social isolation, his emerging sexuality and his faith in God. Later, he was able to talk about some of the emotional conflicts that first began to torment him in his youth: "I get an erotic feeling in my penis that associates with my erotic feeling of having intercourse with my mother . . . I put myself in a fantasy condition; I withdraw and things do not seem as real as they should be. I am constantly tense and anxious, mostly when in population because I feel they are going to harm me or punish me . . . There is a conflict between my desires of having sex with my mother." This conflict (love and attraction versus guilt and resentment) would manifest itself no more clearly than on the morning when he set about, but could not carry through, braining his mother with the wrench.

Unruh's Oedipus complex was not his only adolescent worry. In contrast to his sexual desire for Freda, he suffered, according to one doctor, "vague, half-conscious feelings . . . of fear, anxiety and disgust in his dealings with girls his own age." His brother suspected he was homosexual. He would later tell investigators that Howard once made advances to him while they were sleeping together. As if his anxieties about his sexuality were not torment enough, Unruh, the avid Bible reader, was appalled by what God might think. He can hardly have believed that his sexual desires pleased the Lord.

His thoughts—for all their sparking emotionality in the one hemisphere, and rapidly-expanding store of factual information in the other—were rarely evident to those around him. Like Wagner von Degerloch, Unruh was a master of repression. His neighbours considered him a quiet, unremarkable young man, leading a quiet, unremarkable life. He accompanied his mother to St. Paul's Evangelical Church every Sunday without fail, and attended Monday night Bible classes, where he was known as a keen student of the scriptures who would often mark his favourite passages for further study.

In 1939, he graduated from Woodrow Wilson High School and got a job at the naval base in Philadelphia. He began dating a girl, whom he had met at church, and he treated her with the politeness and respect that folk had come to know him for. His belle, in fact, found him a mite *too* polite for her liking. Even kissing and holding hands were best avoided to Howard's way of thinking. For him, the relationship was a charade. It was just another sacrifice to peer pressure, another component in the protective conformity capsule, which he had built around himself and which he now inhabited as a virtual prisoner. Later, after his rampage through the neighbourhood, he was questioned about his relationship with the girl and spoke of it with complete indifference:

"Did her kisses make you feel passionate?"

"No."

"Did you ever have any sexual desires for this woman?"

"No, but she did for me."

"Have you ever had sexual relations with her?"

"No."

"Have you ever had sexual relations with any woman?"

"No."

Unruh was infinitely more interested in the developing war in Europe. He had always followed world events closely, particularly those involving large-scale destruction, but the Second World War was in a league of its own. He filled a scrapbook with newspaper clippings, which he read and re-read, methodically collating the mass of information before committing it to memory. Military equipment, weapons in particular, held not only a special place in his mind, but a special place in his heart. In 1942, he enlisted in the army.

As a soldier, Unruh discovered that he was quite a talented marksman. He earned the rifleman rating of sharpshooter, a peg below expert. It was a revelation and his interest in weapons grew immeasurably. His colleagues found it impossible to say which was his greatest love—the Bible he read with fervent ardour or the rifle he field-stripped and cleaned with religious devotion. When, after his training, he joined the war in Europe, it was with the Good Book in one hand and his M-1 carbine in the other.

In the midst of war, marksmanship was not an abstract talent but the very real power over life and death. For a young man whose impact on people had never been anything other than negligible, this was a heady power indeed. Unruh embraced it passionately. In his usual methodical way, he began to keep a diary, detailing Germans he shot: times, dates, places, and even how the bodies looked in death. In his three-year service with the 342nd Armored Field Artillery, he revelled in killing. His favourite job, apparently, was the number one cannoneer position on his unit's 105-mm howitzer. He loved setting the sights on the target, which was usually within visual range, but most of all he loved firing the gun. He moved with his unit from Italy, through France and Belgium, and on to the finish in a shattered, post-apocalyptic Germany—experiencing first-hand a scale of destruction that previously he had only read about in his Bible.

When the war in Europe ended, H.B. Unruh, private first class, was honourably discharged from the United States Army and returned home to live with his mother in East Camden. He smuggled back with him the weapons and souvenirs he had collected as a soldier. He followed the final stages of the Second World War—combat in the Far East—at a distance but with great interest.

Meanwhile, he tried to pick up the threads of the life he had left behind in New Jersey in 1942. He was now 24 years old, six-foot tall, lean and fit, but to his mother and others in the neighbourhood, he seemed very much the same mild-mannered, quiet young man who had gone off to war three years earlier. As in the past, he accompanied his mother to church on Sundays and attended Monday night Bible classes. Behind the public persona, though, there was a growing bitterness.

Unruh had always been a nonentity in his home community. What had changed, and the reason he now found his lowly status hard to stomach, was the sense of self-worth he had discovered as a soldier. For the first time in his life, he saw himself as a man to be reckoned with. His neighbours, unfortunately, did not and he fiercely resented them for it. Who were they to treat him, Pfc. Unruh, killer of Germans, as an inconsequential nobody? Had he not earned the right to a little respect, a little status? "Hey, you—can't you be

more quiet with that gate?" the pharmacist's wife, Rose
Cohen, shouted at him. What he resented most, he later
revealed, was the use of the phrase "Hey, you." People
thought so little of him that they did not even have the
common decency to address him by name. It was not fair
and Unruh could not understand it. When he looked at his
neighbour, John Pilarchik, for example, he saw a man the
same age as himself, a man who, again like himself, had
been away to war and returned home to New Jersey when
the war ended. Pilarchik, though, had a place in the community, was well thought of by his fellows and had built up
a successful business—in fact, he possessed all the things
that Unruh felt he himself was entitled to.

Unruh made one known attempt to achieve something
within his home community that his neighbours could
understand and admire. He took some refresher courses at
Brown Preparatory School in Philadelphia, and then, under
the GI Bill of Rights, went on to Philadelphia's Temple
University to study pharmacology—the trade of his highly
respected next-door neighbours the Cohens. Unfortunately,
he was not the least bit interested in the subject, found it
impossible to concentrate, and quit the programme after just
three months.

For sustenance, Unruh drew on his self-respect and his
pride in his marksmanship. He surrounded himself with
reminders of his army days. Apart from his stamp album
and train sets, a book on astronomy and volumes concerned
with what a detective termed "sex hygiene," his bedroom
was a shrine to war and weapons. The walls were decorated
with crossed bayonets and pictures of armoured artillery in
action; he had books on weaponry and military strategy,
clips of 30-30 cartridges for rifle use, a pistol, ash trays
made from German shell casings and a host of other war
souvenirs. In the cellar of the house, he set up a shooting
range and practised regularly.

Meanwhile, his loathing of those around him grew.
Howard and his gun were worth any ten of them and

one day he would prove it. He would have his revenge for the slights and insults that he felt were being aimed at him from all sides—for the great injustices that he felt were being done him by his neighbours. The list of grievances he had against them was long and detailed: "I had trouble with the barber because in building his store next to our place he excavated for the cellar and spread dirt over the vacant lot to the rear which increased the rise of the land and prevented the free drainage of heavy rainfall, and as a result the water was diverted into our cellar, flooding it. Then there was the shoemaker who . . . not only buried considerable trash in the backyard close to our property, but also kept throwing trash over into our yard on many occasions." The manager of the American Stores grocery "had always been nice to me, until a clerk that he hired had difficulty one time with me over some change and since that time forward the manager was never nice." The pharmacist, Maurice Cohen, "shortchanged me five different times," and Cohen's wife, Rose, "was always talking about me and very belligerent towards me and seemed to take pleasure in bawling me out in front of people."

Just as he had during the war, Unruh started to keep a diary—not a death tally of German soldiers this time, but a list of the petty grievances he had against his neighbours. The diary entries were invariably followed by cryptic notes: "Ret. W.T.S."—an abbreviation for "Retaliate when time suitable," and "D.N.D.R."—"Do not delay retaliation." He was obsessed with the idea of retaliation; the word itself appears close to 200 times in the diary.

In the course of the painstaking interrogation of Unruh after the massacre, his reply to one of the least probing questions led to one of the most significant discoveries. He was asked if he had ever been sick or in hospital and answered that he had once been treated for gonorrhoea. Prosecutor Mitchell Cohen (no relation to Unruh's pharmacist neighbour), remembering his earlier assertion that he had never slept with a woman, asked him how he came to contract the disease. Unruh replied that he had been an active homosexual since 1946.

His first homosexual encounter apparently took place in a Philadelphia cinema when a man, whom he had never before met, masturbated him during the film. Thereafter, he became highly promiscuous and, with his customary attention to detail, kept a diary of his sexual encounters, listing names, dates and places. Although he confined his activities to Philadelphia, and even rented a room to ensure maximum discretion, he became convinced—just as Wagner had—that the people of his home community knew his secret. "The tailor . . . circulated the story that he saw me 'go down on somebody in an alley one time,' " Unruh alleged. He also said that he had heard muttered comments from neighbours who passed him in the street: "You can get him to stay all night with you," and other pointed remarks. He began to fear that he would be physically attacked by his neighbours, and took to arming himself against the possibility. He claimed to have heard people plotting against him: "One time they said they were going to gang up on me." Another time, they said, "Let's give him a chance to use his gun."

One of the psychiatrists who later examined him noted: "It must definitely be acknowledged that this patient has a very high index of suspicion, a very marked tendency to refer to himself apparently indifferent acts perpetrated by his neighbours and a general paranoid tendency to resent real acts which a normal person would pass off as harmless pranks or part of the everyday friction inevitable between families who live closely together."

As Unruh plotted his revenge, he endeavoured to maintain his public composure. His brother, James, by this time married and living nearby in Haddon Heights—thought Howard was a little nervous at that time but could not put his finger on exactly what form the nervousness took: "He just seemed changed." Neighbours who had once considered him quiet and polite now saw him more as quiet and *moody*—but that was all. No one was even remotely aware of the true complexion of the world inside his head.

Early in 1947, Unruh added another gun to his collection. It was a German Luger 9-mm pistol, which he purchased in Philadelphia. Later the same year, he bought a mail-order machete from L.L. Bean's, in Maine, after fantasizing about cutting off the Cohens' heads.

By the spring of 1948, he was no longer accompanying his mother to church on Sundays or attending Monday night Bible classes. His years of study and what Dr. Harold Magee described as an "obsessive rumination concerning his relations to the Deity and his responsibility for right and wrong behaviour" had done little but awaken him to grand biblical themes of apocalypse—themes he could readily adapt to legitimize in his own mind his mass-murderous mission.

On Monday 5 September 1949, he went into Philadelphia and spent the evening at the cinema, sitting through several showings of the double bill presentation, *I Cheated the Law* and *The Lady Gambles*. In the early hours of the morning of Tuesday 6 September, he returned home by bus, arriving at around three o'clock. Someone had removed his backyard gate from its hinges. The time for revenge had finally arrived. He resolved there and then, he told the county prosecutor, to shoot the people who had "talked about me," and he figured 9:30 A.M. would be a good time to do it because most of the neighbourhood gossip-shops would be open by that time. Before he went to bed, he left a note on the kitchen table, instructing his mother to wake him at 8:00 A.M. Having made the decision to end his torment once and for all, he apparently enjoyed a good night's sleep.

Life After Death

"For sheer horror, the massacre which occurred in Camden . . . was without parallel in the criminal annals of this country . . . The very wantonness of the killings and their number caused concern in the minds of a great number of people as to [Unruh's] sanity," county prosecutor Mitchell Cohen told reporters. The case made national headlines and aroused enormous public fear and outrage. "I'm sure Unruh is crazy, nevertheless I say kill him," a man from Alabama wrote in a typical letter. One of Unruh's neighbours told the *New York Times*, "He was a quiet one, that guy. He was all the time figuring to do this thing. You gotta watch them quiet ones." Theories for why he committed his deed were many and varied. Disturbingly, some responses were from people who sympathized with the killer and who said they knew how he felt.

After his arrest, Unruh was questioned intensely by Mitchell Cohen at police headquarters. "I deserve everything I get, so I will tell you everything I did and tell you the truth," he stated at the beginning of the interview. He lived up to his word. His answers to the prosecutor's questions were brutally honest, brief and to the point. As the first interview was terminated, a bloodstain left on the chair he had occupied betrayed the wound he had received from Frank Engel's .38. A bullet was lodged near his sacroiliac and he was taken to Cooper Hospital. Later in the day, he was transferred to the New Jersey State Hospital, at Trenton, for psychiatric tests. He continued to co-operate fully with both the county prosecutor and a legion of psychiatrists. One doctor described him as being "unexcited, entirely free from any objective demonstration of anxiety or guilt." Unruh's recollection of the murder of John Pilarchik illustrates the point: "I had levelled the gun at him, neither of us said nothing, and I pulled the trigger. He had a funny look on his face, staggered back, and fell to the floor. I realized then he was still alive, so I fired into his head."

Unruh spoke of the shootings like a soldier being debriefed after a successful military operation. Only on a few occasions did his matter-of-fact narration falter. He was extremely uncomfortable talking about threatening his mother and was reduced to tears on several occasions. He was also less than ebullient when talking about the children he killed. He repeatedly tried to impress upon his interrogators the idea that the children's deaths were accidental. He claimed to have no recollection of shooting Orris Smith: "It must have happened while I was trying to get a clear shot at the barber." Similarly, little Thomas Hamilton was "a shadow behind the apartment [window] and it was moving. Not realizing who it was or what they were doing, I fired several times." Neither, he claimed, did he deliberately shoot John Wilson: "I walked up towards the car and fired at the woman driver. I must have missed because I saw a child between the women with blood running down its face."

Throughout the questioning, Unruh insisted that he knew the difference between right and wrong. "I was not justified at all," he said. "I retaliated and tried to settle the score. Murder is sin, so it's wrong. I knew it was wrong before I did it. I expect to get the chair . . . I should get the chair." Mitchell Cohen, however, felt that the killer was emotionally unconnected to the sentiments he expressed. Unruh consistently spoke of himself as the primary victim of the whole affair and what remorse he did show was strictly limited: "I was in perfect control when I started out. In the excitement I shot others I did not plan to kill." Ultimately, when asked if he would follow the same course of action if given the chance again, he did not hesitate to say that he would: "And I would handle it the same way. [Only this time] I would get the Sorg boy, the restaurant man, the tailor and the man and wife in the apartment house." On one occasion he said, "I'd have killed thousands if I'd had bullets enough."

On 7 October 1949, Mitchell Cohen made a statement to the press:

> My duty required me to determine whether this man legally could be tried for his acts of Sept. 6, 1949. If

he were mentally competent to stand trial then the law of this state as well as my conscience demanded that he pay with his life for the thirteen which he so wantonly took. Unruh has been examined by four of the most eminent psychiatrists in this section of the country, all men in whom I have the utmost confidence . . . these experts have examined Unruh on numerous occasions since his arrest. Some of their examinations have been individual, some collective. They have studied his case over a period of weeks. Now these experts, in whom I have implicit confidence, unanimously declare he is suffering from dementia praecox [schizophrenia]. While the mental examinations were being conducted, my office completed an exhaustive investigation of the killings. The state was prepared to try this case at once if Unruh could be placed on trial. Under the laws of this state, however, an insane person cannot be tried. There is no alternative but to have Unruh committed to the state mental hospital. I here and now serve notice on Unruh and his family that so long as I live I shall vigorously oppose any attempt by anyone at any time to have this man released into society.

The Asylum Years

Unruh was raised in the Depression, was a moderate student and did not harbour extravagant ambitions and expectations. A little respect and status in the community of shopkeepers, where he had lived nearly all his life, was the extent of his dreams. After the rampage and his unsuccessful attempts to persuade the authorities that he was a sane man and should be put to death, there was no grand literary career for him to pursue, as there had been for Wagner von Degerloch. He indulged in simple passions, old pastimes that remained open to him—reading and col-

lecting stamps—and enjoyed a measure of status as a distin-
guished member of the hospital élite—patients confined in
the maximum-security Vroom Building. "He's not violent
in any way," a hospital spokesman revealed in 1976. "Once,
maybe twice, the institution's residents had a break attempt
where several of them got out in the yard, and they opened
his cell door and invited him to go along and he wouldn't
do it."

Although Unruh badly missed his mother, a regular chat
with her by telephone kept him in line and he had "the best
single track record" of any patient in the Vroom Building,
according to 1979 testimony of hospital administrator Dr.
Harvey Musikoff. In fact, he assimilated the institution's
ethos and demands so well and harmonized so responsive-
ly with his environment that, according to a 1982 report,
"he spends most of his time walking in a circle . . . [and]
believes he is being treated through the television set by
psychiatrists." Another report noted that "Over the years,
his mental condition has deteriorated greatly. His physical
condition has also deteriorated and he has aged far beyond
what would be expected merely by the number of years that
have passed."

In 1980, the Superior Court ruled that Unruh's constitutional right to a speedy trial had been violated and the
court dismissed the murder and assault indictment pend-
ing against him. The Camden county prosecutor's office
appealed against the decision, to no avail, and failed in
a 1982 attempt to have the charges reinstated. It was a
little more successful in opposing Unruh's 1979 request
to be moved to a minimum-security hospital, in Marlboro,
close to the home of his then 80-year-old mother. He was
eventually transferred in 1983, although not to Marlboro—
only to a less restrictive section of the Trenton facility.

Dr. Edward Yaskin, one of the four psychiatrists who
had originally examined Unruh in 1949, remained uncertain as to whether or not the confessed mass murderer
still posed a threat. Others were convinced he did not.

Dr. Max Pepernick found, on examining Unruh in 1982, "no indication . . . that he is a danger to others." Trenton administrator Dr. Musikoff was of the opinion that "if we don't transfer him before his mother expires . . . he will go downhill very rapidly. I think the environment, coupled with the fact that there's a great distance between him and his mother exacerbates this slow physical deterioration." Dr. Musikoff believed that the consequences of not moving Unruh to Marlboro would be grave: "I think if we don't transfer him he'll die shortly."

At the time of writing, Unruh is still alive and still a patient at the Trenton Psychiatric Hospital. He is 71 years old.

Wagner and Unruh

The Camden and Muehlhausen massacres are the two major cases from the first half of the twentieth century, and for all their geographical distance, there are many parallels between them. The two perpetrators, Unruh and Wagner, were extremely status conscious—but failed to find the social success and respect they felt they deserved. What they did find, however, was an explanation for their failure in their sexual habits—Unruh in ongoing homosexual liaisons, Wagner in a brief pre-marital affair—and both were aided and abetted in formulating their explanations by the societies in which they lived. In other words, their rationale was only viable because they lived in cultures that instilled in homosexuals a genuine terror of discovery and an enormous fear of the consequences.

The puritanism and intolerance of Wagner's Germany had its counterpart in Unruh's America. After the Second World War, when Unruh became active as a homosexual, there was a period of hysterical witch-hunting—the McCarthy era. Communists, suspected communists and anyone else who did not conform to a narrow, conservative

norm (every good McCarthyite knew, for example, that
a homosexual was just about the same darn thing as a
communist), were slandered, abused, harassed, blacklisted,
jailed—in short, had their lives damaged or destroyed. But
unlike communism, which was a crime of the poor or of
dissidents from the higher classes, homosexuality possessed
the unique characteristic of being a crime that could be
committed by an otherwise devout disciple of the society
and its ideology. And here is the key to the strength of
the bitterness of our two killers—they were vilified and
condemned by cultures they deeply believed in and desperately wanted to be accepted by. Except in their sexuality,
Wagner and Unruh were dedicated conformists—two of the
most conservative fellows one could ever wish to meet.
As such, they suffered a rare and profound love-hate relationship with the world in which they found themselves.
It was this that would ultimately lead them to endorse
Oscar Wilde's proposition that "each man kills the thing
he loves," and perpetrate a kind of crime of passion—a
violent assault against society, but formulated in a manner
prescribed by it.

Wagner and Unruh were both adjudged insane, but in
the same way that many of Wagner's ideas coincided with
those embraced by the Nazi Government, so Unruh disturbingly reflected some of the dominant themes of American
society.

Four years before the Camden massacre, President Tru-
man sanctioned the idea of massive retaliation when he
ordered atomic bombs to be exploded on the Japanese
cities of Hiroshima and Nagasaki; contemporaneous to
the Camden massacre, Senator Joseph McCarthy and his
cronies publicly authorized scapegoating as an acceptable
practice.

In such a cultural climate, we have to ask: just how
irrational was it for Howard Unruh, fascinated by the Bible
prophecies, to wish to see played out, in his own small
world, a Day of Judgment where all his enemies would

finally be vanquished? Was Unruh insane, or had he adopted, in terms of the logic of his culture, an entirely rational position?

Mass Murder and Madness

"The mass-murderer," wrote the criminologist William Bolitho in his book *Murder for Profit,* "is almost always found to have had dealings, psychological at any rate, with the institution of War." Although Bolitho's study of mass murderers was limited to those who kill for profit, many of his observations hold true for other mass killers—in particular that the mass murderer justifies himself with doctrine "stolen from the common stock" and that he is "even on the slightest acquaintance nastily like ourselves." We balk at such a proposition, of course, for we would like our killers to be freaks and weirdos, terrifyingly dissimilar to the rest of humanity—and throughout history, we have invented mechanisms to validate the idea.

When religion dominated man's view of the world, it was widely believed that perpetrators of heinous crimes were possessed by the devil, a view that still persists in some quarters today. Then the nineteenth-century criminologist Lombroso measured the heads of criminals and announced the discovery of a criminal physical type—conveniently isolating killers as a distinctly separate strain. When Lombroso's theories were discredited, the new doctors of the psyche stepped into the breach to quarantine killers on the grounds of psychological weirdness.

Unfortunately, mass murderers are rarely the rabid, babbling lunatics we would like them to be. They do, invariably, make a false reconstruction of the outside world, in which they attribute an unreasonable place for their own importance, but this is the common pastime of all men. Their delusions differ from our own not in their fundamental nature, only in degree, and this has much to do with the ongoing dialogue between the individual and the world around him. In certain circumstances, normal people can do crazy things.

On 16 March 1968, a platoon of US soldiers, under the command of Lieutenant William Laws Calley, entered a South Vietnamese village called My Lai. During the course of the morning, they razed the village, torched crops, destroyed livestock and slaughtered women, children and elders. Many of the girls were raped, sodomized, stabbed in the vagina or otherwise mutilated, before being shot. Calley ordered one GI, who was holding a hand grenade to a girl's head and forcing her to fellate him, to stop wasting time, pull up his pants and get on with the killing. After the first sweep through the village, the Lieutenant ordered the survivors to be rounded up and herded into an irrigation ditch. There he opened fire on them with his M-16 assault rifle and commanded his men to follow suit. When the platoon pulled out of the sector, in the early afternoon, they left somewhere between 172 and 347 corpses in the village itself; perhaps as many as 500 in the general area. Atrocities such as those perpetrated in My Lai, or in the infamous Rape of Nanking by the Japanese Imperial Army, are not uncommon. Amnesty International has documented many similar cases. Psychiatrist Henry Dicks has argued persuasively that even such a heinous example of mass liquidation as the Nazi holocaust was not, as the popular belief has it, the work of demented sadists inspired by an insane leader. From interviews with former Nazi SS killers, Dicks concluded that under different circumstances his subjects would hardly have become murderers at all, let alone mass murderers. The general point is made by quoting a soldier who participated in the My Lai massacre. "How do you, a father, shoot babies?" the soldier was asked. He replied, "I don't know—it's just one of those things."[2]

In a similar way, perhaps, does the killer who dwells in the pages of *Berserk!* commit his abominable deeds. If so, then he does not so much lose his mind as surrender his morality to the higher authority of dominant cultural themes—scapegoating as a just and righteous practice, massive retribution as a legitimate response to problems (indeed, sanctioned by God himself), and war as an heroic and noble pastime—themes he can readily use to rationalize a murderous mission that he would otherwise find impossible to justify.

3

The All-American Boy

After the Second World War, the industrial nations moved into an era of unprecedented growth and affluence. There was enormous expansion in all sectors: industrial, commercial and social welfare. The military also prospered, as the Cold War got underway and the arms and space races gathered momentum. The United States, at the head of the alliance of Western democracies, rapidly established itself in a new position of strength and influence in the world. Although there was a perceived threat from communism, Americans, on the whole, believed that the American Way was secure and that the American Dream was there to be realized by anyone who put his mind to work or his nose to the grindstone. In two post-war decades, the people of the United States—people who had known the Depression, who had beaten off the threat of fascism in the Second World War and who were keeping the contemporary threat of communism at bay with constant vigilance—enjoyed a golden age of stability and prosperity. It was in this golden age, in Lake Worth, Florida, a quiet, little city, five miles south of Palm Beach, that Charles Joseph Whitman was raised.

Whitman's Public Face

Charlie was born on 24 June 1941, the first of three boys, to Charles and Margaret Whitman; the second boy was called Patrick and the youngest John. The Whitmans were aspiring, upwardly mobile people—to all outward appearances a model American family—and Charles Jun. was a model American boy, the kind mothers of contumacious youngsters looked at with wistful hearts. Charlie was "high spirited and lots of fun as a child, but gave no trouble," according to Mrs. L.J. Holleran, who lived across the street from the Whitmans' large, ranch-style bungalow. Other neighbours held a similarly high opinion of him.

In his youth, Charlie was an Eagle Scout—at the time, one of the youngest to make the grade—and later he won the Boy Scout "God and Country" award. He was also an altar boy, an achievement that was especially pleasing for his mother, a devout Roman Catholic. Margaret doted on all three boys but had a particular soft spot for her first-born. Charlie had a paper round, delivering the *Palm Beach Post*, and if it rained she would drive him round the route. Charles Whitman Sen., a successful plumbing contractor—a self-made man and proud of it—also indulged his sons: "I was raised as an orphan, and didn't have the advantages my boys did. So I gave them everything I could—cars when they were just kids, that kind of thing." There were, though, strings attached to the father's material generosity: "I was a strict father . . . With all three of my sons, it was 'yes, sir' and 'no, sir.' They minded me." Margaret minded him, too: "I did on many occasions beat my wife . . . I have to admit it, because of my temper, I knocked her around. But my wife was a fine woman and she understood my nature."

If there were certain of his father's predilections that the young Charlie found unpalatable, there were others for which he acquired an immediate taste. Charles Sen. was a self-confessed gun fanatic and there were guns hanging in just about every room of the house. Charlie's training in the use of firearms began just as soon as he was strong enough to hold them steady. He was, according to his father, "always a crack shot" and, by the time he graduated from Cardinal Newman High School, could plug a squirrel in the eye.

On 6 July 1959, twelve days after his eighteenth birthday, Whitman enlisted in the marines. With his powerful physique—he was six-foot tall and weighed 200 pounds—his good looks, and his neatly cropped, blond hair, he seemed the quintessential all-American boy. A successful career in the marine corps looked very much on the cards. To begin with, things went well for him. He gained the rifle rating of sharpshooter, scoring 215 points out of a possible 250, and he qualified for a navy scientific training programme at the University of Texas in Austin, which would have given him the equivalent of a bachelor's degree and an officer's commission.

He began his studies at UT-Austin in September 1961. He was soon dating a fellow student, Kathleen Leissner, a trainee schoolteacher. Kathy was a couple of years younger than Charlie and the only daughter of a Texan rice farmer and real estate man. She was a pretty, brown-haired girl and she and Charlie were "the perfect couple," according to Frank Greenhaw, a close friend. They married in the summer of 1962.

Less than a year after the wedding, Whitman received a setback. In February 1963, he was forced to quit the University of Texas, apparently because of unsatisfactory academic progress, and was posted to the Second Marine Division, at Camp Lejeune in South Carolina. Having blown his chance of a speedy rise in the ranks, he found it difficult to readjust to life as a regular marine. After a string of violations of the Uniform Code of Military Justice, through the summer and early autumn of 1963, he was court-martialled in November. Whitman pleaded guilty to possessing a .25-calibre pistol aboard the USS *Raleigh* in July, and to possessing the same weapon at Camp Lejeune in October, along with two rounds of 7.62-mm ammunition (the standard round for an M-14 rifle); he pleaded guilty to ten instances of lending money for interest and to gambling with a member of his unit. In addition, he denied a charge of "communicating a threat to another marine to knock his teeth out," but was found guilty of that, too. Things had gone from bad to worse for him. Not only had his failure at UT-Austin prevented him from gaining an officer's commission, but the court martial resulted in his being demoted from corporal to private. He also received thirty days' hard labour. On 4 December 1964, Pfc. C.J. Whitman was honourably discharged from the marine corps.

Two years after his failure on the navy-sponsored programme at the University of Texas, he returned to Austin and enrolled in a mechanical engineering programme. Kathy had by this time graduated from the university and was teaching science at Austin's Lanier High School. On a tight budget, the couple took a small brick cottage in Jewell Street, in a modest suburb of the city south of the Colorado River. Charlie hung a stout rope from the pecan tree in the yard, on which he would do his marine corps exercises to the delight of neighbourhood children.

He did not last long on the mechanical engineering course and switched to architectural engineering because, according to his faculty adviser, Dr. Leonardt Kreisle, he felt he "could express his artistic talents better." Study does not appear to have come easily to Whitman. His friend Frank Greenhaw was not the only one to notice how hard the ex-marine had to work in order to maintain a B average for the course: "Charlie would stay up studying all night in the engineering building, sometimes putting his head down on the drafting table for a nap. And in the morning Kathy would come up with his breakfast."

Halfway across the world, meanwhile, the war in Vietnam was beginning to escalate under the auspices of President Lyndon Johnson. The number of servicemen in and around South Vietnam rose tenfold between February 1965 and the end of the year; 40,000 navy personnel, including many of Whitman's former marine corps buddies, were stationed aboard ships in the South China Sea.

In the spring of 1966, Margaret Whitman telephoned her eldest son from the family home in Florida, telling him that she was going to leave her husband. Charlie drove down to Lake Worth, picked her up, and returned with her to Austin. She moved into an apartment across the river from her son and daughter-in-law's house, and apparently took a job as a cashier in a cafeteria.

Pressure was beginning to mount on Whitman. He had less than a year to go to graduation and had registered for an unusually heavy fourteen-hour course load that summer. He quit as a scoutmaster with a local troop, worried that he would be unable to maintain a good grade average, but continued to work part time, about three hours a day (he had a string of casual jobs while at college, including one as a collector for a finance company). On top of the pressures of work and study, he was anxious about his mother. "He took very good care of her and tried to see that she wasn't overworked. She was always over at Charlie's and Kathy's," according to the manager of the Penthouse Apartments, where Margaret lived.

Charlie was also being subjected to a torrent of telephone calls from his father, petitioning him to persuade his mother to return to Lake Worth. Charles Sen. was "not ashamed of the fact I spent a thousand dollars a month on the phone bill, begging her to come back. I loved my wife dearly, my sons dearly, and I wanted our home to be happy. I kept begging Charlie to come back to me, too . . . I promised Charlie that if he'd only persuade his Mama to come back, I'd swear never to lay a hand on her."

Charlie began to suffer headaches and other signs of stress; he complained to friends about overwork and mental strain. Larry Fuess, a fellow engineering student and one of Charlie's closest friends, called at the Whitmans' place soon after Margaret moved to town.

"I walked into Charlie's one morning and he was packing his bags. He said he was going to leave everything—school, his wife, everything—and become a bum." Fuess and Whitman talked a while and in the end Charlie abandoned the plan. He stayed on in Austin but, he was no longer the "happy Charlie" his friends knew.

The Killings

In the early evening of Sunday 31 July 1966, Whitman sat down at his desk in the living room of the house on Jewell Street. The temperature had been up in the mid-nineties during the afternoon and it was still very hot. Outside, the lawns, parched by the summer sun, were full of dust. A month earlier, the United States had begun bombing targets in the demilitarized zone in Vietnam and had launched the first attacks against Hanoi, the North Vietnam capital, and the port city of Haiphong. Whitman put a sheet of paper in an old, portable typewriter and started to type: *To whom it may concern. I don't understand what is compelling me to type this note. I've been having fears and violent impulses. I've had some tremendous headaches . . .*

At about 7:30 P.M. he was interrupted by a visit from Larry Fuess and his wife, Elaine. The Fuesses asked him what he was writing and he replied, "Letters to old friends," and put the sheet away. Larry Fuess would later recall that Charlie "was in good spirits. It didn't seem like anything at all was bothering him. In fact it was strange because he had a test the next day and usually he was very tense before tests . . . Looking back, it seemed that he was particularly relieved about something—you know, as if you had solved a problem." Whitman and the Fuesses chatted generally for an hour or so, and at one point the conversation turned to Vietnam. Whitman "said he couldn't understand why boys from the United States had to go over there and die for something they didn't have anything to do with."

When Larry and Elaine left, Charlie returned to his type-writer. *I intend to kill Kathy. I love her very much*, he wrote. *I intend to kill my wife after I pick her up from work. I don't want her to face the embarrassment that my actions will surely cause*. He did not elaborate on what these actions might be, but did write: *I am prepared to die*.

At about 10:00 P.M. Whitman drove into town to pick up Kathy from the Southwestern Bell Telephone office where she was working the summer as an information operator. He dropped her off at home and then went out again to visit his mother. At the Penthouse Apartments, he stabbed his mother in the chest and shot her in the back of the head. Margaret may have put up a struggle because several bones in her left hand were broken with such force that the band of her engagement ring was driven into her finger. Detectives would find her body the next day, together with a letter in her son's neat handwriting: *I have just killed my mother. If there's a heaven, she is going there. If there is not a heaven, she is out of her pain and misery. I love my mother with all my heart*. He left the Penthouse Apartments at around midnight, pinning another note on his dead mother's door: *Roy, mother ill and not able to come to work today*. Then he drove home.

In the first hour of the morning of Monday 1 August, Whitman appended a hand-written note to the letter he had earlier composed on the typewriter: *12:30 A.M.—mother already dead*. At 3:00 A.M. he added his final remark: *Wife and mother both dead*. He had stabbed Kathy three times in the chest, apparently as she slept, and carefully wrapped her naked body in a bedsheet. At 5:45 A.M. he telephoned Kathy's supervisor at Southwestern Bell. She was scheduled to start a shift at half past eight that morning. He told the supervisor that she was ill and would not be in for work.

At 7:15 A.M. Whitman drove to the Austin Rental Equipment Service office and hired for cash a three-wheeled dolly, used for moving crates. At the drive-in window of an Austin bank, he cashed two $125 cheques; one of the cheques was on his account and nearly depleted it, and the other was on his mother's. At the Davis Hardware store, he bought a reconditioned Second World War .30-calibre M-1 carbine, and at Chuck's Gun Shop, several magazines for the M-1 and ammunition for it and for other rifles. He paid the bill by cheque for which there were now insufficient funds in his account. A clerk inquired, with friendly interest, what he wanted all the ammunition for and he replied, "To shoot some pigs." The clerk thought nothing of it; plenty of Austin hunters liked to shoot wild pig.

At 9:30 A.M. Whitman appeared at the large, modern Sears Roebuck department store in downtown Austin. He bought a twelve-gauge shotgun on credit and during the next hour sawed off part of the stock and barrel. He put the shotgun in his old marine corps footlocker, together with the M-1 carbine he had bought. Then, he added a 6-mm Remington bolt-action rifle with a four-power Leupold telescopic sight, a .35-calibre Remington pump rifle, a 9-mm Luger pistol, a .25-calibre Galesi-Brescia pistol, a .357 Smith & Wesson Magnum revolver, and well over 500 rounds of ammunition. Some of his guns, including two Derringer pistols, he decided to leave at home. All his weapons were legally owned.

In addition to the firearms, he also packed into the footlocker a Bowie knife, machete and hatchet, two jerry cans—one filled with water, the other with petrol—matches, lighter fuel, adhesive tape, rope, a flashlight, a clock and a transistor radio, various canned foods, including Spam and fruit cocktail, packets of raisins, a bottle of deodorant and a roll of toilet paper.

It was about 11:00 A.M. and 90 degrees Fahrenheit when Whitman's Chevrolet rolled into a parking area reserved for executives at the northwest corner of the 307-foot tall Main Building of the University of Texas. The granite tower, housing the university's library and administrative offices, and the Hogg Foundation for Mental Health, dominated the campus of otherwise low, Spanish-style buildings with terracotta roofs. Whitman, wearing a grey, nylon boiler suit over his blue jeans, white shirt and tennis shoes, loaded his marine corps footlocker onto the rented dolly and wheeled it into the Main Building. He smiled at a receptionist, who assumed he was a maintenance man, and headed across the marble hall towards the two automatic lifts.

The lift went as far as the twenty-seventh floor, and Whitman hauled the trunk up the last few flights of steps to the top floor. Mrs. Edna Townsley, the receptionist on the top-floor observation deck, apparently approached him to see what it was he wanted. Whitman smashed her over the head with the butt of a rifle, with such force that part of her skull was torn away. He then dragged her limp body behind a couch in the reception room, put a bullet in her head and left her for dead. She actually died some two hours later.

As Whitman manhandled the footlocker over to the door that led out onto the open walkway around the top of the tower, a group of sightseers arrived in the lift on the twenty-seventh floor: M.J. Gabour, a gas station operator, his wife, Mary, and their two sons, 19-year-old Mike, a cadet at the Air Force Academy, and 15-year-old Mark. Accompanying them were Gabour's sister, Mrs. Marguerite Lamport, and her husband, William. The two teenage boys were the first members of the party to reach the top floor, a few steps ahead of their mother and aunt. The women's husbands trailed a little behind. "Mark opened the door to the observation deck and a gun went off," Gabour later recalled. "Mike screamed." A sawn-off shotgun was discharged twice in rapid succession. Mary, Marguerite, Mike and Mark, Gabour said, "came rolling down the stairs. Whoever did the shooting slammed the door." Gabour and Lamport hauled the four victims down to the twenty-seventh floor. Mark was already dead.

Whitman, meanwhile, had barricaded the door from the stairs to the reception room and now had the entire observation deck to himself. He went out onto the open walkway and looked over the chest-high, stone parapet. Immediately above him, the south clock face was reading ten to twelve. Above the clock was the bell tower and above the bell tower nothing but clear blue sky. Mapped out below him was the 232-acre university campus, the whole of the city of Austin and sixty-five miles of Texas countryside in whichever direction he looked: to the south and east, lush farmland; to the west, distant, mist-veiled mountains and the road to the LBJ Ranch where one night, five years earlier, he and a couple of companions shot a deer after it became trapped in the headlights of their car. Someone had noticed the automobile, with the young buck lashed to the back of it, and telephoned the licence number to the Texas Game and Fish Commission. At 4:30 A.M. on the morning of 20 November 1961, Game Warder Grover Simpson and three Austin police officers found Charlie and his roommates dressing the deer in a dormitory bathroom. Now, five years on, Whitman was poaching people. He opened fire from the top of the tower and the huge bell, twenty feet above his head, began to chime. It was high noon in Austin.

A newsboy, 17-year-old Alec Hernandez, suddenly teetered and fell from his bicycle. Denver Dolman, a bookstore operator on the edge of the campus, unaware that a high-velocity bullet had just drilled through the newsboy's groin, looked on—bemused by what appeared to be an inexplicable cycling accident. Then, he heard gunshots and all around him "people started falling."

Claire Wilson, 18 years old and eight months pregnant, had just left a first-year anthropology class in the company of a fellow freshman, Thomas Eckman. The pair were strolling across the sun-drenched South Mall when a bullet struck Claire in the lower abdomen, tearing into her womb and shattering the skull of her baby. Claire survived, but the baby was stillborn. As the horrified Eckman knelt beside his wounded friend, a second shot was fired, killing him instantly. Robert Boyer, a research physicist and lecturer in applied mathematics, had just left the Main Building to meet a friend for lunch. As he walked out onto the South Mall, heading away from the tower, he suddenly collapsed, a bullet in his back. Seeing the first victims fall, Charlotte Dareshori, a secretary in the Dean's office, rushed outside to help—but was soon under fire herself. She found refuge behind the concrete base of a flagpole and crouched there, under Old Glory, for ninety minutes, isolated but safe— one of the few people to venture out onto the exposed South Mall and survive.

Outside the Rae Ann dress shop, in a street bordering the campus to the west, chemistry student Abdul Khashab, his fiancée, Janet Paulos, and a friend Lana Phillips, all fell wounded within a few seconds of each other. A jewellery shop manager was just leaving the building to go to the aid of another trio of wounded victims on the pavement, when the shop windows shattered and bullet fragments tore into his leg. Harry Walchuk, a political scientist and graduate student working towards his doctorate, suddenly gasped, staggered backwards clasping his throat, and collapsed by a newsstand, mortally wounded. A block away, 18-year-old Paul Sonntag, a summer lifeguard at the municipal pool, was strolling north with Claudia Rutt, also 18, when Claudia suddenly clutched at her chest, cried out and slumped to the pavement. Seconds later, another bullet brought Sonntag down beside her.

Most of Whitman's victims were shot during the first twenty minutes of sniping and he relied mainly on the 6-mm Remington rifle with the four-power scope, a weapon and sight configuration with which even a moderate marksman can consistently hit a target the size of a human head at 300 yards. Thomas Karr, a senior from Fort Worth, was shot dead at just about that range to the west of the tower. Thomas Ashton, a Peace Corps trainee was shot dead to the east. North of the tower, Associated Press reporter, Robert Heard, running at full tilt, caught a bullet in the shoulder. It was a painful wound, but not sufficiently serious to prevent him from marvelling "What a shot!"

South of the tower, one of the first police officers on the scene, 23-year-old patrolman Billy Speed, took up a position behind the stone columns of a balustrade. Leland Ammons, a law student, saw the young cop suddenly go sprawling. "The shot hit him high in the shoulder," Ammons said later. "It must have either ricocheted or the bullet came through one of the slits between the fence pillars." Whichever way he was hit, it made no difference to Speed; the shot killed him.

At the top of the tower, Whitman frequently changed his position, each time finding fresh prey in his sights. Karen Griffith, a 17-year-old Austin girl, was shot in the chest and died a week later from the wounds. Four students were wounded on Twenty-fourth Street, north of the tower. Three people were wounded on the roof of the Computation Center, just east of the tower.

Meanwhile, over 100 law enforcement officers had responded to the trouble signal that had gone out over all police channels, soon after the sniping started. City cops, highway patrolmen, Texas Rangers, and even US secret servicemen from Lyndon Johnson's Austin office, had converged on the tower. Off-duty officers began showing up, as news of the shooting spread. Patrolman Ramiro Martinez was at home cooking steak when he heard a newsflash on the radio. He buckled on his service revolver and rushed to the scene. Local gun-owning citizens materialized and started shooting at the tower. A cop angrily demanded of one such public-spirited citizen what the hell he thought he was doing. The man, reportedly dressed in battle fatigues and with an M-14 rifle set up on a tripod, replied, "Just helping out."

Police desperately tried to seal off the area around the tower but Whitman's wide shooting radius and easy access to all points of the compass made the task impossible. Three blocks south of the tower, Roy Dell Schmidt, an electrician with a service call to make in the area, got out of his van to find out what a police roadblock up ahead was all about. Told to leave the area, Schmidt retreated to where a group of onlookers was gathered on the sidewalk. Suddenly, a bullet tore through his chest. "He told me we were out of range," the man who had been standing next to him revealed later.

The dead and the dying were scattered over an ever-widening area as Whitman looked farther afield for his victims. A police marksman, Lieutenant Marion Lee, was sent up in a light aircraft to try to pick the sniper off. Rescuers in an armoured car worked to retrieve the wounded from the dangerous no-man's-land of the South Mall. Unintimidated by the sharpshooting cop above him or by the barrage of fire coming from the ground below him, Whitman first forced the plane to retreat, with a few accurate shots at its fuselage, and then turned his attention back to zeroing in on his human targets.

Three blocks north and two blocks west of the tower, a basketball coach, Billy Snowden, was just stepping into a barbershop when a bullet crashed into his shoulder. Way over to the southeast, two students sitting near windows were nicked by bullets. An ambulanceman, trying to help some of the wounded to the west of the tower was himself shot and wounded.

In the meantime, the hail of police bullets ricocheted from the bell turret at the top of the tower, peppered the clock faces, or chipped away at the stone parapet around the walkway—but failed to find the vulnerable flesh of the sniper's body. Whitman stayed low. Utilizing the narrow drainage ducts as gunports, he was virtually impossible to hit.

If an architect had set out to design a building with the express intention of it being used by a sniper, he could have done little better than produce the blueprint of the University of Texas tower. For more than one and a half hours, Whitman's position was unassailable. He had such an unobstructed view of the campus and its environs that police were unable to rush the building, and he was so well protected that they were unable to shoot him down at long range. It was not until a few, resourceful officers found themselves together in the tower, after gaining entry by various means—through underground conduits or by zig-zagging from building to building—that the initiative switched to the police.

Ramiro Martinez, the off-duty patrolman who had abandoned his steak dinner to come to the scene, was joined by a handful of other officers, including Houston McCoy and Jerry Day, and by a civilian, Allen Crum, an employee of the university and a former air force tailgunner.

Crum was deputized on the spot. The group took the lift to the twenty-sixth floor because, Crum later explained "we didn't want to take a chance of running into [Whitman] if he was waiting for us on the twenty-seventh." Cautiously, they made their way up the final flights of steps. On the twenty-seventh floor, they came across members of the Gabour and Lamport families, some dead, some wounded and the remainder grief-stricken. While their colleagues tended to the victims, officers Martinez and McCoy, and the newly deputized Crum, continued up the stairs to the observation deck.

The door to the reception room was still barricaded. Carefully, the trio pushed against the door, easing back the desk that blocked it, until there was a sufficiently large gap to squeeze through. They were advised, by radio, of the sniper's position—he was on the north side of the roof—and Martinez crawled out onto the walkway on the south side, and began moving stealthily eastwards. Crum and McCoy followed, Crum turning to the west and McCoy backing up Martinez. Martinez rounded the southeast corner of the tower, onto the east walkway. If Whitman was in the position he was supposed to be, Martinez would find him when he turned the next corner. He made his way towards it.

Crum, meanwhile, had turned onto the west walkway. Suddenly, he heard footsteps up ahead. He fired a shot from his rifle into the northwest corner to prevent the sniper from bursting around it and shooting him. On the other side of the tower, Martinez turned cautiously onto the north walkway. Fifty feet away crouched Whitman, the M-1 in his hands, waiting for Crum at the opposite corner. Martinez raised his .38 service revolver and shot into Whitman's left side. "He jerked up the carbine toward me," the patrolman later recalled. "He couldn't keep it level. He kept trembling, going up instead of coming down with it. I don't know how many shots I fired." In fact, he fired all six, emptying his revolver. McCoy moved up, stepped around him, and blasted Whitman with a shotgun. Martinez grabbed the shotgun: "That guy was still flopping and he had that carbine in his hands . . . and I ran at him and shot at the same time. I got to him and saw that he was dead." Crum took a towel from Whitman's footlocker and waved it above the parapet signalling to the men on the ground that it was all over.

The Aftermath

Whitman's body, in which, the autopsy showed, there was no sign of alcohol or other drug abuse, was brought down from the tower at 1:40 P.M., a police officer at each limb. In all, Whitman was responsible for seventeen deaths, including his own, which he had sealed as surely as if he had put a gun to his head himself. More than thirty other people were wounded. The impact of the massacre was felt beyond the city of Austin, beyond the state of Texas and beyond the USA. The story was big news as far afield as Europe, the Soviet Union and Japan. In Germany, newspapers and magazines revived the Wagner case from half a century earlier. In England, the *Evening Standard* wanted to know, like everyone else, "Why did it happen?" Governor John B. Connally Jun. of Texas—no stranger to a sniper's bullets (he was riding with President Kennedy, in Dallas, when the President was assassinated and was himself hit)—ordered "a complete and thorough investigation" into the massacre. The investigation would, he hoped, "shed light on the background and causes and give some clues on preventing future occurrences of this nature."

As ever, there were those for whom a brief glance at the number of victims involved provided conclusive evidence of the gunman's insanity. Austin Police Chief Robert Miles, on the other hand, had access to more data than most in the immediate aftermath of the shootings and was considerably more cautious about drawing hasty conclusions. Miles was struck by the fact that the killer "was very rational in his notes."

Whitman's friends and neighbours were of one voice when confronted with the news that Charlie was responsible for the massacre. The reaction of Agnes Fabris, who had known him since his childhood, was typical. "Oh no, it just couldn't be Charlie," she said. Charlie was "very dependable" and "the kind of boy you would want for a son." He was "a thinker who never went off half-cocked. Completely normal, just one of the guys," according to Frank McCarty, an old high school friend. Kathy Whitman's father, Raymond Leissner, agreed. His son-in-law was, he said, "just as normal as anybody I ever knew." According to University of Texas academic adviser Dr. Leonardt Kreisle, Charlie was "more mature than most people his age." From Lake Worth, to Needville, to Austin, it was the same story.

If the portrait that emerged from the testimony of Whitman's friends and neighbours was hardly the classic one of a violent psychotic, the most interesting revelation concerning the state of his mental health came from a professional source; Dr. Maurice Heatly, staff psychiatrist at the University of Texas. Whitman, who had gone to Dr. Heatly for a consultation on 29 March, shortly after he had been persuaded by Larry Fuess not to abandon his life in Austin, is one of the few mass killers to have been seen and assessed by a psychiatrist shortly *before* going on the rampage. Rather bewilderingly, given that killers are so frequently found to be insane when examined by psychiatrists *after* their murder sprees (Wagner and Unruh being cases in point), Heatly found Whitman to be afflicted with nothing more serious than a minor personality trait disturbance. He dictated a report for the clinic's records, of which these are extracts:

This is a new student referred by one of the general practitioners downstairs. This massive, muscular youth seemed to be oozing hostility as he initiated the hour with the statement that something was happening to him and he didn't seem to be himself.

Past history revealed a youth who . . . grew up in Florida, where the father was a very successful plumbing contractor without an education, but who had achieved considerable wealth. He identified his father as being brutal, domineering and extremely demanding of the other three members of the family . . . He expressed himself as being very fond of his wife, but admitted that his tactics were similar to his father's and that he had on two occasions assaulted his wife physically.

The real precipitating factor for this initial visit after being on the campus for several years seemed to stem from the separation of his parents some thirty days ago . . . Although he identifies with his mother in the matter . . . his real concern is with himself at the present time. He readily admits to having overwhelming periods of hostility with a very minimum of provocation. Repeated inquiries attempting to analyze his exact experiences were not successful with the exception of his vivid reference to "thinking about going up on the tower with a deer rifle and start shooting people."

He recognizes, or rather feels, that he is not achieving in his work at the level of which he is capable and this is very disconcerting to him. The youth could talk for long periods of time and develop overt hostility while talking and then during the same narration may show signs of weeping.

OBSERVATIONS: This youth told numerous stories of his childhood and of involvement with his father

[Heatly made no notes on these] . . . and it was felt that this relationship . . . is largely responsible for his present predicament. The youth has lived for the day when he could consider himself as a person capable of excelling his father in high society in general. He long ago acknowledged that he had surpassed him in educational fields, but he is seeking that status in virtually all fields of human endeavor. He was self-centered and egocentric, and at the same time he wants to improve himself. The degenerated state of affairs with his parents plus his repeated recent failures to achieve have become extremely frustrating to him.

No medication was given to this youth at this time and he was told to make an appointment for the same day next week, and should he feel that he needs to talk to this therapist he could call me at any time during the interval.

Whitman did not see the doctor again. After the massacre, Heatly was questioned intensely about the content of his report, particularly about Whitman's reference to the tower. Heatly maintained that the remark was not, in the context in which it was made, especially disturbing. Other doctors agreed that the kind of sentiment Whitman expressed is commonplace. University of Chicago psychiatrist Robert Davis said, "Thousands of people—and I mean literally thousands—talk to doctors about having such feelings." Even with the knowledge that Whitman did ascend the tower and shoot people, Dr. Heatly was unwilling to revise his original assessment: "I could not say now that he was a psychopath." The minor personality trait disturbance was the only thing approaching a mental abnormality he was able to confirm, and he was, he stated, at a loss to "account for the chain of events on a simple psychiatric basis."

While Heatly, the only professional mind analyst to take

a first-hand look at Whitman's, was unable to explain the massacre in terms of gross pathology of the psyche, his counterpart analysing the physical structure of the brain, sought a biological answer. Dr. Coleman de Chenar, of the Austin State Hospital, performed the autopsy on Whitman. He found that his subject was an excellent physical specimen, except for a tumour, the size of a pecan nut, in the brain. The tumour was in the hypothalamus, near the stem of the brain, and there was no evidence of a generalized increase in pressure in other parts. If there had been, in an area crucial to cognitive behaviour, for example, and if Whitman's carefully planned and sustained violence had been brief and transitory (in keeping with a behaviour-altering tumour), then the discovery may have been significant. As it was, most brain specialists thought it unlikely that the tumour had sparked the murder spree. According to the *Merck Manual of Diagnosis and Therapy* brain tumours are found in around one out of every fifty autopsies. Unfortunately, for those who have sought to explain heinous crimes as the result of diseased brains, tumours in mass murderers appear to be no more nor less common than tumours in the general population.

The committee of investigation appointed by Governor Connally was unable to formulate any real explanation for the massacre. The report concluded with the sadly vague observation that Whitman had been "living under conditions of increasing personal stress from which he felt he could not escape and which he could not master."

Whitman's War

All who knew him recognized that his father had a profound influence, directly and indirectly, on the way young Charlie lived his life. His influence went way beyond introducing a boy of tender years to guns and wife-beating. "The youth has lived for the day when he could consider himself as a person capable of excelling his father in high society in general . . . He is seeking that status in virtually all fields of human endeavor," Dr. Heatly noted. Whitman's close friend Larry Fuess was of the opinion that "His whole life was like an escape from his father. He left home after high school and just built himself up completely—his mind, his body, his career, everything. He was like a computer—he would install his own values into the machine, then program the things he had to do, and out would come the results." Other friends noted that "he was mortally afraid of being like his father," and that "He hated himself when he did something like his father."

Like many mass killers, Whitman was an aspiring model citizen. A Manhattan psychiatrist, speaking in the wake of the Austin massacre, suggested that such folk frequently "live the opposite of what they feel. They become gentle, very mild, extremely nice people, and often show a compulsive need to be perfectionistic." They are, like Wagner von Degerloch and Howard Unruh, among the most conservative citizens one is ever likely to encounter. Such was young Charlie Whitman, Eagle Scout and altar boy. Although the burden was squarely on his shoulders, as the eldest son, to challenge his authoritarian and violent father, he responded not with confrontation or rebellion but with submission. Charlie, named in pop's honour, simply became the perfect youngster his father demanded he be. Evidently, though, his early life was permeated by feelings of impotence and frustration—guilt, too, probably—which he kept carefully concealed. When he began to plot against Charles Sen. his revenge was also suitably camouflaged. He vowed to be a better person than his "brutal, domineering and extremely demanding" father and to out-succeed the allegedly semi-literate but successful and respected businessman.

What would become a lifelong covert war for Charles Jun. began well enough with his early successes and his marriage. He was serious, he studied hard and he thought constantly of getting ahead. In the post-war era of massive expansion and prosperity, individuals with even the most limited talents could envisage for themselves successful careers and a rise in the social hierarchy. Whitman may not have reached quite for the stars, but he did set his sights high. The powerful US myth of the ease of social advancement—the American Dream—and the rampant optimism of the post-war era, not only encouraged him in his belief that he could rise above his father in society, but fostered in him a high *expectation* of doing so. His self-belief was further reinforced by his particular family circumstances: if the flawed Charles Sen. could amass considerable wealth and status, then, in a just America, how much more could a perfect Charles Jun.—as his doting mother insisted he was—achieve?

It can only have come as a bitter blow to Whitman when he was forced to withdraw from the navy-sponsored programme at UT-Austin after failing to come up to scratch. Suddenly, the future did not look quite so promising for a young man who listed on a confidential personal data form, at the university's Mental Hygiene Clinic, his main interest in life as "how to make money." When, significantly partly through his entrepreneurial efforts, Whitman was court-martialled and demoted, the future looked bleaker still. The chance of his ever earning sufficient status as a marine to rival his father was slim, and his eventual honourable discharge is of little surprise. "It is unusual," a Pentagon spokesman revealed, "but Whitman's conduct and proficiency marks before and after the court-martial were high"—Charlie the model citizen.

In truth, the final year in the marines was one of torment for him. Detectives going through his effects, after the massacre, came across two pages of old notes. At the top of the first page, Whitman had written more recently (presumably not long before his rampage), "These notes were made in 1964 when I was feeling very much as I am now." Police Chief Miles summarized the themes of the notes: "He was having headaches and wanted to do strange things" and "he felt impulses that were quite contrary to his whole way of thinking."

Whitman was not prepared to admit defeat yet, though, and soon pulled himself together. Evidently aware of when and where the life he had planned had gone off the rails, he returned to Austin and enrolled in an engineering programme at the University of Texas—an obvious bid to get himself back on the right track. Although Dr. Heatly noted that he had "long ago acknowledged that he had surpassed [Charles Sen.] in educational fields," this was not, in fact, true. Until Charlie actually graduated from university, he would hold, like his father, just high school qualifications.

Whitman seems to have been convinced that a college education was the key to his status battle with Charles Sen., a perfectly logical belief, given the son's inability to beat his father at his own game—Charlie was a hopelessly inept entrepreneur. In Austin, although he was "always trying to make a fast buck," as a friend put it, he had little, if any, success. After the shootings, more than one person would claim to be holding a bad cheque given by Charlie in a poker game, while an Austin businessman would tell reporters that he had been hounded by Whitman with a business proposition—"He said he had a nice supply of pornography"—which also came to nothing.

It was, therefore, essential to Charlie's campaign that he succeed at university and, as staff and friends testified, he worked tremendously hard to do so. He insisted on working part time—to have been supported entirely by Kathy was probably unthinkable to him, given that one of his father's more meritorious achievements was to have kept his family materially well provided for.

In spite of the sacrifices, Whitman struggled. Although his college records show that he consistently managed above-average grades, he was not a naturally talented student. His father-in-law, Raymond Leissner, noticed that Charlie had to work "awfully hard at his grades," while friends commented on the gruelling study regime he imposed upon himself. What success he did have was down to inordinately long hours of sheer hard work and the single-minded determination to outdo his father.

If, as his friends said, Charlie was like a computer, then the system was already close to overload when Margaret Whitman walked out on her husband. Margaret's arrival in Austin was like a bug in the program, sending Charlie haywire. His first reaction was to abandon everything and become a bum, but this was never a realistic option for a young man who had dedicated himself to model citizenship. Instead, he soldiered on, fretting about his mother (an additional responsibility no dutiful son could shirk), tormented by the stream of phone calls from his father, working at a part time job, and trying to keep on top of a punishing fourteen-credit-hour academic schedule. His studies suffered and the spectre of academic failure loomed again. The model citizen was beginning to crack.

By the early summer of 1966, Whitman had twice assaulted Kathy (he was no better than his wife-beating father), felt himself to be on the verge of failure at university (no better than his high school educated father), and had proved to be a completely incompetent entrepreneur (a good deal inferior to his successful businessman father). All his ambitions had come to naught and his whole *raison d' être* was rapidly evaporating. Police Chief Miles believed he "had just decided that this world was not worth living in." So he had. But he had also decided that there were accounts to be settled before he bowed out.

Charles Whitman, the model citizen, a young man who had always tried to do the right thing, who had tried to do everything his society demanded of him, wound up a loser. He nominated the University of Texas campus as the location for a spectacular final gesture. He perceived the university as the central source of all his problems—a stubborn obstacle that had kept triumph beyond his reach, ever since his first failure there back in 1962—and, with the exception of some non-target-group casualties (inevitable in "war"), his victims would be students; the very people on the threshold of the kind of life he so desperately desired. His motive for murdering Margaret and Kathy may, as he claimed, have been to protect them from the embarrassment of his later actions. It seems equally possible, though—as it was with Wagner—that he killed them in the belief that they carried some of the blame for his failure.

In the final analysis, Whitman became a man of action. While his predecessors had to go out and hunt down their chosen targets, Whitman's mission was simplified by the presence of the University of Texas tower. Here, as *Time* magazine put it, "somewhat like the travelers in Thornton Wilder's *The Bridge of San Luis Rey*, who were drawn by an inexorable fate to their crucial place in time and space," Whitman's victims came to him.

Like the heroes of popular American novels from Wilder's era, and like the heroes of popular movies from his own—*A Fistful of Dollars, For a Few Dollars More*— Charles Whitman was, for the people of Austin on that hot August day, the nameless man, the stranger, the fast gun who takes the law into his own hands and stamps his will on a hostile world. That the archetypal American hero parallels so closely the pictures that gunmen have of themselves, is surely not without significance—for in such a way, perhaps, do American Dreams become nightmares.

4

THE FAMILY MAN

In the post-war era of opportunity and prosperity, many men were able to realize their dreams. Some were able to realize grand dreams. Charles Whitman's, though, spawned by the intensity of his desire to better himself beyond his father's achievements were so absurdly extravagant, measured against his ability to realize them, that he was destined to fail. If young men like Whitman were something of a rarity, there were others, raised in the same prosperous time but with less grandiose ambitions, who, nevertheless, suddenly found their prospects fading as the economies of the industrial nations began to contract in the late 1960s and early 1970s.

There were middle-aged men, too, who came to feel betrayed by their governments, their employers, their workmates—by their societies—men who had enjoyed full employment for twenty-five post-war years, who had become accustomed to the idea of a job for life or to moving from job to job (in a world where there was always a new job to go to) in pursuit of their dreams; men who had, in fact, come to feel that they had a *right* to these things. As the closure of the economy began to bite, some of these men—young and old—finding themselves thwarted by forces beyond their control, began to develop new dreams, dreams of revenge. Some turned their dreams into reality.

Through the 1970s, the incidence of mass shootings in the United States climbed dramatically, outstripping the rate in other nations, where such crimes remained unknown or infrequent anomalies, by a huge margin.

In New York State, an 18-year-old Honours student, Anthony Barbaro, barricaded himself in his high school, set fires and began shooting at passers-by, police and firemen. He killed three people, wounded eight others and hanged himself in his jail cell with a bedsheet. In New Orleans, 23-year-old Mark Essex shot dead nine people and wounded almost twice as many before being killed in a hail of police bullets. Michael Soles—"a real good boy" according to his aunt—shot dead two people and wounded seven others at the Holiday Inn, in Wichita, Kansas. Emile Benoist, the son of a politician, shot dead six walkers and joggers near Hackettstown, New Jersey, then turned the rifle on himself. Seventeen-year-old Kenneth Wilson died the same way, after firing on a group of picnickers—killing two and wounding two—in Charlotte, South Carolina. Richard Hicks cruised along Interstate 10, between Los Angeles and Phoenix, blasting other drivers with a sawn-off .22-calibre rifle, killing three and wounding six others. Kenyon Pruyn, a 32-year-old, opened fire on a restaurant across the street from his apartment. He killed two people and wounded ten. Other gunmen went on the rampage in Richmond, Virginia, in Greenwater, Washington, in South River, California—there were countless cases all across the United States.

In 1979, 64-year-old Ira Attebury, shouting, "What kind of society is this?" brought the decade to a close when he opened fire with an arsenal of weapons on a crowd of some 5,000 people, gathered in San Antonio, Texas, for the annual Battle of the Flowers parade. It was more like the Battle of the Alamo. Attebury hit about sixty people in sixty minutes, two of whom died from their wounds, then shot himself dead with a .38.

This dramatic increase in the incidence of mass shootings continued in the 1980s, the economy now in recession and the golden age of the fifties apparently lost forever. When James Huberty decided, in 1984, to go out "hunting humans," it was hardly an original idea. The massacre he perpetrated, however, was one of the most destructive of all time.

The McDonald's Restaurant Massacre

On Wednesday 18 July, at about 4:00 P.M., Huberty, a 41-year-old unemployed man, walked through the golden arches of a McDonald's restaurant in the town of San Ysidro, on the California-México border. He was dressed in combat trousers and a black T-shirt. Matching accessories included a semi-automatic rifle slung over one shoulder, a canvas bag full of ammunition over the other, a 9-mm semi-automatic pistol with a fourteen-shot clip tucked in his belt, and a twelve-gauge shotgun in his hands.

A McDonald's assistant, 16-year-old John Arnold, standing by the service counter, glanced up and found himself looking straight down the barrel of the shotgun: "Guillermo [a fellow employee] said, 'Hey, John, that guy's gonna shoot you,' " Arnold later recalled. "He was pointing that gun right at me. He pulled the trigger, but nothing happened. Then he brought it down and started messing with it." Arnold turned and walked away, disgusted by what he thought was a sick joke.

Of the customers who had noticed Huberty's entrance, some headed immediately for the door, some shifted nervously in their seats and some, presumably thinking Huberty was a harmless zany "character" of one sort or another—a kiddies' entertainer, perhaps, or a Rambo lookalike contestant—simply went back to reading the overhead menus, eating their Big Macs or drinking their milkshakes.

Outside, across the street, 11-year-old Armando Rodriguez was staring intently at the restaurant. He had been kicking a football about a few minutes earlier, but had left off the game when he noticed a black Mercury Marquis pulling into the McDonald's car park. A heavily armed man had climbed out of the car and walked into the restaurant. Now, as the bemused Armando watched, the man with the guns was motioning with his hand for the people in the building to get down on the floor. Some witnesses were reported to have said that Huberty shouted, "I'm going to kill you all"; one young boy reportedly said he yelled, "I killed thousands in Vietnam, and I want to kill more," but police who interviewed the survivors believed he simply ordered everyone to lie down. Armando Rodriguez was still watching from outside. He saw a woman running for the exit and the gunman turn and fire. The woman dropped to the floor.

John Arnold, who had walked away when Huberty first entered the restaurant, was nicked by a shotgun pellet in the opening volley of shots. A plate glass window shattered, bodies fell all around him and Arnold dived under a seat. "I just pushed my head up against the bricks. I scrunched into a ball. I tried not to breathe. I just thought 'Oh, please, don't come over here.' " He would remain in that position, thinking that same thought, for the next seventy-five minutes. Griselda Diaz and her young son, Erwin, also dived to the floor during the first volley of shots. They managed to crawl to a side door and safety.

Many other customers were not so lucky. Huberty calmly fired off round after round. When one gun was empty, he moved on to another. Most of the victims were hit within the first few minutes of shooting. The first emergency call, from a McDonald's employee, was logged at 4:03 P.M. Other calls quickly followed. Betty Everhart, a retired nurse who lived opposite the restaurant, had, like many people, mistaken the first shots for a car backfiring. But two men ran to her door, telling her that somebody was shooting a gun and to call the police.

Meanwhile, McDonald's employees in the kitchen, wondering what the commotion in the restaurant was all about, soon found out. Alicia Garcia was cooking chips when Huberty walked in. She turned and ran downstairs to a cloakroom, taking two of her colleagues with her. They were joined by other employees with the same idea. The small group huddled together nervously while, upstairs, the firing continued.

Huberty shot dead the manager, Neva Caine, and rooted out four other employees who had tried to hide. He fired on them from close-range and two girls were killed instantly. A third, wounded, tried to crawl away, as did a young man, Albert Leos. Huberty pumped more bullets into the girl, killing her, then found himself with an empty magazine. He returned to the service counter, where his bag of ammunition sat, and began reloading. Albert Leos, terrified that the gunman would return at any moment to finish him off, tried to get to his feet but was unable to do so. He had been shot four times—in the left arm, the right arm, the right leg and the abdomen. Desperately, he dragged and pulled himself across the kitchen floor, heading for the steps to the basement.

But Huberty had plenty more targets to aim at—in the restaurant, and in the playground and car park outside. Three youngsters, Joshua Coleman, David Flores and Omar Hernandez, pushing bicycles along the pavement in front of the building, suddenly collapsed in a heap. Rafael Meza, an employee of an all-night grocery chain just up the street, had run down to the McDonald's soon after the gunfire started. He tried to reach the boys but "somebody was shooting at me with a pistol. Then all the windows started breaking. I hid behind a truck . . . There were bullets flying everywhere . . . Everybody was screaming and running around, they were just running for their lives . . . You could see people getting shot and falling down, just like in a shooting gallery that you couldn't get out of, just like in the movies." A couple and their 4-month-old daughter were hit, as were a couple in their seventies, the oldest victims of the massacre.

When the first police car arrived at 4:07 P.M., its windscreen and emergency lights were shattered in a barrage of gunfire. The police officer alerted radio dispatch that a major siege was in progress and requested a SWAT (Special Weapons and Tactics) team. Inside McDonald's, though, bodies already lay everywhere. Some people played dead. Most weren't playing. "It's an absolute massacre," Police Commander Larry Gore later told reporters. "It's a total disaster inside the facility." Huberty had systematically killed staff and customers with no more concern than a slaughterman killing cattle.

Victor Rivera, a maintenance man, had taken his wife and daughter to McDonald's. It was the little girl's favourite restaurant. Victor was shot dead. His wife and their 4-year-old daughter were both wounded.

Jackie Wright Reyes, her 8-month-old son, a friend, and Jackie's 11-year-old niece, had stopped off for a snack. The niece was the only one of the quartet to come out of the McDonald's alive.

Ron and Blythe Herrera had been on vacation with their 11-year-old son and were on their way home. Mother and son were killed. Ron suffered seven gunshot wounds but survived.

Lawrence Versluis, a 62-year-old truck driver, was having his coffee break. He had worked for the same local company for almost forty years and was due to retire at the end of the week. Huberty shot him dead.

In the restaurant and outside—in the car park and the playground, among the comical pirate statues and other figures familiar in McDonald's advertisements—twenty-one people lay dead or dying and nineteen lay injured. Out on a nearby eight-lane freeway, Interstate 5, a motorist was shot and wounded. Meanwhile, inside, burger cook Albert

Leos had managed to haul himself down to the basement. His colleagues, hiding there, tended him as best they could. Upstairs, Huberty continued to roam the restaurant, firing sporadically.

Outside, the police closed off six blocks of San Ysidro Boulevard and the Highway Patrol shut down Interstate 5. By 4:55 P.M. the SWAT team had assembled and taken up positions at the post office to the south of the restaurant, at a doughnut shop to the north, and on San Ysidro Boulevard to the east. McDonald's tinted windows, many of them now patterned with dense spiders' webs of fractures, gave appalling visibility for officers trying to assess the situation inside. To make matters worse, from a tactical point of view, Huberty was occupying high ground: when the restaurant was built, it had been elevated some three feet, with a retaining wall running around three sides. SWAT field commander Jerry Sanders was in a difficult position and, until he could gain more information on the situation inside the restaurant, had no option but to maintain a "red light" condition: no firing unless the gunman tried to escape.

By 5:13 P.M. Sanders was sufficiently clear on the position to proceed. There was just one man with a lot of guns. Many people were dead, too many for witnesses even to begin to estimate the number, but others were still alive. The gunman was no longer shooting at the customers, though. He had turned his attention to police officers outside. He was coming closer to windows and doors and, as he continued to shoot, more and more glass panes were falling out of their frames. He was leaving the interior of the restaurant—and himself—increasingly exposed. Sanders changed the red light condition to green—any sharpshooter seeing a clear shot at their man could take it.

SWAT sniper Charles Foster and his spotter Barry Bennett had taken up a position behind a parapet on the roof of the post office. There was a shot from the restaurant and another pane of glass exploded outwards. Bennett caught a brief glimpse of the gunman. The description matched the one he had just heard over his walkie-talkie. "All right, mister, now we can do it," he said. Chuck Foster gave his .308-calibre sniper rifle one final check.

At 5:17 P.M., four minutes after receiving the green light, Bennett spotted the gunman again. He told Foster, "There he is, right in the window. It's him." Foster rose smoothly up from behind the parapet and found Huberty in his sights. He drew in a breath, held it, and gently squeezed the trigger. The single bullet crashed into Huberty's chest just above the heart, and tore through his body, shattering the spinal column. A bullet fired simultaneously from an M-16 by an officer below Foster, and two bullets fired by a third officer with a .38 revolver, all missed. Foster's single shot was sufficient, though, and Huberty dropped to the floor. In the eerie silence following seventy-five minutes of gunfire, officers with binoculars observed Huberty's prone body (found to be alcohol- and drug-free at the subsequent autopsy), waiting to make sure he was dead. Once they were satisfied he was, SWAT personnel entered the restaurant.

The scene that greeted Jerry Sanders and his men would come to haunt them. "It was like an awful still life," Sanders told *The Times* later. "One of the little bodies I picked up . . . was about the same age as my daughter . . . I went through nightmares . . . So did a lot of the other guys . . . You can never put that vision out of your mind."

The Killer's Life

James Huberty was born in the early 1940s and raised in the golden post-war era. As a young boy in Canton, Ohio, he contracted polio and, according to his father, Earl, suffered from crooked knees and mild, spastic paralysis that occasionally caused numbness throughout his body: "His whole nervous system was hurt. It screwed him up. It made changes in him when he was little. Maybe he would get quick-tempered." The debilitating disease was not, however, the only, or indeed the most acute, source of pain for the young Huberty. When he was 7 years old, his mother, Isel, heeded a "calling" and became a missionary. By 1950, she and Earl were divorced. Their boy was deeply affected by the loss of his mother. According to David Lombardi, Pastor of the Trinity Gospel Temple in Canton, "His father raised [the family], and Huberty got embittered by it . . . [He] blamed God for taking his mother away from him."

Bertha Eggeman, who lived down the road from the Huberty farmhouse, recalled, "Jimmy was a loner—not a bad boy but someone who spent most of his time by himself . . . He just did not want to mix, he didn't want to talk to people." According to Mrs. Eggeman, guns were about the only thing that interested him. Alte Miller, an Amish farmer, agreed: "He was always a shooting guy . . . he'd shoot five heads of cabbage and pick one." After the massacre, Huberty's wife, Etna, gave her impressions of his formative years in a letter to KFMB-TV, in San Diego. "He had a very unhappy childhood. He was very sad. He came from a broken home. He was always very sad and very lonely. His only close friend was his dog Shep."

Whatever the pain and sadness of his childhood, Huberty's adult life developed happily enough. In the prosperous postwar era, when social advancement beckoned for even the least talented, Huberty, whom David Lombardi described as "halfway intelligent," made the most of the opportunities. He enrolled at Malone College, a small humanities school in Ohio, where Etna was also studying. He graduated and began training to obtain a state licence as an embalmer and funeral director. A fellow embalmer, Reverend Dennis Dean, noticed that the young Huberty possessed "a considerable ballistics knowledge . . . He was a gun collector . . . he was preoccupied with weapons and the things which various calibres could do to the human body." Loquacious on the subject of firearms, Huberty was otherwise very reserved.

In 1965, he and Etna were married at the Trinity Gospel Temple. The ceremony was performed by Pastor Lombardi, who knew both the families well. Etna's parents were active in the church and Isel Huberty had attended on occasions, too—until she received her calling to missionary work. Lombardi also knew Etna and James, although "with him you always felt a little uneasy about the way he harboured something inside. He was pent up; he was a loner and he had kind of an explosive personality."

Pent up or not, Huberty's life was progressing well. In 1971, he and Etna moved into a large, red-brick house in a middle-class section of Massillon, Ohio, about ten miles west of Canton. They redecorated the house extensively and furnished it well. Huberty had received a licence from the Pittsburgh Institute of Mortuary Science in 1965, but had not taken up a career in the funeral business. Instead, he took a job at the Babcock and Wilcox utility plant in Canton. Don Williams, the owner of the funeral home where Huberty served his apprenticeship, had "told him he was in the wrong business. He was a good embalmer but just didn't relate to people. That's why he was better as a welder. He could just pull that mask down and be by himself."

Huberty's job with Babcock and Wilcox was a good, steady one and backed up by Etna, or "propped up by a strong-willed lady," in the words of Arlen Vorsteeg (a psychologist who sat in on some of the post-massacre police interviews), the couple were able to make the payments on what Etna called their "good home," as well as on an investment property; a six-unit apartment building adjacent to the house. Huberty's career ambitions extended only as far as earning enough to provide a reasonably comfortable life and home in a nice section of town for himself and his wife—and, in time, their children—and by 1971, he had just about realized his dreams.

Huberty placed a particularly high value on a good and happy family life; the concept was extremely precious to him. When Earl put the final nail in the coffin of the old Huberty family unit by remarrying in 1972, James, who, according to his father, "didn't like that too well," set about expanding the new model and by the early 1970s they had two daughters, Zelia and Cassandra. He severed nearly all links with his father (Earl said he got to see his granddaughters just twice in the years ahead), and invested all his love in the family that he himself had created—a family which, if he was a good husband and father, would provide him with all the joy that had been absent in his childhood.

Outside his family, Huberty had no friends to speak of. He was not one for socializing, did not mix easily, and didn't appear even to like other people. "Maybe he was a good father, but he was not able to relate to people," the psychologist, Versteeg, surmised. Home and family provided him with his whole *raison d'être* and he was fiercely protective of the dream he had constructed within the four walls of that red-brick house.

He was a fanatical devotee of the conservative cultural principles relating to the sanctity of private land and property ownership and a devout believer in a man's right to circle his wagons and defend his patch of soil. He read about survivalist movements and was fascinated by them. He raised what a Massillon Police Department spokesman called "attack dogs." He put up a "No Trespassing" sign outside his property and was ever-vigilant for transgressions by people or their pets. Heated dog-related disputes between Huberty and his neighbours were common. Cindy Straight, who lived across the street, witnessed one confrontation Huberty had with her father. A stray dog had defecated on Huberty's front lawn and "He went after this poodle with a big gun and came running across the street to my dad's alley and was getting ready to shoot it when my dad stepped out. My dad convinced him not to shoot and then he told my dad never to set foot on his property or he'd kill him." According to Etna, her husband was always "a nervous person who could not take much pressure."

Aside from the continual bickering with the neighbours, Huberty and his family enjoyed a decade of generally good and happy years. With reference to their lives in Massillon, Etna wrote in her letter to KFMB-TV that her husband "felt that he was a worthwhile individule [sic]."

Everything changed, however, in the early 1980s when hard times came to the region. The Babcock and Wilcox plant was badly hit and forced to shut down. "My husband was terminated on Nov. 15, 1982," Etna wrote. "His world came crashing in around him. I immideately [sic] tried to sell the properties. The real estate person made a fraudulent purchasing agreement on the apartment house. My husband was very angry and disalusioned [sic]. Five and one half months later he got another job . . . [but he] was laid off again." Huberty remained unemployed through most of 1983 and at one point, according to Etna, tried to kill himself: "He had this little silver gun in his hand. He always played with guns. He raised it to his head. I grabbed his arm. I pried his fingers off the gun. I left the room to hide the gun. When I came back, he was sitting on the sofa crying."

Much of Huberty's aggression, however, was not self-directed but aimed at others. Terry Kelly, a former colleague, told the *Akron Beacon Journal* that Huberty once said to him, "Hey, I got nothing to live for. I got no job or anything . . . He said that if this was the end of his making a living for his family, he was going to take everyone with him. He was always talking about shooting somebody." Another former colleague, James Aslanes, recalled that Huberty "felt the country wasn't treating him right, that everything was being done against working people." He blamed his predicament on such far-off forces as the former President, Jimmy Carter, the Trilateral Commission, high interest rates and the Federal Reserve Board. His bad-mouthing of government institutions led some people to believe he was a communist. Etna disagreed. "If anything, he was a Nazi," she said.

As 1983 went on, Huberty became increasingly frustrated and bitter. In September, he was involved in a car crash. It was one of a series of accidents and vehicle-associated altercations (he was arrested for disorderly conduct at a filling station in 1980). According to Etna, the injuries he received in his September accident exacerbated the lingering pains of childhood polio and left him with a tremor in one hand.

Whereas previously it was those outside the family who bore the brunt of Huberty's wrath, now Etna and the two girls also found themselves in the firing line. In turn, Huberty, the devoted family man, only became more frustrated and bad-tempered. It was a vicious circle. He knew he had to do something, and fast—take off, uproot, anything but remain in the hard-times town of Massillon, Ohio, where the cherished dream of a happy family life was evaporating before his very eyes.

In the autumn of 1983, he and Etna were still trying to work out deals to unload the properties when, "holding a great deal of paper and seeing very little money, my husband had the idea to move to . . . California and live reasonably." Neighbours remember hearing that the Hubertys "wanted to try it out west," then, all of a sudden, the family was gone, the situation with their properties in Massillon still not resolved.

James, Etna and the children wound up in the border towns of southern California, down below San Diego. They moved more times—from apartment block to apartment block—in less than ten months than they had in the previous ten years. At the Cottonwood Apartments, where they took up residence in January 1984, they were the only Anglo family amid Spanish-speaking tenants. According to Etna, her husband "did not fit into the Mexican community. He knew no Spanish. He felt lost, rejected and hopeless . . . To his mind, everything in Ohio was done right and he could not adjust to the way things were done in California. I asked him if he wanted to go back to Ohio but he said no that there was nothing there but cold winters and high utility bills."

According to Sandra Martinez, the assistant manager of the Cottonwood Apartments, Huberty was "a quiet man who seemed like he was always mad at somebody. He was always frowning." A neighbour alleged that one night somebody tried to steal Huberty's motorcycle and that Huberty fired a shot to scare the thief off. Versteeg, the psychologist, revealed that he had also, on occasions, threatened Etna and the children with a gun, but that Etna had not taken the threats seriously: "She saw him not as mentally deranged but as isolated and lonely." She also saw that he was becoming increasingly obsessed with war.

Crushed by the loss of the good family life he had once known, Huberty found a kind of bitter joy in the idea that the whole world was going to end anyway—and, he believed, sooner rather than later. Fascinated by guns and gun magazines, violence and destruction, warfare and survivalist movements, he found it easy to picture cataclysmic scenarios; modern equivalents of Wagner von Degerloch's bloody dramatizations of apocalyptic biblical themes. At the same time, though, he seems to have been aware that this thinking was not altogether healthy and that he needed some kind of help. According to Etna, her husband walked up to a police car in San Ysidro one day, claiming to be a war criminal. The police interviewed and released him.

In June 1984, Huberty moved his family out of the Cottonwood Apartments and into another block in San Ysidro. He was no happier there. According to the *New York Times*, the apartment block "struggled to maintain a middle-class air in a down-at-the-heels neighborhood," and so did Huberty. According to other tenants, he was a clean-cut dresser, "like an executive" and virtually unapproachable. One of his new neighbours, Tim Keller, would say hello to him in passing but Huberty never responded. "He came across to me as cold. He looked like your average guy except for his facial expression. I never saw a smile on him."

Huberty had been hunting for work all around the south
San Diego area. He had applied for a job as a security guard
with the Bernstein Security Service in Chula Vista, but, said
company secretary Marianne Sides, "he didn't get hired
here. In fact, there was a big 'No' about four inches high
written on his application by the people who interviewed
him. I understand he had an attitude problem." He did,
finally, find a job with another security company, guarding
a condominium complex, but he was fired just a few weeks
later, on 10 July. By this stage, though, he seems to have
been past caring. He had "found nothing but frustrations
and broken dreams in San Diego," said Etna, and he had
already told her a month or two earlier, referring to his
suicide attempt, that she should have let him kill himself.

Around this time, Huberty received what in the event
was a final letter from his estranged father. It contained a
photograph of a mural that Earl had just finished painting
at his local church; a scene of the River Jordan flowing into
the Sea of Galilee. "I was hoping he would come by and
see it one day," Earl told reporters. "It's too late now."

On Tuesday 17 July, Huberty told his wife that he had
tried to make an appointment at a mental health clinic. He
said the clinic was going to call him back. He stationed
himself by the phone but no call came, and eventually he
got fed up of waiting and told Etna he was going to ride to
Imperial Beach on his motorcycle. When he left, Etna went
through the telephone directory, calling clinics, but no one
knew anything about a Mr. Huberty having phoned.

Investigators would also later try to verify Huberty's
claim, but with no success.

The following morning, the morning of Wednesday 18
July, the Hubertys drove up to San Diego, to the traffic court in Clairemont Mesa, where James was "favour-
ably treated," according to Police Chief William Kolender,
while disputing a ticket. Afterwards, they went to a nearby
McDonald's for lunch and then on to the San Diego Zoo. It
appears to have been at this point, while wandering among

the caged animals, that Huberty finally decided his fantasies of revenge and destruction would become a reality. "Society had their chance," he told Etna and they drove home to San Ysidro.

Some reports suggested that Huberty and his wife argued on the day of the massacre but these were discounted by police. In the afternoon, the couple were sitting in the bedroom of their apartment when Huberty got up and pulled on camouflage pants and a black T-shirt. He said he was going out. "Where are you going, honey?" Etna asked him. "Going hunting humans," he replied. He finished dressing and, as Etna wrote to KFMB-TV, "When he left the house about 3:45, he said, 'I will not be going far.' I said, 'Do you not want to stay here with us?' He said, 'No.' I called to him and told him that I had talked to Mr. Smith, the man who bought the house in Massilon [sic] Ohio, and he advised me that he would refinance the house and pay us off in October and we could buy a business. Then he left."

Etna had offered her husband a final straw to clutch at, but it was of no interest. Huberty either no longer believed in, or was no longer prepared to wait for, some possible rosy future. His life, so far as he could see it, had come to the end of the line.

When robbed, in Massillon, of his role as provider for, and protector of, his family—a role that was everything to him—he had uprooted and headed west in pursuit of his rapidly vanishing dream. In San Ysidro, he was just about as far west as a man could get and, riding his motorcycle over to the Pacific Ocean at Imperial Beach, as he took to doing, it can have been only too clear to him—looking out off the edge of the world—that he could pursue the dream no further.

With revenge in his heart, Huberty climbed into his battered old Mercury Marquis—its bumper sticker reading "I'm not deaf. I'm just ignoring you"—and headed for McDonald's, a block away on San Ysidro Boulevard.

The restaurant possessed particular qualities as a fitting location to Huberty for a grand, final gesture. First, it faced the teeming Mexican border town of Tijuana and the right-wing Huberty had a big downer on Hispanics. They had the jobs he felt he should have had and they confidently patronized what he considered to be a white middle-class restaurant. Secondly, the outlet was, after the often long wait to pass through US customs, a welcome first stop for returning American day-trippers, before speeding on their way north to the eight-lane freeways and the good life (which Huberty had failed to find) in southern California. Thirdly, McDonald's was one of the biggest corporate pedlars of idealized family life—an intoxicating never-never land of perpetual fun, laughter and happiness for mums, dads and kids, a dream world created with an annual $400 million advertising budget, a world that stood in polar opposition to Huberty's world and that cruelly, if unwittingly, mocked *his* family dreams.

"The fact is that a McDonald's restaurant was the site of the killings," said Charles Rubner, a spokesman for the company, in the wake of the massacre. His comment was intended to address the question of adverse publicity for the McDonald's Corporation, but he inadvertently highlighted a key clue to understanding the killer's twisted logic. In precisely the same way that Charles Whitman, whose dreams revolved around a college education, nominated the University of Texas as the location for a last pitched battle, so James Huberty, the disenfranchised family man, nominated a McDonald's.

Unfortunately, Rubner's perceptive comment was soon lost in the tide of impotence that was the public response to the massacre. "This could happen anywhere," said Carlos Lopez, the grandfather of one wounded victim.

5

THREE MORE MIDDLE-AGED MEN

The Florida Shopping Mall Rampage

The major themes of James Huberty's life reappear time and again in the biographies of other middle-aged gunmen. In 1987, 59-year-old William Cruse was living in semi-retirement in Palm Bay, Florida, a bright, sunny city, thirty miles south of Cape Canaveral. Cruse and his wife, a near-invalid, had moved to Florida from Kentucky two years earlier. Like Huberty, Cruse had a quick temper and few friends. His home was his life and he was obsessively concerned with the protection of his property. In Kentucky, he had a history of minor altercations with neighbours and other folk—on one occasion he was arrested for assault—and he seems to have moved to Palm Bay with the dream of enjoying a quiet and trouble-free old age.

The property he purchased was charming; a cream-coloured, stuccoed house, trimmed in redwood, with a garden full of beautiful plants and immaculately manicured shrubs. He fell in love with the property—but not with Palm Bay. Although the city continued to attract in the 1980s, as it had in the past, many retired people who shared the dream of a peaceful existence in their sunset years, an increasing number of upwardly mobile young families were also moving into town, lured by the good salaries paid by the dynamic, new high-tech industries that had sprung up in the area. Palm Bay had become, in fact, by the time Cruse moved there, one of the fastest-growing communities in Florida.

The young families were the bane of his life. The children had no respect for his property, wandering onto his lawns without so much as a second thought, and the parents were unable or unwilling to control their delinquent broods—that was the way Cruse saw it at any rate. As in Kentucky, his contact with his neighbours was largely limited to confrontations resulting from incursions onto his land. Neighbours were forever complaining about him yelling at and hounding their kids. Ron Stearn reported him to the police for allegedly chasing his 6-year-old son. Others reported him for driving after their children in his car. "He really disliked children very, very intensely," according to one neighbour, Marguerite Hall. "He was out there the minute they came home from school, to make sure they didn't bother his property, didn't walk across it."

Within months of arriving in Palm Bay, Cruse put his house up for sale. Either he could not sell it or he changed his mind about wanting to; possibly he decided that he had not come all the way to Florida only to be driven away again. Whatever the reason was, he stayed put and his resentment grew. Teenager Derek Saurez, who lived nearby, told reporters that on one occasion Cruse wrecked a swing set in a neighbour's yard and that another time he fired pistol shots in the air when children went near his garden. Other neighbours claimed that on at least two occasions Cruse had been sighted with a rifle in his possession, shouting "Get off my land." In the fall of 1986, some residents signed a petition asking that the authorities take action against him, but nothing came of it. The tense situation in the neighbourhood festered and finally came to a head on Thursday 23 April 1987.

In the early evening, two youngsters cut across Cruse's

lawn and Cruse came out of his house armed with a gun, yelling and firing. One of the teenagers was reportedly nicked by a bullet but not seriously wounded. Marguerite Hall, at home at the time, heard Cruse screaming and saw him drive away.

A short while later, a white Toyota bearing Kentucky licence plates pulled into one of the car parks that served the Sabal Palms and Palm Bay shopping centres about half a mile from Cruse's home. The retail complex was a focal point for the community—one of the few places where the otherwise dispersed residents congregated in large numbers. Young parents came to the twin shopping malls for reasonably priced goods and services; teenagers came to hang out. In fact, there was nowhere in the city quite like the malls for attracting the kinds of people William Cruse so passionately despised.

Cruse in a shopping mall was like a fox in a chicken house. Brad Roshto was closing up his jewellery store when he heard a rapid burst of shooting and turned to see an old-ish man with greying hair standing twenty feet away, firing a semi-automatic rifle. "The look on his face," Roshto said, "was like suicide." According to Gene Romanelli, owner of a pizza restaurant, "It was just pop, pop, pop and before you knew it people were running everywhere."

Waiter Ray Mendoza saw a Ford pull into the car park and bullets smash into the windscreen. The jeweller, Brad Roshto, saw a man shot in the back. A grocery store employee saw two other victims cut down in similar fashion: "He shot both of them. They were lying on the ground and he just kept shooting them." Checkout girl Jodie Pearson watched in horror as two dogs in a truck were shot. Other witnesses saw a woman in a car and a little boy get shot.

Marion Ames, a young mother who was shot in the abdomen, later described her ordeal from a hospital bed. "It was like we was ducks at the fair," she said, but she was relatively fortunate: six of the sixteen people shot by Cruse were in no position to say anything to anybody. The dead included the first police officers to arrive at the scene.

A witness said, "I looked to my left. There was this man with reddish grey hair, aiming his rifle at the cop behind the wheel before the car stopped. He was just standing there calmly squeezing off shots into the windshield. The cop never had a chance. He just slumped over the wheel." When a second police cruiser pulled into the car park, that officer did not stand a chance either.

By the time 200 officers from neighbouring communities, backed up by US Air Force canine units, converged on the shopping malls, Cruse was holed-up in a supermarket and had taken several hostages. Paramedics arriving at the scene struggled to reach the dead and wounded sprawled in the car park because of sporadic gunfire coming from the store. Police spokeswoman Louise Brown told reporters that there were thirty people on the ground but was unable to say how many were simply taking cover. The Holmes Regional Medical Center was prepared for the worst and called in its full complement of general surgeons and specialists.

Witnesses to the massacre who managed to escape out of range were ferried away in buses to a nearby store for interviews and then to City Hall for reunions with relatives. Two citizens were detained during the evening. One, who exchanged gunfire with Cruse, was released; the other, wearing a police hat, badge and revolver, was sent to a mental facility. In the streets around the shopping centres, people tuned in to TV and radio news bulletins. A taxi driver, cruising the neighbourhood, noticed "a lot of people . . . sitting around drinking beer like it's some sort of holiday." One local resident was sitting out on his porch with a shotgun across his lap.

A police negotiating team set up a telephone link and worked on Cruse throughout the evening. It was heavy going. "[He] was incoherent, rambled [and] talked about getting a car," Police Chief Charles Simmons subsequently disclosed. "He went from melancholy to fits of rage."

The negotiating team suggested he communicate with them via a hostage if he found it easier that way. Cruse nominated a young, female store clerk. "He said he was sorry he had to do this to me. Then he had me go ask the police officers [by phone] how many people were killed. That's what he wanted to know." As the siege continued, "He opened up to me. He said I was his friend. He told me he wanted to get revenge on everybody who bothered him . . . He told me he knew he was going to be dead because he had killed and paralysed people." When he started talking about committing suicide, she told him to go somewhere else to do it.

By 2:00 A.M. Cruse was still barricaded in the supermarket but had let all his hostages go free. He threatened to commit suicide and a SWAT team went in, preceded by tear gas and stun grenades. Cruse stumbled out of a rear exit where he was met by other officers, who pursued and subdued him.

Cruse was thoroughly interrogated on Friday morning but, according to Police Chief Simmons, did not appear at all concerned about what he had done. He was charged with six counts of first-degree murder, ten of attempted first-degree murder and numerous other counts, including kidnapping. Later in the day, he made a brief appearance before a Brevard County judge, Harry Stein. He gave rather oblique responses to questions about his financial status. "I had a car," he said. "I don't know what happened to it."

The Oklahoma Post Office Massacre

For James Huberty and William Cruse, a job was little more than a means to an end—both men's hearts lay in their homes—but there were other older men, with no allegiance to home and family (and deteriorating prospects of ever forming one), for whom a job was in itself an end, for whom work was the central element of their lives.

In 1986, 44-year-old Patrick Sherrill was living, as he had for most of his life, in Oklahoma City, in the heart of America's Bible Belt. He was very much like Huberty and Cruse in that he had difficulty relating to his fellows, but in one respect he was very different: he had never married and there was no warm bosom of family to compensate for his isolation from the wider society. He lived alone and his life revolved to a large extent around his job, and various hobbies—notably pistol shooting—which filled the long lonely hours outside work.

Sherrill was born on 13 November 1941. He was a strong, stocky youngster, although quiet and a little bit shy. He enjoyed sports, football in particular, and he made the Harding High School first team as a defensive lineman, substituting an injured player. According to the coach, Byron Roberts, he was a passive sort of boy who tried hard but lacked star quality. When Don Roberts, the coach's son, saw Sherrill some years later at a team reunion, "He just seemed quiet, easygoing, normal. He smiled a lot. But he was a loner."

Sherrill joined the marine corps in January 1964. He maintained a good record, as a weapons expert, until his discharge on 30 December 1966. In years to come, he would boast that he had served in Vietnam; in fact, he was stationed in the US throughout his service.

Like Howard Unruh, when Sherrill left the military, he returned home to live with his mother. Also like Unruh, he came back obsessed with warfare, guns and military apparel. "Whenever you'd see him when he first came home, he'd always be in those army fatigues," neighbour Charles Thompson recalled. "There were always guns and live ammunition and hand grenades lying around that house."

The golden post-war era was only just beginning to lose its shine in the late 1960s. To a large extent, it was still possible for a man to move relatively freely from job to job in pursuit of his dreams, and this is what Sherrill did. The list of employers he worked for included such community-orientated organizations as the Oklahoma City municipal authority and a local chapter of the American Cancer Society. Of course, as the years passed, the economy contracted and things became more difficult, but for a long time he was able to maintain his independence and his freedom of movement.

At work and in his neighbourhood—a modest community of small, neatly kept homes in the northwest of Oklahoma City—he made some attempts to foster friendships, but was handicapped by his poor social skills. He found it hard enough to form superficial bonds with people, let alone intimate relationships. "He used to whistle at me and thump his legs like he really was hot for me," according to one woman, but he made little impression on her or on any other potential partners. His most successful sexual relationship seems to have been with an extensive collection of pornographic magazines. A neighbour, Jane Thompson, told reporters that one of her abiding memories of the neighbourhood was Sherrill riding around on a "bicycle built for two—never with anybody in the second seat."

In the late 1970s, Sherrill's mother died. He had lived with her for more than thirty years and her death affected him deeply. She was the one person with whom he had experienced anything remotely like a close relationship. Janet Cox, the lawyer who handled his mother's will, had the impression that he was extremely lonely. She did a lot of work with juveniles and said he had the same look in his eyes as a newly orphaned child.

For the next eight years, Sherrill lived alone in his mother's house. The crutch of a job was more important to him than ever. He was now middle-aged—acutely aware of it judging by his sensitivity about his rapidly developing baldness—and the economy was in recession. It must have been patently clear to him that any dreams he harboured of a dynamic working life were no longer viable; secure employment was about the best he could hope for and even that was hard to come by these days.

By 1985, though, he had found a job that fitted the bill nicely—letter carrier with the United States Postal Service. His job, which was based at a large office in Edmond, twelve miles outside of Oklahoma City, filled up much of his time, and also provided the funds for him to pursue a range of hobbies and interests to fill up the rest. His home was becoming shabby through neglect, but it was stuffed with expensive electronic hardware: a computer and its accessories, and citizens' band and short-wave radio equipment. His interest in radio gave him some contact with other people, albeit at long range, but, "He wasn't well liked by anybody in the ham radio community," according to one enthusiast and was apparently refused membership of a local club.

Weapons, however, were Sherrill's greatest love. Guns and ammunition, as well as stacks of magazines like, appropriately enough, *Guns and Ammo*, littered the house. He had even set up a shooting range. It ran from the end of a hallway to the back wall of a bedroom, where targets were mounted, and he practised diligently. He was a member of the Oklahoma Air National Guard (he had joined in October 1984) and was one of its best marksmen. According to Major General Bob Morgan, "He was a quiet person, but he served the military well." He received awards for good conduct and for 100 per cent drill attendance.

As a letter carrier, however, things were not going nearly so well for him. Under increasing pressure from private courier companies, the US Postal Service was responding with stricter management and policies aimed at getting greater efficiency and productivity from employees. "It's so doggone hard to fire anybody," Hugh Bates, the President of the National Association of Postmasters, complained in 1986, citing the four levels of appeal that employees facing dismissal could go to. Military veterans like Sherrill could go a stage further, to the Merit System Protection Board. "Some people feel," Bates added, "[that] if they work for the Federal Government they can do as they please and not be fired." Sherrill can only have been relieved to have found himself in such an apparently secure position.

According to Vincent Sombrotto, the President of the National Association of Letter Carriers, complaints from his members of management intimidation and harassment were on the increase, particularly allegations of verbal abuse and threats of dismissal. Sherrill was vulnerable. According to Karleen White, a non-union carrier, "The guy couldn't carry mail—he couldn't do the job. I think if anything the union is partly to blame. I think sometimes they protect too much. This guy should have gone a long time ago."

By the summer of 1986, Sherrill had been spoken to a number of times about his poor performance and suspended at least once. He confided in a colleague, "They'll be sorry. They'll be sorry and everyone's going to know about it."

On Saturday 16 August, he was issued with two .45-calibre pistols and 200 rounds of ammunition by the Oklahoma National Guard. He was scheduled to participate in marksmanship competitions at Arcadia, Oklahoma (sponsored by the National Rifle Association), and at Little Rock, Arkansas (a National Guard contest). He was one of just a dozen Oklahoma Guard members authorized to take away weapons and ammunition. On Sunday 17 August, he was issued with another 300 rounds, ostensibly for additional practice.

Two days later, Sherrill again found himself in trouble with his supervisors at the post office. According to police, one of the supervisors involved, Bill Bland, told them that he threatened Sherrill with dismissal if his work did not improve. According to a post office spokesman, also claiming Bland as his source, there was no threat of dismissal and the meeting was classified as a "counselling" session, the lowest level of corrective action. Whichever way it was, Sherrill was sufficiently worried to telephone union officials twice to see if they could get him transferred from the Edmond facility to Oklahoma City.

On the morning of the following day, Wednesday 20 August, Sherrill drove out to Edmond, arriving at around 7:00 A.M. He was wearing his full letter carrier's uniform but his mailbag contained his two .45-calibre pistols, a .22-calibre pistol and many rounds of ammunition.

When Sherrill reached the heart of the building, he pulled out the guns. "He was in the centre of the room with two .45s blazing away," according to Larry Vercelli, one of the hundred or so people who were in the building, sorting mail and preparing for the day's deliveries. The first to die included a Vietnam veteran, one of the supervisors who had disciplined Sherrill the previous day. The other supervisor, Bill Bland, was not in the building, having reportedly overslept.

Ernest Bingham, who had been with the Postal Service for eighteen years and who had helped train Sherrill, did not realize what was happening at first. Then he saw two bodies lying by the supervisor's desk. "That's when I leapt over the counter and out the front door," he later told reporters. "All I could think [of] was getting out of there. There were several that didn't." In fact, there were many that didn't.

Mail carrier Diane Mason "got down on the floor and curled up in the smallest ball I could. I was just praying to God that when he got to me, he'd kill me quick and it wouldn't hurt. He shot and killed people to the left of me, to the right of me, all around me. I don't know how he missed getting me." When Sherrill moved away, she scrambled over the service counter and ran. "It was a miracle . . . but I almost got hit by a car when I was running across the street."

Inside the building, meanwhile, the slaughter continued. In the space of ten minutes, Sherrill shot dead fourteen people and wounded six others. Finally he killed himself with a bullet to the brain.

By the time police had sealed off the area and a SWAT team had assembled and taken up positions, there was nothing but an ominous silence emanating from the building.

Police made attempts to contact the gunman by telephone, unaware that he was already dead.

At 8:30 A.M., having failed to make contact with the gunman, the SWAT team entered the building with weapons drawn. "There was a lot of blood, a lot of bodies," Lieutenant Mike Woolridge later told newsmen. "With fourteen people, you're going to have a lot of blood."

The Kentucky Printing Plant Massacre

Joseph Wesbecker, like Charles Whitman, James Huberty and Patrick Sherrill, was born in the early 1940s. His father, a construction worker, was killed in a fall in 1943 when Joseph was little more than a year old and he was raised, an only child, by his mother, Martha, with a lot of help from grandma, Nancy Montgomery, and a host of aunts in Louisville, Kentucky.

Wesbecker was a moderate student and left high school just as soon as he could. In the prevailing climate of opportunity and prosperity, this did no serious damage to his prospects and by 1960 he had a steady job as a pressman in a printing plant. The following year he got married. The marriage produced two sons, Joseph Jun. and James, but did not last, ending with an acrimonious divorce and a bitter battle over the custody and support arrangements for the children.

In 1971, Wesbecker moved to a new job in the printing industry, also in Louisville, with the Standard Gravure Corporation. Standard Gravure, although quite a sizeable outfit, was very much run as a family business and the employees were, for the most part, content in their work and felt themselves to be "part of the family."

In marked contrast to Wesbecker's tumultuous personal life—he married a second time in 1983, but was divorced again just a year later—his working life was extremely stable. By 1986, he had spent more than twenty-five years in the printing industry, the last fifteen of them with Standard Gravure. His work record, in what was an otherwise ill-starred life, was one thing about which he could feel justifiably proud.

In 1986, though, everything changed when Standard Gravure's owners, the Bingham family, sold up. The new management's priority was to shed any excess fat on the company and to sharpen its teeth and claws, making it fit to fight in the dog-eat-dog economic climate of the day. One of the first things to go was the feeling the employees had that they were part of a family. Their futures were no longer certain.

Faced with demands from his company for greater efficiency and productivity, Wesbecker was found wanting, and he sought the help of his union. "Almost from the beginning, on the very first day, he laid it out cold and told me he was a manic depressive and was taking medication," union lawyer Herbert Segal revealed. "Some days he had good days and other times he didn't and talked about conspiracies to harass him." Whereas, previously, Wesbecker's deficiencies had been accommodated with a measure of tolerance and compassion by Standard Gravure, few allowances appear to have been made for him under the new management.

Wesbecker became obsessed with the tense labour situation. His grievances with the company encompassed the general—the relocation of an employees' car park farther from the plant and a ban on the ink-stained pressmen from using the lifts to the administrative offices—and the personal: he had been assigned to running a mechanical folder in the printing of advertising supplements but felt he could not cope with the precision and timing of the work. He complained of stress and asked to be returned to his old job, operating the ink-running wheels, but his request fell on deaf ears.

Finally, in May 1987, he lodged a complaint with Louisville's Human Relations Commission, charging that, in view of his mental disability, Standard Gravure had discriminated against him. Commission investigators confirmed that Wesbecker—by this time on sick leave—was a manic depressive and found reasonable basis for his charge of discrimination. "The rule in discrimination cases involving mental or physical disabilities is that the employer is required to reasonably accommodate the person and the condition," Gwendolyn Young, the executive director of the Human Relations Commission, explained. "As far as we know, the company, without admitting discrimination, agreed to return him to his old position when he was well enough to come back to work."

In the three years following the takeover of Standard Gravure, Wesbecker's work for the company became increasingly sporadic and his outlook increasingly bitter. A police officer who knew him said that in these latter years he became "argumentative and confrontational." Relatives said he attempted suicide on three occasions.

In 1989, Wesbecker was placed on long-term disability leave and his bitterness towards the company grew. "They done him dirty," his aunt, Mildred Higgins told the Louisville *Courier-Journal.* Colleagues knew that Wesbecker "talked about coming back and wiping the place out and how he was going to get even with the company."

Apparently no one in Wesbecker's family knew of his longstanding fascination with guns. A snub-nose .38-calibre revolver, bought from a Memphis dealer in 1974, was probably the first of the many firearms he purchased. Over the years, the collection grew to include a Colt 6-mm revolver, a shotgun and a .32-calibre revolver.

In August 1988, he began adding semi-automatic weapons to his arsenal. His first purchase was a SIG-Sauer 9-mm pistol. In February 1989, he also bought two MAC-11 pistols. Jack Tilford, a gunshop owner, recalled telling him that the MAC-11 cost $249. Wesbecker replied "At that price, I want two." In May, he returned to Tilford's store to buy an AK-47 rifle. Tilford asked him how he liked the

MAC-11 and Wesbecker said he loved it. He told Tilford on each visit that he wanted the guns for target shooting. He had a valid firearms purchase permit and, so far as Tilford could tell, "He was normal in every way."

In the summer of 1989, Nancy Montgomery, the grand-mother who had helped raise Wesbecker, died. By early September, though, his mind was focused back on the situation at Standard Gravure. According to his Aunt Mildred, "He was upset about things at work and said they will get paid back. He said things like that all the time, and I would agree with him and just listen. You know, it was just a figure of speech."

But his aunt was wrong. A week later, on Thursday 14 September, at 8:30 A.M., Wesbecker walked into the Standard Gravure Corporation plant with a sports bag full of guns and ammunition. Employee John Tingle was one of the first people to encounter him. "I told them I'd be back," Wesbecker said. Tingle asked him how he was keeping. "Fine, John. Back off and get out of the way." Wesbecker replied. None of the workers in the vicinity was about to argue. They retreated to a cloakroom and locked the door.

Wesbecker took a lift, in petty defiance of company rules, to the third floor administrative offices. Tingle speculated: "He was up there looking for bosses. He couldn't find the bosses and couldn't find the supervisors. He was just in too deep to turn back. So he just shot anything that was close to him." As he did so, he worked his way back down-stairs. In the snack bar, he fired copper-cased 7.62-mm bullets from the AK-47 rifle into a refrigerator, a vending machine, and into one of the seven people who died during the rampage. Thirteen other people were taken to hospital, most with multiple gunshot wounds, one with a heart attack. Wesbecker ended up in a pressroom in the basement where he killed himself with a shot under the chin from his SIG-Sauer pistol.

When police arrived, a worker sitting in a chair, bleeding from a stomach wound, pointed grimly at Wesbecker's body sprawled on the floor, a few yards away. On or close by the body, police found, in addition to the SIG-Sauer and the AK-47 rifle, Wesbecker's two MAC-11 semi-automatic pistols, the snub-nose .38, a bayonet and hundreds of rounds of ammunition. Standard Gravure employee Joe White told reporters, "This guy's been talking about this for a year. He's been talking about guns and *Soldier of Fortune* magazine. He's paranoid and he thought everyone was after him."

6

A Profile of the Armed Mass Killer

James Huberty had his dreams of a happy, middle-class family life shattered, William Cruse his dreams of retirement in Florida, Sherrill and Wesbecker their working lives. Howard Unruh failed to find respect and status in the community of shopkeepers where he lived all his life, Wagner von Degerloch failed to find literary fame, and Charles Whitman failed to out-succeed his father in all fields of human endeavour. Mass shootings are, manifestly, the grand, final gestures of emasculated and disillusioned men—and in the 1970s, a time of dramatic change in the factors impinging on men's prospects of success, the mass murder rate began to rise sharply.

Many thousands of men, however, have suffered failure, without going out and shooting large numbers of their fellows, and the question remains, why should just a few—a tiny minority—decide to embark upon missions of mass murderous revenge? Why is their bitterness so profound? Their empathy for their fellows in such short supply? And their desire for revenge so overwhelming? Do they share other common characteristics, beyond broken dreams, which might answer these vexing questions?

A Refined Sense of Personal Sovereignty

FBI figures for the period 1976–80 (covering all types of mass murder involving four or more victims) showed over 93 per cent of perpetrators to be male. Clearly, unless we accept that men are in some way genetically more susceptible to mass murder than women, we have to conclude that the cultural definition of the male in our societies is a key component in the creation of our killers. A further cultural dimension is evident in FBI statistics that reveal that although whites commit 50 per cent of all US murders, they are responsible for four out of five mass murders—and the percentage appears to be higher still for large-scale public slaughter. Whatever the factors are, then, that facilitate the evolution of armed mass killers, they are felt most acutely by white males.

But what are these factors? What sets the white male so markedly apart from the majority of black males and from virtually all women, black or white? The answer would seem to be that in comparison to women, with a long history of being culturally applauded for playing a submissive role in society, and in comparison to many non-whites in Western democracies, who have been conditioned to poor prospects and poverty for generations, the white male is raised with high aspirations and the expectation of an active, aggressive role for himself in society. What the white male possesses, as his birthright, is a powerful sense of himself as a sovereign individual. This sense of personal sovereignty, a necessary and valuable asset if a man is to succeed in an increasingly competitive environment, becomes, should he fail, potentially dangerous for the society that instilled it in him—for it is with a highly refined sense of personal sovereignty that the mass murderer commits his abominable deeds. "Intellectually he knows it is wrong to kill," Georgina Lloyd notes, in her study *One Was Not Enough*, "but he feels that his is a special case and it is not wrong *for him* to do so." (This also explains why those of our killers who survive their rampages show so little remorse.)

We can probably never know the precise way, or ways, in which certain men come to develop so profound a sense of personal sovereignty that they can commit mass murder. A factor that seems to be relevant, though, as far as our particular type of killer is concerned, is that he is frequently the only or eldest child of a doting mother. Freda Unruh, for example, even as her eldest boy was shooting dead her neighbours, had no harsh words for him. "Howard, oh Howard, *they're to blame* for this," she cried. Immersed in his mother's love, all his whims and fancies indulged, mom's special boy is likely to be more prone than most to believing he can do no wrong—more prone than most to being so convinced of his own specialness that no matter what evidence to the contrary confronts him in later life, his self-obsession and high opinion of himself remain paramount.

Social Isolation

The same childhood experience that perhaps helps foster our killer's profound sense of personal sovereignty, also often fosters his profound sense of social isolation—another common trait of the mass murderous. Coddled and pampered, and often prohibited from participating in the games and hurly-burly of his playmate contemporaries, he learns few early social skills. By the time he enters school, he is already typically "quiet" or "shy" and will frequently exclude himself or be excluded by his fellows from team, class and school camaraderie. His childhood passes, leaving him deficient in the complex skills of social interaction necessary for success and happiness, and he enters adulthood as a kind of mutant version of the social system's ideal man: he has a sense of personal sovereignty, but *too* strong a sense;

he feels little allegiance to those around him, but *too* little. Nevertheless, to all outward appearances, he is essentially "normal"—certainly not an obvious freak or madman.

An Obsession with Status

The mass killer also possesses, in extreme, another of the key attributes that the modern social system demands of its members; a yearning for status. This preoccupation would seem to grow in large part out of his inability to reconcile his self-obsession with the lack of attention paid him by his fellows; his high opinion of himself with the low opinion they appear to have of him. It also seems to be nurtured, though, by the position in the social hierarchy he tends to occupy.

Killers may, occasionally, like Charles Whitman, come from a first-generation middle-class family—still permeated with all the insecurities of the parvenu—or he may himself be a nervous newcomer from the lower orders, like Wagner von Degerloch. Typically, though, they occupy a position in socio-economic, and frequently geographic, terms between the lowest, poorest classes, which they abhor but into which they themselves can so easily slip if they do not constantly strive to better themselves, and the middle classes, whose solid respectability they aspire towards. In the military, they are typically corporals—the rank, incidentally, of Adolf Hitler before he made himself Führer—or privates first class. They are highly conservative and status-conscious, and are particularly susceptible to the urge to model citizenship.

A Soldier's Sensibilities

A preoccupation with guns, the military and war—with the kind of violence that, in our societies, boys from the earliest of ages are encouraged to see as the highest order of manliness and heroism—is, perhaps not surprisingly, another common thread running through the lives of so many armed mass murderers. The shy and sensitive mother's boy seems to adopt an extreme compensatory bravado and machismo (in his fantasies if not always in his day-to-day life). The intensity of this preoccupation may also be due, in part at least, to another frequently recurring feature in these killers' backgrounds; a hostile or absent father. As the killer-to-be grows towards adulthood, he comes under pressure, being the only or eldest child, to fill the role of man of the house, in cases where the father is absent, or, in cases where the father is present but hostile, to challenge his authority. Either way, the shy and sensitive mother's boy must struggle to don the ill-fitting mantle of manhood, and for such a youngster, associating himself with guns, the military and war is a most direct method of constructing for himself a manly public image.

Failure and Revenge

The killer fails to realize his dreams. As an arch-conservative and conformist who believes deeply in the dominant ideology of his culture, the pain of this social failure and rejection is acute. His love is unrequited and he becomes, like the jilted suitor who grows to hate with an intensity only possible in one who has loved with equal passion, the erstwhile object of his affections. His failure, and his feelings of powerlessness and frustration, are wholly incompatible with his narcissism and highly refined sense of personal sovereignty. He cannot come to terms with the fact that, in the broad scheme of things, he is a nobody. Possibly, if he happens to be a citizen of one of the most powerful nations on the planet, his personal powerlessness is all the more acutely felt. Possibly, if he happens to live in a culture that ferociously propagates the myth of the ease of social advancement, failure is all the more difficult for him to accept, his sense of humiliation all the more severe.

For a nation, there is no greater justification for violent retaliation than a threat to or an attack upon its sovereignty. The mass killer—a devout believer in the rightness and nobility of such a philosophy—adopts precisely the same stance when his personal sovereignty is assaulted. Indeed, it was just this phenomenon that William Bolitho observed among the mass murderous: "When he tries to explain himself," Bolitho noted in his book, *Murder for Profit*, "the murderer invariably appeals to the ethics by which 'the noblest manifestation of a nation in action' is defended."

The dialogue between mass killers and their cultures is a key clue to why their particular life histories culminate in the shooting of large numbers of their fellows—and why the United States has produced more of these killers than any other industrial nation.

The American Nightmare

Ever since the invention of the revolver, it has been a simple matter for one man to commit mass murder in the space of a few short seconds. Since the arrival, not long ago, of sophisticated semi- and fully-automatic weapons, it has become possible for him to murder more people, more efficiently than ever before. Whereas once only the most powerful, determined, or ingenious were able to perpetrate large-scale slaughters, today anyone who has a mind to, and a gun to hand, can kill with consummate ease. Like most commercial gun manufacturers, Sturm Ruger & Co., founded in the United States after the Second World War, has an egalitarian manifesto: "Produce the best-built firearms in the world, and do so at a price that anyone can afford."

Whenever an armed man goes on the rampage, firearms legislation comes under the spotlight. In the USA, many states have had, and still have, very lax laws in the area of firearms acquisition. Attempts to revise legislation have been consistently opposed by the formidable National Rifle Association, a 2.7-million-member organization with a nine-storey headquarters in Washington and an annual budget of $85 million—a powerful lobbying force in maintaining the constitutional right of US citizens "to keep and bear arms." The number of firearms in civilian hands is enormous, running to tens of millions. One-quarter of all households in the United States have at least one handgun, an estimated 135,000 children carry a gun to school *every day*, and handguns are used in 50 per cent of all US murders. In Canada, where legislation is tougher and firearms ownership less widespread, the handgun murder rate is just 10 per cent.

Most analysts agree that the incidence of murder rises with the number of guns in existence. Clearly, in the course of a dispute or robbery, if a gun is readily available then there is always a chance that, in the heat of the moment, it will be used. But this is not the whole story. If the relationship between the availability of guns and the frequency of their use was straightforward, then there would be a more or less direct statistical correlation. Unfortunately, there is not. The per capita acquisition rate for handguns, for example, is about ten times as high in the United States as it is in Canada; the per capita handgun murder rate, however, is almost *twenty* times as high. The contrasting experience of a country like Switzerland is also interesting in this respect. Switzerland operates a citizens' militia and has the highest level of private gun ownership in the world; not just any guns either, but some of the deadliest semi-automatics. The firearms murder rate, however, is low—massacres on the scale seen in the US unheard of.

What would seem to distinguish Switzerland and Canada from the United States, then, is not so much the number of guns in circulation, but differing cultural attitudes towards their use.

The American love affair with guns goes back many years. The first full-scale historical use of snipers was in the American Civil War. Many generals fell to snipers' bullets. Major General John Sedgewick was hit in the left eye at Spotsylvania, Brigadier General William Lytle was shot at Chickanauga and General John F. Reynolds at Gettysburg. Abraham Lincoln had a narrow escape in 1864, when a bullet meant for him was intercepted by a surgeon standing a few feet away.

Throughout the nineteenth century, United Empire Loyalists in Canada observed with disdain the lawlessness and violence of their southern cousins. In 1896, the incoming President of the Loyalists' Association stated in his inaugural address that no one should be surprised by the level of violence in the United States, for "did not the Revolution teach Americans that if your neighbour does not agree with you, you may shoot him, confiscate his property, and injure him to the utmost of your ability?" The violent Caesarean birth of the United States was in marked contrast to the emergence of Canada. In Canada, there was never a "wild west"—the law, in the shape of the North-West Mounted Police (now the Royal Canadian Mounted Police) preceded development. Frontier justice, which so permeated the development of the USA, had no counterpart north of the border.

In the aftermath of the 1966 massacre in Austin, Texas, *Time* reported some of the factors that, it was thought, had a bearing on the creation of mass murderers. "Some of the violence of the frontier still lingers in the American character," was one suggestion. In a sense, this is perfectly true, for although there may not be a frontier gene as such, the continuing propagation of the glory of blood-letting in all forms of popular culture has ensured, as inevitably as if it was genetically inherited, a warm place for violence and its most efficient instrument, the gun, in the hearts of successive American generations. No single characteristic differentiates the United States from other industrial nations quite as markedly as the strength of this cultural predilection. It is difficult to think, for instance, of another Western democracy where opponents of stricter gun controls would fight their case with slogans like "God, guns and guts: they made America great—Let's keep all three." Or another nation that could produce the kind of public response to an armed robbery during which a girl was shot and wounded as the Kansas City *Times*: an act "so diabolically daring and so utterly in contempt of fear that we are bound to admire it and revere its perpetrators." It is surely more than coincidence that mass shootings have been most virulent in a society that shows such overt reverence for the gun.

Another cultural cornerstone that sets the United States apart, and which would seem to have some relevance to its high mass murder rate, is the principal of massive retaliation. Most Western democracies have self-defence laws in the spirit of Section 34 of the Canadian Criminal Code: "Every one who is unlawfully assaulted and who causes death or grievous bodily harm in repelling the assault is justified if . . . he believes, on reasonable and probable grounds, that he cannot otherwise preserve himself from death or grievous bodily harm." The law in the United States, however, in the past and in many jurisdictions today, does not require the innocent party to flee, even if it is safe to do so. As regular highly-publicized cases of vigilantism demonstrate, a man is quite within his rights to respond with a level of violence that may be out of all proportion to the original menace.

This principle, in laws designed to guide individuals in appropriate and acceptable behaviour, has also guided, since the emergence of the US as a superpower, the nation's behaviour on the international stage. The dropping of atomic bombs on Japan, military action in Korea, the Middle East, South America, and Vietnam (where, a few weeks before leading his platoon into My Lai, Lieutenant Calley called in a million-dollar barrage in an attempt to dislodge just one Viet Cong sniper), exemplify the nation's self-defence principles. When the state endorses so enthusiastically the concept of massive, and if necessary pre-emptive, retaliation, can we be surprised that certain individuals, whose personal sovereignty is under threat and who perceive themselves to be persecuted, should respond in the same way? Suspicion, paranoia and feelings of persecution are certainly further significant elements in the psyche of the mass killer. His social isolation makes him more vulnerable than most to these feelings. The world also happens to be, in the late twentieth century, better equipped than ever before for encouraging them. The atomic bomb, which became the single most important fact of post-war national and international life—shaping everything from domestic economies to global politics—also began to shape, in the 1960s, many individual nightmares, as government "Duck and Cover" and "Protect and Survive" assurances were exposed as naive folly. Possible scenarios of nuclear destruction became very real with the discovery, in 1962, of Soviet missiles on Cuban soil, precipitating a major crisis. The undercurrent of anxiety— what might be termed the background level of paranoia— was further enhanced by an historical coincidence: the possibility of nuclear annihilation raised its ugly head towards the end of a millennium—just as religious organizations, both mainstream and obscure, began to trumpet the idea of imminent Armageddon.

Post-1945, and particularly from the 1960s onwards, there were many other new features of life on earth with the ability to kindle fears (legitimate or otherwise), and in this field, as in so many, the United States was in the vanguard: the development of sophisticated information storage and retrieval technology; the birth of industrial robots, and of artificial intelligence and virtual reality systems; the dawn of the space age, with its listening posts and spy satellites; the spread of electronic visual surveillance in all areas from private homes to roads, shopping centres, the workplace and airports; the exposure of the extent of the Central Intelligence Agency's secret surveillance activities; the assassinations of

President J.F. Kennedy, Robert Kennedy and Martin Luther King; the Watergate scandal; the triumph of the architecture of Mies van der Rohe and his disciples; the spread of corporate anonymity, of vast glass buildings concealing watching eyes, of sinister corporate messages—"We're thinking what you're thinking," "Just do it"—beamed direct into individual homes through the new mass medium of television.

Of all the many things that have made the late twentieth century such a breeding ground for fear and paranoia, television seems to be, in the eyes of those most susceptible, a source of particular power and influence. In the early hours of 18 January 1983, 22-year-old Bruce Blackman shot and beat to death his parents, his brother, his two sisters and a brother-in-law. He claimed that he was acting on orders received from TV shows, which had begun when he was watching *The Magic Christian*, starring Peter Sellers and Ringo Starr. He claimed that under the influence of TV programming, he killed his family in order that they might be saved from a "big bang," which he supposed was soon to destroy the world.

So many other people—murderers forming but a small proportion—have made similar claims of enslavement to television that there can be little doubt that it has the ability to exert extraordinary power over certain individuals—and not inconsiderable power over the rest of us.

Human life has certainly been changed out of all recognition by television. In the United States, the average child watches five or six hours of TV every day. There is less communication within families, and between families, than ever before. Today, many of us know more about, and empathize more readily with, television than with the people living next door.

Television has also played an enormous part in fostering suspicion of our fellows and fear of violence, in part because of its inherent antisocial nature and in part because it comprehensively distorts our view of the world. In the

United States, crime on television is over 100 times more likely to involve murder than real-life crime, while TV law enforcement officers kill at an astonishing rate. In a study of eighteen episodes of the police drama *Miami Vice*, for example, the two police characters killed thirty-eight people—five times as many killings as were committed by real police in Miami in the whole of 1985. Against this background of dramatic fictional exaggeration and distortion, factual programmes grossly over-report untypical crimes such as murder, rape and robbery. Small wonder, then, that in surveys of the populace, subjects consistently overestimate the likelihood of themselves becoming a victim of crime—and often those who perceive themselves to be the most vulnerable are those who have least to fear. In California in 1980, for example, young white women were fifteen times *less likely* to be the victims of murder than poor young black males.

That television has been a significant instrument in making us less social and sociable animals than we once were, and that it has also played a major role in the evolution of a more paranoid world, kindling irrational fears—whether it be widespread anxiety about crime and violence, or the more extreme paranoia of a Bruce Blackman—seems reasonably clear. It also seems clear that antisocial and paranoid trends will have made at least some contribution to the spread of many social ills, including, probably, mass murder. Whether or not television's influence goes beyond this, however, has been the subject of heated debate.

Certainly, as the primary cultural medium, TV reinforces with great skill and élan the dominant ideology. It does much to encourage, for example, the social ambition that drives our societies, by its aggressive insistence that being a "somebody" is enormously important and rewarding (and again, this may have some impact on our mass killers, who, as we know, are status-obsessed). Where the debate becomes most heated, though, is on the precise nature of the relationship between screen violence and real-life violence. Some studies have suggested only a tenuous connection between the two; others a very strong correlation. Either way, TV coverage of the Vietnam War—the first full-colour, televised war in history—seems to have been a watershed, violating the last vestige of death's sacrosanctity, and heralding in the modern era of casual TV killings. In the post-Vietnam War era, the kind of "designer violence" that first appeared with the likes of *Starsky and Hutch* and that continues today in shows such as *The A Team* and *Miami Vice*, is not only acceptable, but highly popular with the viewing public. In films with revenge as a theme, revenge is more violent, bloody and massive than ever before. The *Death Wish* film series is a perfect illustration.

If this kind of casual and excessive violence can indeed influence the behaviour of those who immerse themselves in it, then obviously it can have a bearing on the creation of killers. Take the emergence of a new breed of anti-hero, created by conservative drama makers in response to 1960s liberalism, civil rights gains, social protest and unrest. No figure better exemplified the qualities of this new hero than Harry Callahan, the cop played by Clint Eastwood in the 1971 movie *Dirty Harry*. It is easy to see the attraction for ultra-conservative men like James Huberty of a moderately ranked detective, short on social skills, and unappreciated by his peers and superiors, who, nevertheless, by the courage of his convictions and his ability with a gun, stamps his will on a hostile world. In fact, the maverick gun-toting loner and killer Harry Callahan, with his cool moves and one-liners—"Make my day" (echoed by George "Time to pay" Hennard, for one)—is an infinitely more appealing character for our killers than the ridiculous, gibbering psycho-sniper he hunts (or the chainsaw maniacs, lunatic dope-fiends and other deviants, for whom the guardians of public morality reserve their fiercest condemnation). The same can be said of the many dirty cops who followed in the bloody prints left by Callahan's shining cowboy boots.

Even though the studies undertaken to date have not established a causal link between media violence and real-life violence, "it appears that many of the researchers in the area are now convinced that excessive media violence increases the chances that at least some viewers will behave more violently."[1] Certainly, few analysts today are prepared to argue that screen violence has no impact at all on anyone. Consider, for example, the following sequence of events: on 15 May 1972, Arthur Bremer, who wanted to make a name for himself, attempted to assassinate Governor George C. Wallace of Alabama. Reportedly, drawing inspiration from Bremer's diaries, writer Paul Schrader drafted a screenplay, which became a Martin Scorcese-directed movie, *Taxi Driver*, starring Robert de Niro and Jodie Foster. On seeing the film, a young man called John Hinckley became infatuated with Jodie Foster. When Foster failed to respond to his letters, Hinckley decided to impress her, in the style of the film's protagonist, by shooting somebody. He shot President Ronald Reagan, the old film actor.

There has also been cross-fertilisation between life and art in the field of mass shootings. By the 1970s, the mass shooting had established itself as a murder genre in its own right, with its own rules of engagement and mythology (one wonders, for instance, at just what market the makers of the Street Sweeper semi-automatic rifle were aiming their weapon). The cases of Howard Unruh and Charles Whitman had been given enormous publicity and there was a growing body of fictional work with mass murder as a theme: *The Open Square* (1962), a novel by Ford Clarke, features a young man who climbs a tower on a Midwestern campus and opens fire on the people below (the novel pre-dates Whitman's massacre, but there was no evidence he had read it); *Targets* (1968), a film which borrowed heavily from Whitman's life but which has its climax in a drive-in cinema; and, since the 1960s, many others, including *First*

Blood (1982), a film that *Variety* described as "Socially irresponsible . . . there are enough nuts out there without giving them a hero to cheer for."

The potential for copycat cases, following a crime that is given a high media profile, is not inconsiderable. In November 1966, a student, Robert Smith, walked into a beauty parlour in Mesa, Arizona, made five women and two children lie on the floor and shot them all in the back of the head. He claimed that he had been inspired by Charles Whitman's exploits three months earlier. Probably the best example, though, of the way in which one case can inspire a veritable fashion came in 1982. It was not a case of mass shooting but of poisoning.

In October of that year, an unknown person, or persons, went into numerous retail stores in the Chicago area, bought bottles of ExtraStrength Tylenol (a pain-relieving drug), filled some of the capsules with cyanide and then returned the tampered bottles to the shelves. A 12-year-old girl, Mary Kellerman, was the first to die. Within days the number of victims had risen to seven. During the following month, there were over a hundred copycat cases in more than a dozen US states. A man who bought eyedrops, for example, wound up bathing his eyes in hydrochloric acid, while official warnings to children playing "trick or treat" on Halloween failed to prevent a record number being rushed to hospital after eating doctored treats.

Whatever other impact TV may or may not have had upon the world, it is difficult to conceive of the spread of copycat murders and attempted murders on this scale without the complicity of a vast electronic media network that consistently over-reports exceptional crimes.

Composite Portrait of the Armed Mass Killer

For all that mass shootings appear random and meaningless when looked at individually, when the examination is broadened to cover many cases and their location in time and space, patterns emerge. While we are never likely to understand all the matrixes of experiences and dynamics that can produce a mass murderous personality, there are factors known about killers: the kind of society in which they flourish best and which gender and race, in such a society, the killer will almost always come from. It would also seem that particular individual, familial and class characteristics recur with a frequency that chance alone cannot account for. Drawing on the cases and themes examined to date, it should be possible to construct what ought to be a broadly representative model of the pseudo-commando killer. Doubtless when matched against an actual killer, it will not be accurate in every detail, but there should be a reasonable and useful likeness as with a decent Photofit picture.

He will be born a white male in an upper-working-class family; occasionally a first-generation middle-class family. Very possibly he will be the only child or eldest son of a doting mother. Very possibly his father will be absent or hostile. He will tend to be extremely narcissistic, but his high opinion of himself will not be shared by his fellows. He will develop a preoccupation with guns.

By the time he is an adult, he will also have developed ambitions, expectations and a sense of personal sovereignty consistent with his gender, race and high self-regard; possibly even consistent, in an age of opportunity, with his realistic chances of success. Sooner or later, though, because of his modest social origins or his lack of talent, or both, he will discover that his dreams are beyond his means; in an era of recession, he will be particularly vulnerable.

The chasm between his ambitions and achievements will leave him with acute feelings of failure, powerlessness and frustration. Possibly these feelings will be exacerbated if he happens to be a citizen of one of the world's most powerful nations and one that also ferociously propagates the myth of the ease of social advancement.

Because of his unusual degree of narcissism, he will find it impossible to lay any of the blame for his failure at his own door. Rather, he will believe that he is being persecuted, a feeling that may be reinforced by a very specific fear, as with Wagner and Unruh, or, in the late twentieth century, by a more general paranoia (such as Huberty's obsession with such modern, amorphous institutions as the Federal Reserve Board and the Trilateral Commission). Either way, the belief that he is being persecuted will come easily to him, for he will already feel himself to be set apart from his fellows (almost certainly he will have felt this way from as far back as childhood). In addition, and characteristic of members of the military, and ex- or quasi-members, he will tend to have an underlying suspicion and contempt for civilians and civilian life.

His ability with a gun will be one of the few things about which he can feel proud. A national institution may even have recognized and applauded his ability; he may have been honoured with a prestigious marksmanship award (sharpshooter, for example) by the military. Guns will figure prominently in his thinking when his feelings of bitterness, persecution and disillusionment become sufficiently strong for him to consider seeking revenge. He will find self-justification for such a course of action remarkably easy, because he will live in a society that endorses the principle of massive and, if necessary, preemptive retaliation, a society that venerates violence as a noble and manly response to disputes and problems, and a society in which the gun is the most potent symbol of manly power.

It will dawn on him that in making a grand, final gesture ending in his own death, he will not only fulfil his desire for revenge but will achieve that which he so transparently failed to achieve in life; status. He will nominate his targets (either those people he perceives as being directly responsible for his miserable situation or his rivals, who are succeeding where he has failed) and he will select his battlefield (a place that has particular resonance for him).

Much as an aspiring young actor studies the work of the great stars of stage and screen, he may research the classic cases of rampaging gunmen. He will plan meticulously for days, weeks, months or even years, and he will train himself for peak performance. He will be disciplined in his preparations, dedicated to his task and, when the time comes, dauntless in the face of death. He will execute his plans with maximum efficiency and minimum fuss, forcibly seizing, with manly aplomb, a few brief minutes of complete control and power before dying on his chosen battlefield with his personal sovereignty reclaimed.

When all is said and done, he will have left his mark, albeit an ignoble one, upon the world.

7

DEATH UNDER AN ENGLISH HEAVEN

Alfred Ryan was 55 years old and his wife, Dorothy, would not see 35 again when their first and only child, a boy, was born on 18 May 1960. Alfred and Dorothy were overjoyed. Old enough to have been the baby's grandparents, their joy was all the more sweet and their child all the more special to them. They called him Michael, which is the name of the patron saint of soldiers, and gave him the additional kingly names of Robert, Alfred and Henry. They took the infant home to number 4 South View, Hungerford, Berkshire, a red-brick, end-of-terrace council house, where Michael was to live all his life.

According to neighbours, he received the usual overattention of an only child. "His mother doted on him and always bought things for him," said Mrs. Guytha Hunt, who lived next door to the Ryans for twenty-five years. According to Andy Richens, who attended the same school, "He was extremely close to his mother . . . He was very spoilt." Dennis Morley, a family friend, put it less diplomatically. Michael was, he said, a "spoilt little wimp . . . He used to get everything he wanted from his mother."

Alfred Ryan, a building inspector with the Hungerford Rural District Council, was, like Charles Whitman's father, a perfectionist and strict disciplinarian. Nevertheless, he allowed his wife to indulge the boy and had a tendency himself to be overprotective. According to neighbours, Michael was jealously guarded by his father.

Although South View was a quiet cul-de-sac on the outskirts of town where neighbourhood children played together in the street quite safely from an early age, Michael was only an infrequent participant. According to Colin Mason, who lived next door but one to the Ryans, "You could be playing with all your mates in the road and one day he might come and play with you . . . you might not see him again for two or three days."

At Hungerford Primary School, Michael was always on his own and never seemed a very happy child, according to Lyn Rowland, a classmate. Other children tried to include him in their games but he would be moody and sullen, and eventually they left him to his own devices. Chris Bowsher was also at primary school with Ryan: "I remember him holding his mum's hand in the playground. He seemed weak and ineffectual," but, Bowsher noted, "he was mad on Action Man."

The seeds were sown, at an early age, for what would grow into a powerful obsession with the military and war. When Michael asked for an air pistol, his mother bought him one. It was the first of many firearms he was to own. Winn Pask, a neighbour, once caught the 12-year-old Ryan shooting at cows in the pastures beyond South View with a .177 rifle. According to Andy Richens, he was not averse to taking potshots at people either: "I can clearly remember the day when a friend and I were round his house and got into the barn, which was behind the house in a field. We were just playing about like kids do when he picked up an air rifle and shot at us. We jumped out of the barn and didn't worry about it. It was just a joke that day and we never thought any more of it."

Many years later, Constance Ryan, an aunt, would recount an even more disturbing story, told her by her nephew: "He went shooting rabbits one night and he came across a fellow much bigger than himself and he got a little bit stroppy with him so Michael took a gun out of his pocket and held it at him. He said the chap ran away and he said, 'That just goes to prove the power of the gun.' "

In spite of the macho trappings—the guns, the antique swords he collected, the motorbikes his mother bought him, and, later, a series of smart new cars including an Escort XR3i and an Astra GTE—and in spite of the macho posturing recalled by his contemporaries—"He was a bit of a mad driver" and "He was always wearing a combat jacket and tearing around in his car"—Ryan's personality lagged dismally behind the image.

Bob Ponsford lived just around the corner from South View, in Priory Avenue. Ryan was, he said, "a quiet sort of bloke. He wouldn't say boo to a goose." According to David Lee, the headmaster of John O'Gaunt Secondary School, "He was unremarkable, an anonymous sort of lad." Schoolmate Andy Richens said, "He was very, very quiet and hardly mixed with other people . . . [he] was a loner really." Other schoolfellows recall, "He never mixed with anyone. He could not play football and he was picked on a lot" and "The other lads used to pick on him because he was small, but he didn't get into fights. He wouldn't have been able to stick up for himself."

If Ryan's social record at John O'Gaunt was poor, then his academic record was just as bad. He was a C-stream pupil of below-average achievement and he left school in 1976 at sixteen years of age with no qualifications. There had been little incentive for him to do well. He did not get along with his fellows, he was raised in an era when it was still just about possible for a man to carve out a successful career for himself without much of a formal education and, aside from anything else, his mother was only too happy to provide him with all his material needs.

Newcomers to the neighbourhood, Kevin and Linda Drinkwater, who moved into number 1 South View, were not slow in forming the same impression of Ryan as those who had known him all his life. Linda, who worked with Dorothy Ryan as a dinner lady at Hungerford Primary School, noticed that Michael "kept himself to himself . . . he never seemed to have any friends. And I do know that it caused a lot of people to ridicule him for being so lonely and I don't think he appreciated that very much." She would sometimes see him "with an air rifle stuck out of the back bedroom window, aiming but not firing."

Ryan, as a young man, seemed to prefer guns to girls and fast cars to friends. Linda Drinkwater "never saw him with a girlfriend," Andy Richens thought it "unlikely he had a girlfriend. He never seemed that interested in girls," and Kevin Drinkwater noticed that "like somebody would think of his wife, he thought of his car. He idolized his car and even the kids couldn't go nowhere near it. They only had to go past it and he'd be out swinging at them or sending his mother, telling them to get away from it."

When Ryan first left school, he seems to have been keen enough to make his way in the world. He enrolled in a City and Guilds building skills course at Newbury College of Further Education. According to tutor Robin Tubb, "He paid attention and he was a real tryer, but he wasn't very good. I got the feeling he was frustrated with his inadequacy . . . If you showed him how to use a chisel you would have to say 'now hit it.' " Ryan failed to gain the qualification and his life began to drift. He took what menial jobs he could get. At the same time, events at home and in the wider world were conspiring against him.

Alfred Ryan, who had retired in 1974, was now in his seventies, suffering with progressive arthritis, and a shadow of his former self. Michael was under pressure to fulfil the obligations that fell to him as the fit young man of the house, and to live up to the hopes that his mother and father had invested in their special boy. If he was not ideally equipped for such a role on leaving school, then the outlook was soon to get very much bleaker for him. In 1979, the Conservative Party, promising to modernize radically

Britain's economy and release the nation from the bondage of high taxes and inflation, captured the imagination of the voting public and swept to power.

In the building of a new England, the Prime Minister, Margaret Thatcher, looked to the United States for inspiration: "that source and model of an enterprise culture," Jeremy Seabrook wrote in *New Society*, " . . . whose variegated and colourful products include the promotion of militaristic fantasies, cults of heroes, machismo and survivalism, a vast sex and violence industry that masquerades as entertainment, a worship of fame, respect for 'the power of the gun'; and, of course, mass murders." The Prime Minister took pride in fostering a "special relationship" between Britain and the United States.

In the 1980s, the Manhattanization of London would begin; the old market town of Hungerford would come to sit in the new high-tech corridor that stretched west out of the capital along the M4, and which came to be known as Silicon Valley; the government would violently beat the trades unions down as a threat to individual liberty; Britain would embark upon probably its last colonial war, over the sovereignty of the Falkland Islands in the South Atlantic; and, in the battle against inflation, the number of unemployed would rise to unprecedented levels.

In this cultural schism, Michael Ryan, with his highly developed sense of personal sovereignty, was trying and failing pitifully to take on the mantle of manhood. He suffered long periods of unemployment. What work he did find rarely lasted longer than a few months: a job at a local health club, a job at Downe House Girls' School in Cold Ash near Newbury, where, according to gardener Fred Hayes, "He once shot a green woodpecker, which the rest of us found very offensive."

He began to lose touch with the few people from John O'Gaunt School who, at a stretch, he might have termed friends. They got married or moved out of the area. Ryan became increasingly isolated. "He didn't mix socially in the town and always went out of the town," according to one neighbour. He would occasionally be seen drinking alone in public houses to the east of Hungerford, towards Newbury and the US Air Force base at Greenham Common. Ryan was a frequent enough visitor to the Red House pub in Marsh Benham for landlord Peter Bullock to recognize him as a familiar face. "I don't think he was a loner by choice," the publican told reporters. "He just seemed inadequate." In the autopsy, Ryan's liver would show some signs of fatty tissue consistent with long-term alcohol abuse.

Meanwhile, Alfred Ryan finally succumbed to illness and died at 80 years of age. Michael tried all the harder to take on the role of man of the house. The supreme title of breadwinner continued to prove elusive, but in other areas he had his little successes. For years, his mother had made regular visits to the village of Calne, where she had been born and where her sister and brother-in-law, former Calne mayor and mayoress Steve and Nora Fairbrass, still lived. Michael dutifully took over the job of driving her out in the car to see them. "He used to drop my auntie down here for the day and have a cup of tea," his cousin, David, later recalled. "He was a quiet sort of chap, kept himself to himself."

In January 1986, Ryan began a job as a general labourer for millionaire entrepreneur Peter de Savary, working on the £6 million conversion of the nearby Littlecote estate into an American-style theme park. It was to be an historical fantasy world; at its centre was the Great Hall, decorated with well over 100 Civil War guns. Ryan worked conscientiously at the job. According to John Taylor, the Littlecote project manager, no one ever had any cause to complain about his work. Staff observed only that "he was terribly over-mothered and always dreaded going home to her."

By the early summer of 1986, the first construction phase of the theme park was complete and Ryan was once again unemployed. He would remain so for the rest of the year. He suffered a recurring and evidently psychosomatic lump in the throat, which his GP put down to stress. Ryan was worried about going bald. More tellingly, he was suffering ongoing anxiety about the death of his father and about his own miserable lack of success in filling Alfred's shoes.

If, as Linda Drinkwater said, Dorothy was "a doting mother who spoke about what her son did like any mother would," then increasingly his achievements, which Mrs. Ryan faithfully relayed to friends and neighbours, were nothing more than fantasies. Dorothy told one friend, Eileen North, that Michael had met a 95-year-old colonel, living near Hungerford, who had promised him a Porsche, Ferrari or Range Rover, and who had invited him to his tea plantation in India. Others heard that Michael was working for the colonel and was so successful in the job that he had offered Dorothy a trip to Venice on the Orient-Express and the chance to move into a five-bedroom house.

Ryan made other extravagant claims: that he had served with the 2nd Parachute Regiment, that he had a pilot's licence, that he ran an antiques shop in nearby Marlborough, and that he was engaged to be married. Eileen North heard that the fiancée was the wealthy colonel's nurse. According to Connie Ryan, Michael's aunt, "He was supposed to be married but when I phoned up after they invited us to go, his mother said, 'He doesn't know whether he wants to be married or not. First of all it's on and then it's off.' She told me, 'I'll let you know when he's made up his mind.' I didn't hear any more." Some folk heard that Ryan ended the relationship because his fiancée had refused to buy his mother a birthday present. Gun dealer Edred Gwilliam heard a slightly different story. Ryan claimed he was married to an Irish girl who had borne his child, but that she had returned to Ireland with the infant after he had caught her in bed with an elderly uncle.

Police would later be unable to discover any trace of a retired colonel, child or fiancée/wife. David Fairbrass was almost certain that the fiancée never existed: "Even his mother never once saw the girl." Ryan's other claims, about a pilot's licence, a career in the paras, and an antiques shop, were all later discovered to have been bogus. The life that he was leading people to believe he enjoyed was as unreal as the theme park he had once helped to construct. In reality, he was a failure—unemployed, unsociable, and unloved, except by his mother.

The tireless Dorothy, who had taken all sorts of jobs over the years to keep her boy in princely style, was now in her sixties, and working as hard as ever. She continued to shower money and gifts on him, extravagances like a Vauxhall Astra GTE. "She paid for his new cars every year," according to Dennis Morley. Morley also alleged that Ryan "used to hit his mother a lot." Ryan's relatives could neither confirm nor confute the claim. "We have heard these stories that he used to beat up his mother, but I don't know about that," his cousin, David Fairbrass, said. "If he did, her pride would have stopped her saying anything to the family." If Ryan was assaulting Dorothy, then had he perhaps learnt this behaviour from his father?

Although Leslie Ryan, an uncle of Michael's, insisted that Michael had been devoted to Alfred, there seems to have been some ambivalence about his feelings. Elderly patriarchs appeared in Ryan's fantasies as both benevolent and malevolent figures—on the one hand, there was the retired colonel who had promised him the world, and on the other, there was the lecherous old uncle who had displaced him in the marital bed. These, and his treatment of his mother, are juicy images for the speculation of Freudians.

But what we do know, without a shadow of a doubt, is that Ryan's long-standing obsession with guns became more profound in the autumn of 1986. He had possessed a shotgun licence from as far back as 1979, but in November 1986 he joined the Dunmore Gun Club, twenty miles north of Hungerford, in Abingdon, Oxfordshire, and applied for a general firearms certificate. As part of the screening process, he was visited by PC Ronald Hoyes, a community beat officer. PC Hoyes had worked in Hungerford for thirteen years but had never had any dealings with Ryan. So far as he could tell, Ryan was a fit and responsible person to hold a firearms certificate—and the licence was granted him on 11 December, coincidentally, the anniversary of the brutal killing of two policemen in 1876—the last murderous incident to have rocked the otherwise peaceful town of Hungerford.

In the nine months between December 1986 and August 1987, at a time when he was mostly unemployed, Michael Ryan would purchase over £1,000 worth of firearms and accessories and would succeed in having his firearms licence amended to cover his ever-growing collection.

The spring of 1987 found him still without a job—he had been out of work for almost a year by this time—and he felt obliged to take a place on a Manpower Services Commission programme for the long-term unemployed. He began his decidedly undistinguished new career, earning little more money than he had received in state benefits, in April. According to the project manager, John Gregory, "He was quiet, respectful and did his work well," but "he was not a good mixer."

As ever, Ryan tried to compensate for his social inadequacies with swaggering machismo and bravado. He boasted to colleagues that he always carried a pistol and offered to supply anyone with a gun of their choice. His colleagues were not impressed. Three months into the year-long programme, Ryan quit. He said he had found a new job with better pay, but he simply signed on again as unemployed. Four days later, on 13 July, he joined a new gun club, at the Wiltshire Shooting Centre, in Devizes. He paid the £50 fee for probationary membership by Barclaycard. As is often the case in the weeks leading up to a massacre, there was a significant increase in Ryan's shooting practice and weapons purchases. There was also a qualitative change in the type of weapons he was buying.

On 15 July, he bought a Kalashnikov AK-47 semi-automatic rifle for £295 from a gunshop in Westbury,

Charles Whitman, the University of Texas sniper, who killed sixteen people and wounded thirty others in 1966. (Associated Press)

Whitman climbed to the top of this tower on the campus and opened fire on the crowds below. (Associated Press)

Smoke rises from Whitman's gun during his ninety-minute shooting spree. He was finally shot dead by police. (Associated Press)

James Huberty, who in 1984 claimed twenty-one lives at a McDonald's restaurant in San Ysidro, California, before being shot dead by a SWAT sniper. (Rex Features Ltd.)

Bloodied and in shock, a woman sits outside the restaurant. (Rex Features Ltd.)

Police and paramedics assist other survivors of the massacre. (Rex Features Ltd.)

In 1973, five years after this high school photograph was taken, Mark Essex gained notoriety as the New Orleans Sniper. Essex shot dead nine people at a downtown hotel, before dying in a hail of police bullets. (Associated Press)

William Cruse, who claimed six lives when he went on the rampage at a Florida shopping center in 1987. (Associated Press)

Patrick Sherrill, who slaughtered fourteen co-workers and shot himself dead, at a post office in Edmond, Oklahoma, in 1986.
(Associated Press)

Joseph Wesbecker, who shot dead seven co-workers before killing
himself at a printing plant in Louisville, Kentucky in 1989.
(Associated Press)

Wiltshire. The owner of the shop, Peter Michels, would later reveal, "We have only ever sold two, one was to Ryan and the other to a policeman." Ryan's application for the addition of the 7.62-mm rifle to his firearms licence prompted another visit from police. On this occasion, PC Trevor Wainwright, whose house backed onto South View, was the visiting officer: "From local knowledge I knew he was not a yob or mixed with yobs. He was not a villain and I knew he did not have a criminal record. He was a loner but you could not hold that against him." PC Wainwright checked that the weapon would be securely housed, and Ryan's application went through without problem.

On 12 August, Ryan purchased for £150 from the Wiltshire Shooting Centre shop, a reconditioned, US-made M-1 carbine, and fifty rounds of ammunition. According to Andrew White, one of the gun club's directors, "He was a very articulate and polite man. We talked about his M-1 carbine and he seemed to know the history of the weapon and that it was used in the Second World War and Korea." Another director, David Barnard, observed, "He had obviously learnt how to handle a gun safely and was a reasonable shot—not a marksman, but possibly better than the average in the police . . . He asked all the right questions if he needed any advice."

In addition to the M-1 and AK-47, Ryan was the proud owner of three shotguns, a 9-mm Beretta pistol, a Bernadelli pistol, a CZ pistol, and an air rifle. All his weapons were legally held.

Through July and August, he practised shooting virtually every other day. On 6 August he bought more 7.62-mm ammunition, on 8 August, the M-1 and fifty rounds, and on 12 August another box of .30-calibre cartridges for the M-1.

A mission of one sort or another was evidently developing in his mind. He was preparing himself for peak performance. By the middle of August, all his energies were devoted to the task in hand. He no longer had the time or inclination to drive his mother out to Calne for her regular visits with relatives. Steve and Nora Fairbrass had not seen Dorothy for several weeks.

Ironically, at just about the same time that Ryan was embarking upon his period of intensive training, local author Christopher Priest was writing to W.H. Smith, objecting to the company stocking the kind of magazines of which Ryan was an avid reader and in which he was an occasional advertiser (an issue of *Gun Mart* carried an ad reading: "New bullet proof flak jackets. Proof up to .357 Magnum hand gun. M. Ryan, South View, Hungerford"). Priest objected to W.H. Smith on the grounds that "these magazines are pornographic in the pure sense of the word. They are written to arouse response and to encourage participation . . . The overall message throughout the editorial and in the advertisements is that killing is morally justified when performed by 'experts.' "

Ryan had what would prove to be his final training session, at the Wiltshire Shooting Centre, on Tuesday 8 August, beginning at 2:00 P.M. As a fellow club visitor, Peter Browning, a Royal Marine, would remember it, Ryan was wearing military boots, plain green fatigue trousers, a green jumper, and a shooting duvet: "He was very polite— just another guy at a gun club, a nice pleasant lad who liked to talk to people about guns."

That same day, Ryan was spotted in the Savernake Forest (a popular haunt of survivalists), on the A4, between Marlborough and Hungerford. Jean Bennett, the landlady of the Jenny Wren public house in Calne, was driving through the forest with her two children when she noticed him standing by the side of the road. He was dressed in combat clothing. He had a holster and bullet belt around his waist and he was carrying a rifle. "I looked at him and he stared back, and put his hand on the gun in his holster. I said to my son 'I don't like the look of him. He doesn't look right.' " Mrs. Bennett thought about reporting the incident to the police, but thinking about it was as far as she got. She would subsequently tell newsmen, "I feel guilty that things could have been different if I'd done something but I was just a motorist on the road, driving to see friends, and now I'm having to take the brunt for all those people who must have actually known him."

Massacre in Hungerford

The sun rose in a blue sky on Wednesday 19 August 1987. It was a fine, English summer's day. In the village of Burghfield, near Reading, Brian Godfrey, a computer technician with Racal, one of the high-tech companies that had given Silicon Valley its name, said goodbye to his wife, Susan, and his two children, Hannah and James, and left for work. Susan, a nurse, got the children ready to go out on a picnic. She dressed 2-year-old James in his Thomas the Tank Engine T-shirt and tied pink ribbons in 4-year-old Hannah's hair. The pair, as always, looked a picture.

Life had been kind to Susan Godfrey. She had a devoted husband with a good job in a boom industry; she herself, after working for a spell at the Battle Hospital, Reading had moved to the more lucrative private sector and a job in a BUPA hospital; she had a lovely home, in an affluent village, and two beautiful children. When she packed Hannah, James and the picnic into her black Nissan saloon on that morning, she had everything to live for. She drove westwards, away from Reading, along the M4 corridor, following the thread of shimmering computer company buildings, and the River Kennet back upstream, towards Newbury, Hungerford and Marlborough.

Colin, Janet and Alma, the children of Sheila and Roland Mason, had long since grown up and flown the family nest at number 6 South View, Hungerford. Today, Sheila's children had children of their own and, as was her habit on market day, she made her way to the High Street to buy sweets and comics—the little treats she always had in, ready for her grandchildren's weekend visits. The High Street clock tolled its slow, even note, a symbol of permanence and predictability, of ancient traditions and abiding serenity.

Susan Godfrey's black Nissan skirted the northern edge of Hungerford and then headed away west, on the A4, in the direction of Marlborough. Three miles out of Hungerford, near Froxfield, the family made a brief toilet-stop, at the Golden Arrow service station. A few miles before the town, they turned off the A4, into the 2,000-acre Savernake Forest. Now, the great beeches climbed around them in a dark canopy. Driving deeper into the forest, they passed tall pines, big-bellied oaks, and plantations of younger trees. Susan chose a quiet spot for their picnic and pulled the car off the road.

In Hungerford, Sheila Mason finished her shopping and made her way home to South View, laden with treats. Dorothy Ryan was also heading home, from the Elcot Park Hotel, where she had worked as a part-time waitress for the past twelve years. It was her day off but she had called in anyway, just to say hello. When Sheila arrived home, she laid out her purchases of comics and sweets on the kitchen table. Nobody knew it, but the clock in Hungerford High Street had now begun ticking away the last minutes of peace in the town.

In Savernake Forest, Susan Godfrey and her children had finished their picnic and returned to the car. Another car was now parked nearby: a silver-grey Vauxhall Astra. As Susan finished strapping Hannah and James into their seats, she was startled by the sudden appearance of a man at her shoulder. He was armed, and he took the family's blue groundsheet from the car and marched Susan 75 yards into the forest at gunpoint. No one knows what words, if any, passed between Michael Ryan and Susan Godfrey as they walked through the trees. Clearly, though, Susan— "a tiny little thing who would not hurt a fly," according to one of her Burghfield neighbours—was helpless under

Ryan's gun. One and a half hours later, police would find her body on the forest floor. The groundsheet was spread out ten yards away and there were scuff marks between it and the body. Susan had not been sexually assaulted, but she had been shot ten times in the back, had collapsed through a barbed wire fence, and then been shot a further three times.

Hannah and James, strapped in the Nissan, heard the gunshots and saw the man return to his vehicle and drive off. After a while, they managed to extricate themselves from their safety harnesses and climb out of the car. They wandered the forest until they were found, about half an hour later, by Myra Rose, a pensioner from Bournemouth who was visiting friends in Marlborough. As Mrs. Rose strolled along Grand Avenue, Hannah and James came down a hill towards her: "The little boy took my hand and the little girl who acted as spokesman said, 'A man in black shot my mummy. He has taken the car keys. James and me cannot drive a car and we are going home. We are tired.' " It was around 1:15 P.M. The murder of Susan Godfrey, brutal though it was, had been but the prelude to a massacre that was already in bloody progress, ten miles away in Hungerford.

When Ryan had driven out of Savernake Forest, he had turned right onto the A4, heading eastwards. Shortly after 12:30 P.M. Mrs. Kakaub Dean, the cashier at the Golden Arrow service station, glanced up as his Vauxhall pulled onto the forecourt. She recognized the car, and the driver as one of her regular customers. For as long as she could remember, he had called in every other day, putting a couple of gallons of Elf four-star into his car, always from the same pump. Today, the routine was slightly different. He had appeared from the opposite direction to usual and, as she watched, he opened the car boot and took out a Jerry can. He pumped just over a gallon of petrol into it, returned it to the boot, and then filled the Astra's tank.

The operation seemed to be taking him an inordinately long time. Finally, though, as the only other customer at the isolated filling station departed, he snapped the hose back on the pump, and walked towards the cashier's window, rummaging in his pockets as if searching for his wallet. Mrs. Dean turned her attention to the till. When she looked up again, she was staring down the barrel of a gun. Ryan fired, the kiosk window shattered and she dived to the floor. The bullet ricocheted around the kiosk but failed to find its target. The terrified Mrs. Dean crawled further under the counter and remained as still as she could, listening. She heard the shop door open, the sound of footsteps coming towards her, and then "his gun go click-click four or five times. I don't know if his gun jammed or he ran out of bullets." She pleaded, "Please don't, please don't," but her terror was such that it was a barely audible whisper and she would later be unsure whether he had even heard her. Presently, the gunman walked away. Mrs. Dean heard his car engine start up and, still shaking, climbed to her feet. The Vauxhall sped off, Ryan looking back over his shoulder, scowling at her. She dialled 999 and reported the incident. It was 12:40 P.M.

In South View, at about quarter to one, Margery Jackson saw Ryan's Astra pull up outside number 4. She watched him get out of the car. "He looked at me in a very vague frame of mind as if he had been upset or angry and he went inside the house." The next thing Margery knew, gunshots were echoing around South View, the air was tinged with the stench of cordite, and Ryan was back out in the street. He was armed with his Kalashnikov AK-47 rifle, his .30-calibre M-1 carbine and his 9-mm Beretta pistol. He was shooting at anything that moved.

Pensioner Dorothy Smith, who was deaf in one ear, came out of her house and began upbraiding him for disturbing the peace. "Is that you making that noise? You are frightening everybody to death," she told him. He looked at her with "a funny sort of grin on his face," and she shouted at him that he was a "stupid bugger," before Margery Jackson dashed across to her and hustled her indoors. Ryan shot and wounded Margery in the back. "He was jogging up and down. Quite a few bullets came into my home. He was running and jogging and firing . . . It was very quick fire," she recalled. Margery managed to reach her telephone and call her husband, Ivor, at work. Meanwhile, the first of a flood of 999 calls from South View was logged at 12:47 P.M.

Next door but one to Ryan's house, Roland Mason was shot six times in the chest and his wife, Sheila, was shot in the head. Ryan's immediate neighbour on the other side, Alan Lepetit, was shot and wounded in the upper arm. In a garden farther up the street, 84-year-old Abdur Khan was shot in the chest and died where he fell. In a garden backing onto Ryan's, Jane Wainwright had a narrow escape when a bullet missed her head by inches. Her husband, Trevor, was the police constable who had visited Ryan when he had applied to have his firearms licence amended to cover the Kalashnikov rifle.

At number 13 South View, 14-year-old Lisa Mildenhall and her 12-year-old sister, Marie, heard the noise in the street and ran outside to see what was happening. Robert Pascoe, a playmate of the girls, "saw Michael Ryan. He just poked the gun at Lisa and went Der! Der! Der!" As Lisa recalled it, "[Ryan] smiled at me. I fixed my eyes at his eyes and he then crouched down and aimed the rifle at me . . . He fired . . . It must have been about four shots." She was hit in the stomach and both legs, but "didn't think he had actually shot me. I thought he was messing about and my blood was a blood capsule." For a moment she stood bewildered. Then she staggered indoors and through to the kitchen. "Mummy, mummy have I been shot?" she wanted to know. Jenny Mildenhall stared in horror at the bloody apparition that was her daughter. "Everything happened so quickly . . . I said 'I don't know.' I didn't know what was going on. There was blood all over her leg . . . I just thought, I must get Sylvia." It was only when Lisa saw the look on her mother's face that she realized she had indeed been shot, and feeling suddenly weak, she fell to the floor. Jenny ran to the house of her neighbour, Sylvia Pascoe, a member of the St. John Ambulance Brigade.

By the time Margery Jackson's husband, Ivor, arrived in South View, driven by a workmate, George White, Dorothy Ryan had appeared in the street. Margery heard Mrs. Ryan shout out to both her boy and to Mr. Jackson, but to no avail. George White's car was hit eleven times in an arc of fire from Ryan's Kalashnikov. George, who had come through national service in Cyprus unscathed twenty years earlier, died from gunshot wounds to the chest and head. Ivor was hit several times in the chest, near his armpit, and once beneath the ear. He was alive, but his only chance of staying that way was to play dead. The ploy worked. Ryan moved back down the street—and shot his 63-year-old mother twice in the stomach. Dorothy fell face down in the road. He walked up to her, pointed the Kalashnikov at her back and fired two more shots into her at close range.

Farther down the street, at number 13, Jenny Mildenhall made it safely back home with Sylvia Pascoe and another neighbour, Fiona Pask. "Lisa was in the kitchen when I got there," Sylvia later recalled. "Blood was gushing from her thigh. She was being very brave. She seemed more concerned about her pink trousers . . . She's one of my cadets and she knew what to do. She told me where it hurt. I got her leg up and held padding on it to stop the bleeding." It would be forty-five minutes before an ambulance was able to reach them. In the meantime, as Jenny said, "the shooting was still going on. It was so loud. It sounded terrible, like firecrackers one after another."

PC Roger Brereton was the first police officer to respond to the emergency. Nothing in his fourteen years' experience with the Thames Valley Force had prepared him for the carnage he was about to encounter. When he turned his patrol car off Fairview Road, into South View, he found himself in the middle of a bloody battlefield. All of a sudden, Michael Ryan appeared in the rear-view mirror, and opened fire. The vehicle was raked with twenty-four bullets. The police radio controller received the message, "18. 10-9. 10-9," the code for "Urgent assistance required. I have been shot," then heard no more. PC Brereton was dead at the wheel.

The first ambulance on the scene also came under fire. Linda Bright and Hazel Haslett had been called out to what they thought was a shotgun injury. As they made their way along Fairview Road, they heard a repetitive noise like machine-gun fire. Nevertheless, they continued towards their destination. As they reversed into South View, Hazel suddenly caught sight of Ryan. He opened fire and she yelled at Linda to drive off. The windscreen shattered but, fortunately, deflected the bullet and Linda slammed the accelerator to the floor. The ambulance sped away up South View. Once back in Fairview Road, Linda pulled the vehicle to a halt. Hazel radioed in that they had come under fire and then they took refuge in a nearby old folks' home.

A pall of thick, black smoke was now rising above South View. Ryan had set fire to his mother's house and the flames had begun to spread to other houses in the block. Fire crews were unable to tackle the blaze for fear of being shot. The first engine on the scene had attracted gunfire and quickly retreated on police advice.

The emergency services had been overwhelmed with telephone calls and continued to be so. There were far too many coming in for the information to be quickly and accurately collated. Reported sightings of the gunman often contradicted one another. Nobody knew for sure exactly where Ryan was at any given moment during the rampage— except those who were unlucky enough to cross his path.

He made his way south, along Fairview Road, towards Priory Avenue, nipping in and out of side streets as he went, leaving dead and wounded in his wake. Ken Clements, a former soldier, was shot in the stomach as he walked his dog along a footpath near South View. He died clutching the dog's lead; it would still be in his hand when the pathologist examined him later.

Three residents of Clarks Gardens, a street running parallel to South View and backing onto it, were shot and wounded: Linda and Alison Chapman and pensioner Betty Tollady. Betty was in her house when she heard the sound of gunfire. Her first thought was that children were messing around with fireworks. She went out into the garden, shouting, "For God's sake, stop that noise, it's getting me down." Ryan turned around and shot her. The bullet entered at her groin, shattered part of the pelvis and sciatic nerve, before exiting from her back. Betty fell to the ground with no feeling in one leg from the knee down. She managed to crawl back into the house and dial 999.

Retired publican Douglas Wainwright and his wife, Kathleen, had driven from Strood, in Kent, to visit their police constable son, Trevor. As they drove along Fairview Road, their windscreen suddenly shattered. "Automatically my husband put his foot on the brake," Kathleen would later recall. "As we stopped, there was this man right opposite my husband's window on the pavement. I heard about six or eight shots . . . It was this man, he had a blank expression on his face. The gun was pointed at my husband's window. I heard my husband groan twice. I looked at him . . . Blood trickled down his nose and out of his mouth and he fell to one side." Kathleen had also been hit but felt nothing more than a stinging sensation in her breast and hand. She looked up as Ryan walked to the front of the car and started reloading his gun. She thought he was going to fire at her again, but he just kept walking past the car and off down the road. Kathleen ran in the opposite direction. She had been wounded in the chest and one of her hands was mutilated. Her husband was dead, buckled over in the driving seat of their bullet-riddled car. PC Trevor Wainwright would later learn of his parents' fate as he worked frantically at the police station, preparing maps and street plans for the armed officers who would be coming from Newbury, Oxford and Reading. Ryan, meanwhile, had Hungerford at his mercy.

Craftsman Eric Vardy, who worked for the Norland Nursery Nurse Training College, was on his way to a building supplies company in the college's van, when the windscreen suddenly shattered. Eric's body "jumped up and slumped," according to passenger Steve Ball. Then the van careered out of control, mounted the pavement and smashed into a telegraph pole. Ryan moved off down Priory Avenue. Chris Bowsher, who had taken cover in a nearby property, came out of hiding and rushed over to the crashed van, but there was little he could do to help: "The driver was in a dreadful state with most of his face and throat shot away." Eric Vardy, who had only recently nursed his wife through a life-threatening illness, died of a massive haemorrhage.

As the sound of gunshots receded, other people in South View and Fairview Road ventured into the street again. Ambulancewomen Linda Bright and Hazel Haslett left the old folks' home to go to the aid of the wounded. Outside, according to Linda, "there was mayhem." The Norland van was skewed across the pavement, just opposite, and over towards South View two more bullet-riddled vehicles sat in the street, Douglas Wainwright and George White slumped dead behind their steering wheels.

In South View itself, where the fire in the first block of houses was now raging out of control, PC Brereton's patrol car sat gathering soot, along with Ryan's Astra and deceased mother—all three ravaged by bullets. In the boot of Ryan's car, police would later find an extensive survival kit: a NATO poncho/groundsheet, a waterproof jacket and trousers, battledress trousers, body armour and thermal underwear; a respirator mask, a balaclava, ear defenders, a shoulder holster, a Swiss Army knife and waterproof matches; a flask of brandy, wound dressings and other first-aid equipment.

Still Ryan roamed the streets of Hungerford, killing and

maiming, picking off vehicles and their occupants, pedestrians on the streets, and people in their homes. Plant fitter Kevin Lance was shot and wounded in his van. The bullet hit him in the right wrist, travelled up his arm and lodged near his elbow. He accelerated away to the safety of a side street, ditched the van and ran back to his company office nearby. It was his twentieth birthday and he would spend the rest of it in hospital. Two people had narrow escapes when Ryan's bullets shattered their windscreens, but they remained unhurt.

Carl Nethser, from Suffolk, was visiting friends in Hungerford. He was walking down the road when he saw Ryan coming towards him. Ryan opened fire, the shot missed and Carl found refuge in a garden. Jennifer Hibberd got a close look at the gunman when he passed within twelve feet of her: "His face was sweaty with red blotches. I could see he had a smile on his face, half grinning."

Ryan went on a short detour into the streets near the war memorial, cricket ground and swimming pool. Seeing and hearing his approach, three swimming pool employees, Carol Hall, Michael Palmer and David Sparrow, shepherded about two dozen children to safety. Meanwhile, a burst of gunfire raked a taxicab. The driver, Marcus Barnard, who had lived in Hungerford all his life, was hit in the head. The swimming pool employees went to his aid, but he was already dead.

In the war memorial gardens, a man who was walking his dog was shot, Ryan firing again at the prone body. Bystander Leslie Bean tried to help the victim. Kenneth Hall, a local government officer, had also witnessed the shooting. "I could not believe what I had just seen. [Ryan] threw the gun to the floor in front of him as if in disgust. He looked down at the gun and shook his head from time to time." The weapon that the killer abandoned near the war memorial was, ironically, the Second World War reconditioned M-1 carbine. He had fired just one shot from its fifteen-round magazine before forsaking it and switching back to the favoured Kalashnikov. Leslie Bean tried to staunch the flow of blood from a large exit wound in the victim's back, but it was a losing battle.

Ryan, meanwhile, had moved on to fresh territory. Priory Road, which forks away south from the High Street, was one long and ragged wound by the time he had shot his way through it. Carl Harries, a lance corporal in the Royal Engineers, was on leave and visiting his parents. He heard shooting in Priory Road and encountered Ryan when he went to investigate. Ryan took a shot at him and Carl threw himself into a hedge to evade the bullet. Then, the gunman turned his attention to a Renault 5, driven by a young building society clerk, Sandra Hill. The car came awkwardly to a halt. Ryan moved off down the street and Carl Harries disentangled himself from the hedge and went over to the vehicle. He turned off the engine and the blaring radio. When Martin Pearcey, who lived nearby, came across to help, he saw straightaway that "a bullet had gone into her arm and out of her back . . . She was covered in blood." As Carl Harries lifted her out of the car, she gurgled at him through a crimson mouth: "She kept trying to tell me she was going. I told her she was not, but she died a few minutes later." Martin Pearcey "waited twenty minutes for an ambulance to arrive, but she died in about three . . . She never had a chance."

After doing what he could for Sandra, Lance Corporal Harries made his way farther along the road to help a family in a Ford Sierra: Ian Playle, Chief Clerk to West Berkshire Magistrates, his wife, Elizabeth, and their two children, 6-year-old Richard and 18-month-old Sarah-Jane. According to Elizabeth, as they drove along Priory Road, "The car started making a whirring sound and I turned round to ask Ian what the matter was and there was blood pouring from his neck and we crashed into another car." When Carl Harries arrived, Liz, a nurse, was "holding some kind of rag into the guy's neck screaming, 'He's gone, he's gone.' " In fact, Ian would cling tenuously to life for forty-eight hours before succumbing to the wound at the John Radcliffe Hospital in Oxford. It was an inappropriately violent and early death for the Black Watch Regiment soldier's son who had chosen a civilian life.

Elizabeth Playle would later allege that the family had been diverted by police into the gunman's path. Kathleen Wainwright would tell a similar story, as would Eric Vardy's widow, and a Swindon businessman, Nigel Green. Police, unfortunately, had still been unable to track Ryan down. By the time officers on the ground received information as to his whereabouts, the information was often already out of date; Ryan would be at some new location causing mayhem.

Jenny Barnard, the wife of the cabbie, Marcus, was at home—with their baby son, Joe. A police helicopter was sweeping back and forth overhead and outside she could see armed policemen. She called through the window to one of the officers, "Can you tell me about my husband . . . I think he's been shot . . . he's the taxi driver," but the officer could only advise her to keep away from the window; "I can't tell you anything, I've just been dropped here . . . I don't really know where I am to be honest."

In Priory Road, Carl Harries was discovering more victims. "I walked back up the road and all the way was carnage." In the kitchen of number 60, he made probably his most grisly discovery. It was the home of Victor Gibbs, known as Jack, and his wife, Myrtle. Jack, a retired company director, had served with the RAF in the Second World War, and Myrtle had been an army sergeant. They had first met at Hungerford Primary School. Ryan assaulted the couple so violently that Carl Harries was prompted to say that he not so much shot them as "blew them apart." Jack apparently threw himself in front of Myrtle to protect her, but four bullets nevertheless found their way into his wife's body. Jack died instantly. Myrtle died after a seven-hour operation at the Princess Margaret Hospital in Swindon. She had been ill for several years and, as her son said, "There was never any real hope that she would pull through."

At 1:52 P.M., the caretaker of John O'Gaunt Secondary School, at the opposite end of Priory Road to the High Street, reported seeing a man entering the building. It was Michael Ryan. His rampage through the town was over. He had fired 119 times that police were able to verify, including eighty-four armour-piercing bullets; fifteen vehicles had been riddled with a total of eighty bullets and sixteen people lay dead or dying.

It was only when Ryan began talking with a police negotiator, Sergeant Paul Brightwell, at 5:30 P.M., that the authorities were able to confirm that the man holed up in John O'Gaunt was their suspect. According to Chief Constable Colin Smith, "He seemed lucid and reasonable" as he spoke with the sergeant over the next hour and twenty-three minutes.

"What are the casualty figures?" he wanted to know.

"I don't know. Obviously you know you shot a lot of people," Sergeant Brightwell replied.

"Hungerford must be a bit of a mess."

"You are right. They know you've been through. How many do you think you shot?"

"I don't know. It's like a bad dream."

"It happened. The sooner you come out the easier it will be to sort out."

"I know it's happened. I'm not stupid. How's my mother? She's dead, isn't she?"

Ryan asked repeatedly about his mother. He made no fewer than fourteen pleas to have her status confirmed.

"I didn't mean to kill her. It was a mistake," he said.

"I understand that," the sergeant replied.

"How can you understand? I wish I had stayed in bed."

Although Ryan described the day's events as being like a bad dream, his concern was principally for his mother, his pet Labrador, which he had also pumped full of bullets—"Will you give it a decent burial?"—and himself: "Will I go to prison for a long time? I'll get life won't I?" He implied, on several occasions that things had not gone quite as he had planned. "If only the police car hadn't turned up. If only my car had started," he mused at one point. Several times he talked about suicide. He threw the magazine of a pistol out of the window, but said he had kept one round in reserve. When asked why, he replied "It's obvious isn't it?"

In spite of the threats to kill himself and his claim to have an Israeli fragmentation grenade in his possession, the police were fairly confident of bringing the siege to a peaceful conclusion. As well as the pistol magazine, he had also thrown out the Kalashnikov and confirmed that he was holding no hostages. Sergeant Brightwell urged him not to do anything rash.

"Don't worry," Ryan replied. "I have nothing against you. You have got your job to do."

"Leave all your weapons in the room and come down," the sergeant suggested. Silence from Ryan. "Can you hear me?"

"Yes," Ryan responded.

The pair had now been talking for over an hour.

"I want to think about it," Ryan said. "I'm not coming out until I know about my mother."

He pleaded with the sergeant to use his radio to find out Dorothy's status. He talked about suicide again: "It's funny. I've killed all these people but I haven't got the guts to blow my brains out."

Earlier Ryan had "just popped up at the window" of the upper-storey classroom where he had taken refuge. A police marksman, Sergeant Derek Warwick, had held him in his sights for a full minute, without shooting. "I believe he might have done that so that we would do the business for him," Sergeant Warwick said at the inquest. He defended admirably his decision not to shoot: "If I had fired then I would have been a murderer. I would have been no better than him . . . You have got to have the justification. The justification wasn't there . . . We were there to bring that man before a court; we are not judge, jury and executioner all in one."

In the event, Ryan killed himself. At 6:45 P.M., he broke off the conversation with Sergeant Brightwell. There were seven minutes of silence, then the sound of a muffled shot. It was turned eight o'clock when police finally entered the classroom. Ryan was slumped against the wall, his legs splayed, his chin on his chest. Tied to his right wrist with a bootlace was his Beretta. Splashed up the classroom wall were his blood and brains. He had fired a single shot from the Beretta into the right side of his head. The police, alert to the possibility that he may have booby-trapped his own body, gingerly tied a rope to one leg and retreated. They tugged the rope and the corpse toppled harmlessly over.

For Ryan, the bad dream had come to an end. For the people of Hungerford, it was to continue. As one young girl said, "I think that Michael Ryan is still alive. I think that he's going to jump out on me from anywhere and just kill me."

The Aftermath

In the late afternoon of Wednesday 19 August, Hungerford was not only on its knees but was being trampled while it was down. Hordes of newsmen were stampeding through the town, retracing Ryan's bloody steps in a kind of grotesque action replay. Press photographers, heavily armed with sophisticated, rapid-fire cameras, semi-automatics and long-barrelled telephoto lenses, television news crew technicians, carrying bandoliers of accessories, soundmen, aiming boom microphones from the hip and cameramen levelling cameras from the shoulder—were all advancing through Hungerford, shooting any unfortunate victim they chanced upon.

For hours, many of the dead lay where they had fallen. In a garden on Fairview Road, George Renwick kept a solitary vigil beside the body of his father-in-law, Abdur Khan, until the body was removed later in the evening.

Jenny Barnard, who had been worried about Marcus all

afternoon, finally had her worst fears confirmed at about 7:00 P.M. She packed a few things in a bag for herself and baby Joe, "And then we left here, and as we were going to the car Mum said, 'Now you're going to have to be very brave, because we have to actually drive past Barney's car,' and she said, 'Just put your head down and just don't look.'" But Jenny could not help herself; she had to see.

Barney's cab stood in the day's last light. The driver's door was open and a police photographer fluttered around like an enormous moth. In the road, lay the black, pupa-shaped form of a body bag. Jenny stared at it in horror. "It was just his hand, you know, that's all I could see of him." A policeman hastily waved them past, but it was too late. Jenny could no more dislodge the image from her brain than her husband could the bullet from his. It would come to haunt her. She would see it again and again in TV news broadcasts, which she could switch off if she wanted to, and in nightmares, which she could not.

Colin Mason was at the Three Swans Hotel when he finally learned that his parents, Roland and Sheila, were among the dead. Colin had been working near South View when the shooting started. He had telephoned his mum and dad, but the phone had not been answered. He had tried to drive to see them but the road had been blocked by an ambulance. Breaking the news to his children would be heart-rending—"We'd better take a blanket up to Nanny and Grandad, because they'll be cold," little Laura would say—but at least the family were able to grieve together.

For many people in Hungerford, the night of Wednesday 19 August was the longest of their lives. The dawn of Thursday brought little relief. The grief and bewilderment were still there, and there was anger, too, at the media, the emergency services and, in the absence of Michael Ryan, at his corpse. "If Ryan's body is put in any churchyard in Hungerford it will be dug up and thrown out," said one relative of a seriously wounded victim.

In contrast, those who had crossed Ryan's path and

escaped in one piece, experienced a strange kind of euphoria. The overall mood in the town, though, in the first days after the rampage, was best described by social worker Don Phillip: "People are bumping their cars and wandering around like zombies at the moment . . . we are all being very absent-minded as a result of the tragedy. The advice is to be careful about driving and be very tolerant towards one another."

In a town full of policemen, television crews and ghoulish tourists armed with newspaper clippings, wounds were slow to heal and the scars were big and ugly. At the Princess Margaret Hospital in Swindon, Ivor and Margery Jackson refused to return to the South View house where they had lived for fifteen years, and asked the council to rehouse them. "My father fell apart in hospital when he heard they had to go back before the council would help," Susan Hayes, the Jacksons' daughter disclosed. "My parents just cannot face it. They cannot even bear the thought of getting into a car and driving up the road." The Mayor of Hungerford, Ron Tarry, revealed, after visiting Ivor, the full, wretched picture of an utterly broken man: "Mr. Jackson said he'd rather go to an asylum than back there."

A month after the massacre, the first four burnt-out homes in South View had been bulldozed by Newbury District Council and four of the remaining twelve houses lay empty, their occupants having moved out in the wake of the killings. At John O'Gaunt School, Room 6 was as profound a source of terror for some children as Room 101 was for the citizens of Oceania in George Orwell's novel *Nineteen Eighty-four*.

A year after the massacre, there were still many wounds stubbornly refusing to heal. PC Roger Brereton's widow, Liz, told *Woman's Own* that only concern for her children had prevented her from killing herself. She still talks, she said, to her husband's photograph. A year and three lengthy operations after the massacre, wounded pensioner Betty Tollady revealed "I haven't been able to cry since this happened."

The Lessons of Hungerford

"We must learn the lessons of the Hungerford massacre," the authorities quickly asserted in the immediate aftermath of the tragedy. This was, however, something of a Trojan horse. In the new Britain of the 1980s the move to define Ryan solely in terms of bizarre, individual psychopathology was swift and overwhelming.

On the very day of the massacre, Dr. Anthony Clare, armed with only the sketchiest details of Ryan's life history, told *The Times*, "He appears to have been a loner with an odd personality who was unbalanced by the death of his father and eventually went mad." The agenda was thus firmly restricted to the area between Ryan's ears and the debate to ways of what the *Sunday Times* called "Disarming the deranged." There was only one, inevitable conclusion to be reached from such a debate and Conservative MP John Wheeler expressed it as succinctly as anyone: "The law and licensing cannot stop people from going mad." The only lessons to be learnt, then, as far as the state was concerned, had to do with the best ways of helping victims grieve and "come to terms" with the trauma of such tragedies.

Chris Hunter, the director of the Park Lane top security hospital in Liverpool, was one of the few people publicly to voice criticism about the idea of simply labelling Ryan insane and terminating the debate there: "People would like to think that someone who would [commit mass murder] will fit into a category because that makes them feel more comfortable. It doesn't serve any scientific purpose, but it satisfies a need that we have to render something understandable that appears to be inexplicable."

Certainly, there were puzzling features to the Ryan case. The killing of Susan Godfrey, for instance. Although Susan, with her good looks, elegant car and two beautiful children, could not have been a more attractive representative of the self-assured, middle-class world that Ryan so coveted and to which he aspired in his fantasies, there are almost endless possibilities for what he was actually intending at this early stage of his mission. Possibly, he planned to rape Susan, kill her and then commit his massacre. Did he feel he was entitled to lose his virginity before going to war? Possibly, he planned to rape her, but not kill her, before going on the rampage—and only killed her because she put up a struggle. Perhaps, he never intended to rape her at all. Was he simply testing his ability to kill in the relative safety of the forest? And what did Ryan mean when he said, "If only the police car hadn't turned up. If only my car had started"? But such questions were not even posed in the public debate, for they were well outside its narrow purview.

That a mass shooting could have occurred at all was bewildering enough; that it occurred in a Berkshire town, in the very heart of England, was downright incomprehensible. And yet the evidence of the experience in the United States already pointed clearly to the fact that this type of crime has little to do with inner-city deprivation and terminal poverty—that Hungerford was, in fact, exactly the kind of small, decent community where one might *expect* violence of this kind to explode.

Similarly, Ryan possessed all the key characteristics of his American counterparts. All that was needed was a social shift to bring British cultural values more in line with those of the United States and he could plunder doctrine from the common stock to build for himself the identity of avenging commando-killer.

By 1987, the post-war political, economic and military partnership between the smaller Western democracies and their big brother, the United States, had also become, to a large extent, a cultural alliance. Britain, like other nations in Europe and Australasia, had assimilated vast amounts of US culture; everything from Big Macs and milkshakes to .44 Magnums. Through Michael Ryan's teenage years, not only did the video age dawn and the import of American TV programmes grow, but the indigenous entertainment industry also began embracing American values. A pilot programme for a new police series, in 1974, opened with a dawn raid by gun-toting "dirty cop" Jack Regan. *The Sweeney* (interestingly, the original title was *The Outcasts*), broke new ground for home-produced gun-glorifying dramas such as *The Professionals* and *Dempsey and Makepeace*. One of the consequences of this new fast gun, kick-ass diet could be the phenomenon that Anthony Beevor noted in *Inside the British Army*: "Sergeants were . . . dismayed at the change in the recruits they had been getting since about 1987. (Right across the army almost everyone puts their finger on that year, although nobody can give a satisfactory explanation.) . . . [One sergeant] felt that they had little grasp of reality and that their expectations of the army were based on film fantasies."[1]

In the aftermath of the Hungerford shootings, television companies pulled a plethora of violent programmes out of their schedules, to allow the nation a reasonable period of gun-free mourning. In Hungerford, video hire shops removed violent films from their shelves. The owner of the Video Shack, in Reading, however kept violent films—and reported a significant increase in demand for *Rambo* videos: "The films had been waning in popularity but since the massacre, hirings have been above average."

Even more disturbing, Mick Ranger, the sole UK importer of Kalashnikov rifles, reported an increase in sales of the weapon after the massacre. The rise was, however, he said, a pure coincidence. Sales figures for toy versions of the Kalashnikov, which Woolworth's stores were finally shamed into withdrawing at the end of September, are not known.

If the gun, in England, once principally a sporting icon, came to represent something altogether different in Ryan's formative years, then, under the auspices of the government from 1979 onwards, other key components of the type of culture that has proved most sympathetic to the spawning of pseudo-commandos, were resolutely fostered: the fervent exaltation of the individual, the propagation of the myth of the ease of social advancement, the ready adoption of confrontation in preference to consultation and the official sanctioning of force as an appropriate response to disputes and problems whether it be tackling miners in the Yorkshire coalfields, hippies on the plains of Wiltshire, or Argentinians in the South Atlantic. In such a cultural climate, there would need to be only one man, possessing the credentials discussed in the last chapter, young enough to have been raised on cross-cultural US-UK values, and with access to firearms, for a gun massacre to be a real possibility. Michael Ryan's rampage was the most destructive, but there were others.

On Wednesday 6 January 1988, 16-year-old Darren Fowler, the eldest of four brothers, went on a shooting spree at his Northamptonshire school, wounding four people, one seriously, with a shotgun, before being overpowered. Fowler had been expelled from the school four months earlier. He was described as a loner. He had been subjected to verbal abuse from other pupils who called him "smelly" and "gypsy" because of his poor personal hygiene. He was preoccupied with warfare and weapons, and, according to Detective Superintendent David Johnson, of the Northamptonshire police, "had a very great interest in the Hungerford massacre and had studied the case history quite closely. He could discuss the details of that massacre with apparent authority."

On Sunday 30 April 1989, in a suburb of Whitley Bay, a quiet seaside town in northeast England, 22-year-old Robert Sartin went on the rampage with a shotgun. He shot fifteen people, one fatally, having told his victim, "It is your day to die." Sartin, a Department of Social Security clerk, was described as quiet, shy and preoccupied with the Hungerford massacre. He still lived with his parents and on the morning of the shootings, his mother had given him breakfast in bed.

8

The Failed Soldier

*E*ngland was not the only country suddenly to start spawning in the 1980s pseudo-commando killers. Many other countries connected to the international, electronic media network also began to experience the phenomenon. There was a worldwide explosion of cases. The experience of other nations differed from the United States' in just one significant respect. While the list of American armed mass killers included numerous middle-aged men, in Australia, Canada and Europe, the forty- or fifty-year-old gunman was virtually unknown. Like Michael Ryan, they were all young men—men who had been raised in the TV age and been exposed, in their formative years, to a far more substantial amount of US culture than their forefathers.

On 10 November 1988, a 20-year-old former army officer cadet, Julian Knight, was sentenced to 460 years in jail for crimes he committed one August evening, fifteen months earlier, in the Clifton Hill suburb of Melbourne. It took him close to twenty minutes to plead guilty to the charges against him, seven murder charges and forty-six charges of attempted murder.

Julian Knight was born in March 1968 and was adopted

by an army family when he was ten days old. His adoptive father was in the education corps and taught English and maths. For the first thirteen years of his life, Julian was never in one place for very long. The family moved frequently, both within Australia—Laverton, Melbourne and Puckapunyal—and abroad: Hong Kong and Singapore. He was apparently reasonably happy in his early childhood. According to his own testimony, he admired his father, was close to both his parents, but especially his mother, and got along well with his younger brother and sister. He also had a great affinity for the military. He assimilated the whole army ethos with unusual passion and speed, and set his heart on becoming a soldier at an early age.

In 1980, when Julian was 12, his parents separated. He gave most people the impression that he had been expecting the split—and the divorce that followed—and that he was not unduly upset. However, a girlfriend would reveal that as late as 1986 he had still not come to terms with the divorce and would often cry about it. Knight himself would later tell a psychiatrist that he was angry because his parents had kept him completely in the dark about their intentions.

As so often with killers, there was a world inside Knight's head that was rarely glimpsed by those around him. In Knight's case, as with Wagner von Degerloch, beer-drinking bouts would occasionally result in this secret world seeping into the public arena, allowing those present a fleeting look at a psyche that was conspicuously out of harmony with its owner's public persona. In 1982, however, when the newly divorced Mrs. Knight and her three children moved into Ramsden Street, in the Clifton Hill suburb of Melbourne, 14-year-old Julian had not yet taken to heavy beer drinking and his distress about the divorce, as well as the many other facets of his secret world—particularly the extent and the morbid nature of his obsession with the military—remained completely hidden from public view.

In school, according to one friend, Giulia Bagglo, "he

was always the class clown, making jokes, entertaining everybody . . . He was very funny and he was pretty smart, pretty intelligent—always had pretty good marks." According to teachers, though, he was overconfident, and was not altogether convincing as a wisecracking extrovert. His antics earned him a certain amount of popularity with his peers, but at least one teacher felt that his extroversion was rather forced and that, basically, he was a loner.

Knight's love of the military was obvious to all, although no one found it disturbing; he just seemed very committed. He was a school cadet and he often wore army surplus jackets and bought *Soldier of Fortune* and other military magazines. In 1984, he transferred from Fitzroy High School to Melbourne High School, primarily because Melbourne High had the best cadet force in the city. His commanding officer at Melbourne High described him as an enthusiastic cadet who had a good disciplinary record, but little capacity for leadership. Indeed, Knight would never rise above the rank of corporal. In his secret fantasy world, however, he was an altogether more dynamic figure.

He constructed for himself many heroic and honourable death-in-combat scenarios, which he ran and re-ran in his mind. According to psychologist Dr. Kenneth Byrne, "some of his dreams were about himself dying in combat, as the hero protecting his company, or, in other cases, it would be he fighting against overwhelming odds and this is something that provided a lot of gratification to him." Although Knight viewed killing and being killed in very romantic terms, there was also, as psychiatrist Dr. David Sime noted, "a sort of intricate detail about this fantasy life which was very unusual—on and on and on, different battles but actual historical situations and in factual detail." He cast himself in starring roles in the famous last stands of history. He would be, for instance, a German soldier in General Paulus's 6th Army, encircled and doomed at the Battle of Stalingrad.

Often Knight saw people around him not so much as flesh

and blood but as accessories for his fantasies. According to Dr. Sime, "So vivid were his imaginings that he'd be sitting in the schoolroom, for example, and he'd look out of the window and he'd see people walking past and he'd immediately imagine this into an ambush situation and into military terms . . . [It was] very vivid to him." Knight, in fact, had a fundamental lack of empathy for other people—and for some, he had a burning hatred.

The ferocity of his anti-communist, pro-Nazi and racist beliefs is revealed not just by his fantasies—in one of his most persistent and gratifying daydreams he was a South African policeman gunning down blacks in Sharpeville or Soweto—but also by graphic amendments he made to photocaptions in a high school text book, *World Powers in the Twentieth Century*, by Harriet Ward.

Photocaption:	Immigrants arriving in America
Knight:	Send the wogs back
Photocaption:	A Ku Klux Klan initiation ceremony, 1922
Knight:	MY MATES. KKK RULES OK
Photocaption:	Forward to the new utopia
Knight:	KILL COMMIES
Photocaption:	Blacks picketing a Washington bank
Knight:	You stupid niggers. Who do you think you are? Put them niggers in their place
Photocaption:	Russia at war: Russian partisans hanged by the Germans, 1941
Knight:	Ho, ho, ho, MERRY X-MAS
Photocaption:	A Russian poster of 1949 welcomes China into the Communist family
Knight:	It says: Welcome you Asian slant-eyed fuck wits
Photocaption:	The American war in Vietnam
Knight:	LETS GO BACK AND FINISH OFF THOSE COMMIE BASTARDS

He also exhibited, as many other pseudo-commando killers have, an Armageddon fixation, which he revelled in with conspicuous glee.

Photocaption: Late 1950s: An exchange of tactical weapons
Knight: The only way. I LOVE NUKES

Perhaps most interesting of all, though, he pledged undying love for the United States of America.

Photocaption: American Imperialism around 1900
Knight: Australia—Future USA State—I love USA

In seeing so clearly America's insidious cultural colonization of other nations, Knight, who otherwise displayed very little depth of understanding about anything other than guns, showed himself to be not entirely devoid of perceptive ability. In 1989, and with the benefit of hindsight, criminologist Andreas Kapardis would discourse on the same subject in his book *They Wrought Mayhem*: "It would seem that as Australia is becoming more Americanized in its culture we are experiencing the dawn of a new era, the . . . assassination of policemen . . . wanton killings . . . mass murderers."

In the early 1980s, the teenage Julian Knight was living in Australia's most cosmopolitan city, Melbourne, and had access to as much US culture as any US-loving Aussie boy could have dreamt of. He even had a part-time job in that most American of exported American institutions, a McDonald's restaurant. In fact, he was working there when James Huberty shot up the company's San Ysidro outlet on 18 July 1984.

Later, languishing in HM Pentridge Prison, Knight would talk about Huberty and other mass killers as if they were old buddies although, as when Andreas Kapardis visited him, "He was very anxious to convince me that he is the best shot of them all." Knight told Kapardis, "Considering it was dark, I was shooting from a distance at fast-moving targets and I'd had about 13-15 pots of beer, I did a really good job. Good old Chuck [Charles Whitman] did a good job, too, didn't he? He was ex-military like me but I think he had sights. It was easier for Huberty at the McDonald's and Vitkovic in Queen Street because the people they were shooting at were trapped."

Kapardis found himself extremely unsettled by the conversation. Knight's "complete lack of remorse, no mention of any compassion for his victims during our interviews, was very disturbing to me; his logic even more." Perhaps the most disturbing thing about Knight's logic, was that it was derived, in part at least, from an idea that, though indeed disturbing, has, nevertheless, been endowed with much cultural legitimacy—not least by *Soldier of Fortune* and other combat magazines, available from the shelves of all self-styled reputable newsagents—namely that, as a compatriot of Michael Ryan's put it, "killing is morally justified when performed by 'experts.'"

As time went by, Julian Knight, the high school cadet, would become ever more expert in the use of firearms. In 1985, the year he passed his High School Certificate, with C grades in five subjects, he joined the Army Reserve. On a two-week assault trooper's course at Puckapunyal, he was trained in the use of eleven different weapons, ranging from a 9-mm Browning pistol to a .50-calibre machine gun. According to Des McArthur, a fellow reservist, "Most people in the Army Reserve fantasize about walking down the street with an SLR in your hand and feeling the power you might get but no one ever does it . . . you're Rambo when you're out on the army reserve but when you go home, you go back to being a plumber or whatever. Everyone joked around, you know, 'I'm a trained killer.' Julian did, but in a different way. He was more dedicated than anyone else I knew . . . anyone else."

The unhealthy undertones of Knight's military obsession would rise close to the surface in the riotous beer-swilling sessions that army reservists have a fondness for indulging in, and his colleagues were able to perceive, albeit only dimly through the haze of alcohol and general Rambo-swagger, something of the disturbing nature of the world inside his head. Knight was drinking back home in Melbourne, too, and dating girls—a combination that often induced him to spill more of his secrets. Girls with whom he had intimate relationships have testified that not only was he still upset and angry about the divorce of his adoptive parents, but that he also felt profound unhappiness about having been adopted in the first place. Both subjects could reduce him to tears after heavy drinking.

In addition, Knight displayed a tendency to harbour secret grudges over long periods of time—another of the hallmarks of mass killers—which would occasionally result, again after heavy drinking, in physical violence. On one occasion, he began punching a close friend at a downtown disco. The incident that provoked the attack had taken place weeks earlier and Knight had shown his friend no antagonism in between times; indeed, the pair had been drinking together perfectly amicably for most of the evening, before the assault.

For Knight, 1986 had started badly and just seemed to be getting worse. In March, despite his intense yearning for a full-time military career and possibly under pressure from his parents, he had gone to La Trobe University to study French, German history and politics. He had lasted just six weeks. The place was, he complained, full of leftover hippies from the sixties. For the rest of the year his life seemed to drift. He was unemployed, he drank frequently and heavily, fell out with friends as a result, and eventually lost his girl into the bargain.

His one success of the year, and it was a notable one, came when he applied for entry into the military, at the army's Melbourne recruiting office. He was considered a good prospect for the Royal Military College, the Australian equivalent of England's Sandhurst. The opinion of his old CO at Melbourne High, that he had no leadership potential, was evidently either unavailable to, or overlooked by, the recruiting officers who assessed him. He met the required minimum academic standards and was found to be physically fit by a doctor and mentally fit by a psychologist. He went up before an RMC Selection Board, comprising three senior officers and yet another psychologist. He was graded a marginal candidate—the lowest acceptable grade for consideration—but he was in.

In its initial and ongoing assessment of Knight, the army noted, among other things, that Julian was the eldest of three children, that the father was absent, having left the family in 1980, and that Mrs. Knight was very devoted to Julian; she was not altogether happy about his application to the RMC but she was thinking of moving the whole family to Canberra just so she could be near him. It was also noted that Knight was highly committed to the military, that he was over-confident (there was concern among senior staff that his ability might not match his belief in himself), and that he had problems relating to other people and needed to work on developing his social skills. The Royal Military College possessed, in fact, if it had but realized it, a remarkably accurate profile of a typical pseudo-commando killer. The profile was incomplete in just one respect; at the time, Knight lacked the important prerequisite of thwarted ambitions. Indeed, when he entered RMC Duntroon, on 13 January 1987, at the age of 18, he was realizing his life's dream.

After the misery of 1986, the world was now Knight's oyster. He had arrived. He was a winner. He bought himself a fast car. Unfortunately, though, both the car and his dreams would fall apart before the year was out. His immaturity, his high opinion of himself and his fondness for playing the wisecracking extrovert did not go down well with the senior cadets at Duntroon. All new boys are given a hard time in their first year at the Royal Military College, but Knight was given a harder time than most. He drank heavily and performed his duties poorly. Between March and May he was charged with a number of military offences, including four absences without leave and leaving his post while on duty. He failed academic and practical examinations and his leadership ability and other personal qualities were also rated below standard. Weapons expertise was the only area in which he excelled, and he was counselled on more than one occasion about his poor overall performance.

A week before Easter, Knight met up with his former girlfriend in Canberra. According to her, he cried all night over their break-up and because things were not going well for him at Duntroon. He arranged to meet her again, about two weeks later, in Melbourne, so they could have a drink and meal together for old times' sake. There was apparently some confusion about the details of the rendezvous and the girl never showed up at the pub where Knight was waiting. He went on a scouting mission to other local bars and eventually found her drinking with a girlfriend at the Royal Hotel. He suspected she had been deliberately trying to avoid him and he sat at the counter alone, knocking back beer like there was no tomorrow. When, a short while later, she told him she was going on somewhere else and that he could not come along, it only served to confirm his suspicions. He threw his glass across the room and stormed towards the nearest exit. He punched out the window of the inner door but found the outer door locked and turned back into the bar. Now in the red fog of an alcohol-adrenaline rush, he began hitting out at everyone in the immediate vicinity. He was dragged out into the street, where he eventually calmed down, and walked away.

After Easter, Knight returned to Duntroon with his tail between his legs. Nothing was working out right for him. On the last weekend of May, he was confined to barracks

by his sergeant major for one of his all-too-frequent disciplinary offences. By Saturday evening, though, he was fed
up and went out to celebrate a friend's birthday. At around
11:00 P.M., he and some of the other party-goers arrived at
the Private Bin nightclub in Canberra. Unfortunately for
Knight, his sergeant major also happened to be at the club
and he ordered Knight back to barracks. Knight refused.
At about 1:30 A.M., he got into a scrap with the sergeant
major's drinking buddies and was ejected from the building
by a bouncer. He cleaned himself up, sneaked back inside
and drank quietly with his friends until nearly 3:00 A.M. He
then decided to leave. As he was heading for the door, he
passed the sergeant major. Knight pulled out a knife and
stabbed him twice in the right side of the face, near the
ear, and wounded himself in the process when one of his
fingers slid down the blade, severing a tendon.

A short while later, after fleeing from the nightclub,
Knight turned himself in to the Federal Police. He was
charged with assault, malicious wounding and assault
occasioning actual bodily harm. He was bailed to appear
in court on 12 June but the case was subsequently adjourned
to 10 November. His military career was over. The RMC
outlined the options available to him and the only realistic
one was that he resign.

It does not appear to have occurred to the army that
Knight may have been in need of counselling—that his
knifing of a fellow soldier, twice, in the face, was disturbing
enough, without even considering his statement to police
that he had no idea why he did it. The official army view
of the incident, as expressed by General Murray Blake, the
commandant of RMC Duntroon, was that "there were others
involved . . . alcohol was a factor and it's well known that
when alcohol's involved a large proportion of the population, probably, are prone to violence in those situations.
So, there was nothing in his record, there's nothing that he
did that would indicate that he was 'abnormal.'" The army
simply washed its hands of him. On 2 July, he was passed

from Duntroon to the Regimental Supernumerary List. He returned home to Melbourne, his dreams shattered.

On the surface, and to begin with at least, he seemed to cope with the situation extremely well. He was keen to impress upon people that he had learnt from his recent experiences, that his outlook was positive and that he was optimistic about the future. He told friends that alcohol had been ruining his life and that he had decided to give it up for good. He spoke enthusiastically about possible careers with the fire brigade, the Federal Police or customs. In the meantime, he got a job as a storeman, and applied for a place on a security guard training course run by a Melbourne company, scheduled to start on 11 August. On 17 July he was interviewed and accepted for the course. He really seemed to be knuckling down and trying to make something of his life.

It was all show. He knew only too well that a conviction for serious assault would disqualify him from a career with the fire brigade, police force or customs service, and that even the rather inferior man-of-action career of private security guard would probably be closed to him. He had already made the painful discovery that just the fact that there were criminal charges against him—never mind that his guilt had yet to be proved—marked him as a second-rate citizen. He had tried to rejoin his old Army Reserve regiment but they refused to have him, because of the impending trial. What future was there for him? A dead-end job as a storeman? Well, he would see about that.

It was a new and highly unpleasant experience for Knight to see the future not as something to look forward to but as something to dread. And the past continued to torment him, more doggedly now than ever before. Not only was he plagued by the old ghosts—his adoption and the divorce of his adoptive parents—but newer spectres were also haunting him: his ex-girlfriend, his failure at Duntroon and his natural mother. Knight had found out his real mother's name and that she was living in South Africa. He had written her two letters but had received no reply.

Rendered by the past a diffused and ill-defined nobody, and facing the prospect of being absorbed by his newly grey and featureless future, the present became increasingly unbearable for Knight, who had always believed he was a man who would make his mark on the world; a big shot. He soon returned to his old drinking habits, to the old love-hate relationship he had with beer. In the past, the brief, cathartic releases of sentimentality, self-pity and violent anger that the beer facilitated had cost him dearly. These days, they could surely cost him nothing, for his life was about as rock bottom as he thought it could get. He began drinking more frequently and heavily than ever before.

At home in his mother's house, he no longer really belonged. Nearly all signs of his identity as a member of the family had been erased. When he had gone to Duntroon, his mother had converted his bedroom into a sitting room and he slept there, now, with his old duvet and a pillow on a mattress on the floor. His personal effects photos, diaries, army notes and the like—remained packed away in boxes on top of the wardrobe. More of his belongings, including army clothing and equipment, were stored on the landing. Aside from a few clothes and other necessities, the only things he had readily to hand were an album of army photographs and his three guns, which he kept under, of all places, his mother's bed. He owned a .308-calibre M-14 semi-automatic rifle, a Ruger ten-shot/.22-calibre (Model 10/22) semi-automatic rifle, and a twelve-gauge Mossberg slide-action repeating shotgun. The Ruger was a birthday present from an uncle. The M-14 and the Mossberg shotgun he had bought for himself. He had a licence and all three guns were registered.

On Friday 7 August, Knight went out drinking with an old friend. The bender began at the Royal Hotel, at about 7:00 P.M. Midway through the evening, they switched to the Normandy Hotel in Queen's Parade, driving past the house of Knight's former girlfriend, who was having a party to

which Knight had not been invited. They drank heavily at
the Normandy, until about midnight, and then went back
to Knight's house. The following evening, Knight went
drinking at the Royal Hotel, as he had done every evening
for the past week. He whiled away the night trying to chat
up the barmaids and moaning about the fact that he had
not been invited to the party at his ex-girlfriend's the night
before.

It was getting on for midday when Knight climbed out
of bed on Sunday 9 August. A family get-together had been
arranged at his grandmother's that afternoon and, instead of
his usual jeans and shirt, he put on a pair of pleated slacks
and a smart, navy-blue jumper. He drove his little sister
over to their grandmother's arriving at about one o'clock.
His mother and his brother, who had left earlier in Mrs.
Knight's car, were already there, along with assorted aunts,
uncles and friends. Over lunch, Knight drank a couple of
beers and a litre of coke, and talked about the security
officer training course, which he was scheduled to start in
two days' time. He gave a convincing impression of being
excited by it.

At around four o'clock, Knight drove his sister home to
Ramsden Street and went straight back out again in the car.
He called on a friend, told her that the family get-together
had been boring, and then headed back home. On the way
back his car broke down with a gearbox problem. Already
several thousand dollars in debt to the bank, he had been
hoping to raise some capital by selling it. When he got
home, he changed and went out to the Royal Hotel, arriving
shortly before six o'clock.

The pub was reasonably busy but none of his usual
friends were there and he sat at the counter, drinking alone,
chatting up the barmaids. During the course of the evening,
he also chatted to a few of the Royal's regulars. He told a
young apprentice, who was lodging at the hotel, about the
trouble he was having with his car and his ex-girlfriend. He
also talked about his military career. He said that army life

was a hard life but a good one, and that he was a crack
shot with a rifle and had been a big hit with the girls in
Canberra.

Being a Sunday, the Royal closed at eight o'clock. Knight
had one after-hours drink with a couple of the regulars and
left at 8:20 P.M. By this time, he would tell police, exactly
five hours later, he had already made his big decision.

Detective:	So, what you are saying is, about half an hour before you left the hotel—
Knight:	I decided that I'd go home and get my weapons and start shooting.

Nightmare on Hoddle Street

According to police, Knight had drunk no more than five
pots of beer during the evening. According to bar staff, he
drank eight. Knight himself has insisted that he put away
at least thirteen. What is not disputed is the time he left the
Royal Hotel (8:20 P.M.) and the time he arrived home—
according to both his mother and sister, nine o'clock. It
takes less than ten minutes to walk from the pub to Ramsden
Street. Knight has claimed that his mind is a complete blank
from the time he left the pub to the time he got home. In
barely credible contrast, he can remember everything from
9:00 P.M. onwards in extraordinary detail.

He prepared and loaded his three guns. He sorted out
additional ammunition. He clipped a 10-inch sheath knife
onto his belt. He put a single bullet into the left pocket of
his jeans and, at about 9:30 P.M., he slipped quietly out
of the house. He had the Ruger rifle in his left hand, the
Mossberg shotgun in his right and the M-14 slung over his
shoulder.

Ramsden Street was deserted, not a soul to be seen. He
headed west, at a brisk walk, towards the railway crossing.
Instead of using the pedestrian gate, he slipped through a

hole in the wire fence at the side of the crossing, and picked his way over the railway lines, angling off into the darkness. When he emerged, he was on a narrow strip of land that separated the railway track from a parallel-running, four-lane arterial road called Hoddle Street. The buffer strip had been landscaped with grasses, shrubs and trees to give the impression of a natural divide, cleverly hiding the ugly mechanics of the railway—and, on the night of Sunday 9 August 1987, something far uglier still—from the eyes of the suburban car drivers on Hoddle Street.

Knight knelt down by the side of a tree—or "propped," in the military jargon he would invariably employ when talking later about the events of that night—and surveyed the scene before him. The traffic along Hoddle Street was heavy and the nearest vehicles passed within about 20 feet of him. Visibility was reasonable but the cacophony of engine noise and the quality of the light—the low-glare shimmer from the overhead streetlamps and the bright cores and vaporous tracers of headlights and taillights—rendered the world strange and unreal.

Even by the usual cowardly standards of pseudo-commando killers, Knight was extraordinarily spineless. He was unable to embark upon his mission without first dealing himself every last psychological ace from the bottom of the pack. He needed to have his victims comprehensively dehumanized; so he chose the night, when darkness reduces people to mere shadows and silhouettes. He needed to jettison his inhibitions, weaken his conscience and sever completely his tenuous distinction between reality and fantasy; so he loaded himself with beer. Finally, just to be absolutely certain he would not get too close to his victims—that they would remain anonymous, two-dimensional targets—and that the real world and his fantasy world would remain irrevocably fused, he chose, as the location for his rampage, the surreal nightscape of the urban clearway. Hardly surprising, then, that he would later tell detectives, "It was like one big dream . . . It's kind of like you could have been in Beirut and you wouldn't have known the difference."

He took aim with his Ruger rifle at a shadow behind the steering wheel of a southbound car—and then squeezed the trigger. He fired again, and again, and again: "It was just sights, target, BANG, BANG, BANG." He moved north up Hoddle Street, keeping to the trees and bushes, and propped again, beneath the giant Coca-Cola billboard near the Clifton Hill Railway Station. Again he opened fire. The muzzle flash from the rifle was the only visible clue to his whereabouts.

Knight, who had been dreaming for years about seeing action in "East Timor, Irian Jaya, Philippines, Thailand, Burma, Afghanistan, Iran, Iraq, Beirut—especially wanted to go to South Africa—Central America, anywhere there was a shit fight on," but who had failed in the one legitimate career with the potential to satisfy his fantasies, created, in Clifton Hill, Melbourne, on that Sunday evening, his very own combat zone.

The following morning he would retrace his steps, in the company of detectives and a Victoria Police video team. He would be cool and detached, like a soldier being debriefed after a military operation; so much so, that some experts have concluded that he can only have been in a state of post-traumatic shock.

More than twenty people on Hoddle Street were hit by shots from Knight's three guns. The M-14 did most of the damage. Dusan Flajnik and John Muscatt both died from enormous injuries to the chest and neck. Tracey Skinner died from a shot to the head that blew half her face away. Gina Papaioannou died in hospital, eleven days later, from a massive wound to her hip, which looked, according to one of the ambulance officers who attended her, like a shark bite. Hoddle Street was strewn with bodies, bullet-riddled cars and shattered windscreen glass. The air was full of the sound of squealing tyres, screams and sirens. Knight slipped away into the darkness again, following the railway line north.

At the Merri Creek, close to the south end of High Street, he shot and slightly injured a police constable who was busy preventing traffic from heading into the Hoddle Street area. A short while later, a police helicopter swept across the area, its spotlight picking out a figure, crouched in the scrub below the railway bridge. Knight let rip with his M-14. He would say later that it was like a scene from the film *Apocalypse Now* and that "When I shot at the helicopter, I was expecting return fire, because I thought there'd be an SOG [Special Operations Group] marksman in there. I was disappointed when nothing came except it just flew off." He had punctured one of the chopper's fuel tanks and it was forced to make an emergency landing in a nearby reserve. According to Andreas Kapardis in *They Wrought Mayhem*, Knight did not want to die slowly, coughing up blood, with a regular police .38 slug in his heart, but "preferred the SOG to take his head right off." He would not get his wish. As the helicopter veered away, he took to the railway line again.

At about 10:15 P.M., he was running west along McKean Street in North Fitzroy. By this time, he had discarded the Ruger rifle and Mossberg shotgun and had just nine rounds left in his M-14. He was apparently heading for the house of his ex-girlfriend and intended to kill her and then commit suicide or hold the house to siege, "like they do in the films." As he ran along the street, a police car followed in his wake and he ducked into an alley. Senior Constable John Delahunty slammed on the brakes and tried to slide the car sideways to illuminate the alley with the headlights. The stunt didn't quite come off. The car screeched to a halt, but not at the angle the cop had hoped for, and the alley remained shrouded in darkness.

Cautiously, Delahunty and his partner climbed out of their vehicle. Knight, who was crouched by a wall at the alley entrance, emptied his magazine. He was firing at such a rapid rate, he said, that the muzzle flash was overwhelming and he could barely see what he was shooting at. So loud was the sound of the shots in Constable Delahunty's ears, that at first he thought he had been hit in the head: "I crawled along the ground to the back of the car, trying to find cover . . . any cover at all. A blade of grass would've looked good at the time."

Knight, meanwhile, his ammunition exhausted, unclipped the magazine and reached into his pocket for the single bullet he claimed he had kept for himself. The bullet was gone—and he decided to surrender. He rose up slowly from behind the wall. Delahunty "saw his head . . . and I just stood up . . . away from the car, out in the open—and I shouldn't have done that, that was silly . . . and [I] just took an aim at him and fired a shot." Knight ducked back down. As he later remembered it, the police were shouting and Knight begged not to be shot. Delahunty had nothing but contempt for Knight's pleading. Quickly and entirely by the book they arrested, searched and handcuffed him. It was a neat end to the mayhem.

At 7:24 A.M., the following morning, after hours of questioning, Knight would be sitting alone in the police interview room. The video camera would still be running and it would show him drinking from a plastic cup and thumbing through the morning papers.

On hearing about the Hoddle Street massacre, a 22-year-old former law student called Frank Vitkovic would tell people he couldn't understand why anybody would do such a thing. Victoria's Minister for Police, Race Mathews, would tell people that the massacre was an aberration that should remain a one-off indefinitely.

9

Proliferation

Carnage in Quebec

A rented white Pontiac cruised into Quebec City on the morning of Tuesday 8 May 1984. The driver was Denis Lortie, a young corporal in the Canadian Army. He was attached to the Royal 22nd Regiment and stationed at the Carp base, eight miles southwest of Ottawa.

Shortly before 9:30 A.M., Lortie, who was dressed in combat fatigues, walked into the CJRP radio station, in downtown Quebec. He handed a sealed envelope to CJRP personnel, instructed them not to open it until 10:00 A.M. and then left. The envelope bore the legend "The Life of a Person" and contained an audio cassette tape. The staff at CJRP were not predisposed to comply with the 10:00 A.M. instruction. Their suspicions had been aroused by the wicked-looking hunting knife strapped to Lortie's leg and they opened the envelope as soon as he departed. Their hunch that something was amiss was confirmed when they played the tape.

While his regiment, ironically, was charged with the maintenance of Carp bunker, the bolt hole designed for the protection of Canadian leaders should they ever face the threat of nuclear assassination, Lortie promised a no less destructive, one-man strike against those same government figures. He vowed to "destroy the government in power, including René Lévasque [the provincial premier]." He spoke in French; the voice on the tape was calm and composed. "Maybe I will hurt a lot of people," he speculated, "but what do you expect?" The Parti Québécois Government was, he said, "doing much wrong to the French language people of Quebec and Canada . . . What I am doing is for the world of the future and for the French language." He warned: "No one will be able to stop me—not the police, not the army—because I am going to carry out destruction and then I will destroy myself. It will be a first in Canada." By the time CJRP radio had informed the police, the rampage was already underway.

At about 9:40 A.M., at the historic Quebec Citadel, a restored fort, dating back to the 1800s, several tourists were shot at. A short while later, a few minutes before politicians at the National Assembly were due to begin the day's session, Lortie burst into the building through a side door. He carried a pistol and a sub-machine gun. He allegedly yelled, "I came here to kill!" and shot dead two of the Assembly messengers, Georges Boyer and Camille Lepage.

Lortie then made his way to the main chamber and opened fire with the SMG. The ensuing scene was described by witnesses as mayhem. People were screaming and scurrying in all directions, trying to get out of the line of fire. A TV cameraman reported hearing Lortie say to one injured person, "I'm sorry for wounding you, but that's life." More than a dozen other people were also wounded. Ironically, hostesses had replaced army guards in the chamber just a few weeks earlier. For a time, Lortie established himself in the speaker of the parliament's chair.

During a lull in the shooting, René Jaulbert, the Assembly's Sergeant-at-Arms, and a Second World War veteran, put his life on the line by approaching Lortie, shaking his hand and offering him a cigarette. Jaulbert, who had apparently once served with the Royal 22nd Regiment (Lortie's outfit), managed to gain the killer's confidence and presently the two men retired to Jaulbert's office.

The Sergeant-at-Arms' bold move almost certainly saved lives—possibly a considerable number. Ambulance crews were able to get the wounded to hospital for prompt treatment. Quebec provincial police were able to evacuate the Assembly building, seal off the exits and keep Lortie busy on the telephone while they awaited the arrival of a specially trained crisis team from Montreal.

At 2:25 P.M., the Montreal team and local police rushed the building. They overwhelmed Lortie and rescued René Jaulbert unharmed. Lortie was driven away in a fast car—heading for a provincial police station and a life sentence.

Reportedly deeply troubled by the rampage, Jean-Claude Nadeau did not sleep well that night. The following day, 9 May, he went out into a Quebec City street with a gun, and shot and wounded two people.

Australians saw Julian Knight as an aberration and a one-off and Canadians regarded Denis Lortie in much the same way. Lortie had adopted quasi-revolutionary rhetoric to try to justify his mission of self-aggrandizement, casting himself as a political martyr, and it was tempting for Canadians to see him in those terms. The unpalatable alternative would have been to see him as the harbinger of a new phenomenon that, in 1984, was still regarded as an exclusively American problem. Even Jean-Claude Nadeau's copycat shooting the following day could not shake the national belief that Canada was still immune from the violent excesses of her neighbours in the United States.

While it would be five years before Canadian illusions were shattered, Australians enjoyed no such period of grace.

A Second Melbourne Massacre

On Tuesday 8 December 1987, exactly four months after Hoddle Street, and before the nation had even recovered from the shock, Frank Vitkovic shot dead eight people and wounded five others at the Australia Post building on Queen Street, in the city centre. Victoria's Minister for Police, Race Mathews, who, at the time of the shootings, was in a meeting with the Attorney-General in a building diagonally opposite the Australia Post block, told newsmen he was amazed that another massacre could have occurred before the end of the year. He said he felt "sadness for the families in this tragic and unforeseeable incident."

Vitkovic had arrived at the Australia Post offices at 4:15 P.M., dressed in a khaki jacket, chino jeans and running shoes. He went to the Telecom Employees Credit Cooperative, on the fifth floor, asked to see a friend who worked there and then pulled a sawn-off .30-calibre American M-1 carbine out from under his jacket. At 4:17 P.M., one of the tellers hit an alarm button, alerting police and activating a security video camera. Vitkovic began shooting. Outside on Queen Street, "people started looking around everywhere to see where [the shots] were coming from. It was like those films of President Kennedy's assassination with people pointing everywhere," said an eyewitness.

In the course of the next fifteen minutes, on three floors of the building, Vitkovic shot dead eight people and wounded five others. "It was a slaughterhouse," ambulanceman Ian Patrick would later tell reporters. Finally, at 4:34 P.M., Vitkovic leapt to his death from an eleventh-floor window. He was heard to yell, "That will teach you," by Detective Senior Constable Michael Graham.

Vitkovic was born on 7 September 1965, of immigrant parents. His father, a self-employed painter, was from Yugoslavia and his mother, a hospital domestic, was from Italy. At primary school, and later at the Redden Catholic College in Preston, he was considered a bright and conscientious student; a perfectionist even. He was rather quiet and shy, and something of "a mother's perfect kid," according to one childhood friend.

From an early age, Vitkovic set his sights high. He was determined to get top High School Certificate results, get into law school and become a lawyer. His primary motivation seems to have been a strong desire to reward his hard-working parents. He was their only son and he badly wanted to be a son they could be proud of. In his high school years he showed remarkable self-discipline and dedication. Homework was always his first priority. In his leisure time, he watched TV or played tennis, a sport at which he was very good and around which his limited social life revolved. He greatly admired, and modelled himself on the ice-cool Swedish ace Bjorn Borg.

Vitkovic, like Wagner von Degerloch and Charles Whitman, pursued his studies with exceptional commitment and did not socialize nearly as much as his peers. As a result, he failed to develop fully the skills and confidence necessary for building close relationships, and wound up deficient in that most desirable of human qualities, empathy for his fellows. He felt that he did not fit in, that he was not part of the group—that, in fact, other people hated him. On and off throughout his life, he kept a diary that graphically charted his secret torment. Reflecting on his childhood in November 1987, he wrote in his diary, "You are an alien among your own. An outcast. That was how I grew up." He recalled that as early as eight or nine years old, "I had a feeling that people were against me."

Vitkovic's inability to develop and sustain close relationships would plague him all his life. He had particular trouble getting close to members of the opposite sex— "it's hard for a self-conscious guy like me to talk to girls with confidence"—and the one intimate relationship he did experience only ended in tears: "I was 19 she was 16 . . . she was sweet and nice and I liked her a real lot . . . I treated her like a queen . . . and she dumped me for another guy . . . For months I was hurt," he confided to his diary.

In his early teens, Vitkovic meticulously documented his TV viewing habits and these reveal much about him and the situation he perceived himself to be in.

He was a big Jerry Lewis fan and it is not hard to see why he found Lewis, invariably playing the role of the hopeless social misfit who triumphs in the end, such an attractive figure.

Violent horror, murder and revenge films also formed a large part of Vitkovic's viewing and his diary contains many brief plot summaries. Later, in 1987, he would write, "I just like violent films. I don't know why. They make me feel better, all that violence gets me pumped up. The sound of the gun going 'pow.' It's the only fun I know."

Far and away his favourite film, though—it addressed in 100 minutes and with great poignancy *all* of his pre-occupations—was the black-and-white classic *King Kong* (1933), the story of a giant ape, alienated, misunderstood and persecuted, who finally breaks his chains and rampages through New York City. Vitkovic was obsessed with the film and with the hastily made sequel *Son of Kong*.

As his sixteenth birthday approached, Vitkovic wrote in his diary: "I know one thing for certain I am hated very much by many people, but they don't know anything of my hatred which is twice as much as theirs." Although he dreamt about a day when "everyone will pay for their sins," his aggression was confined, in his high school years, mainly to the tennis court, where he usually gave his opponents a good and very satisfying thrashing. Six years later, however, his aggressive urges would be altogether more dangerous. "People think I'm worth nothing . . . I'll treat them as nothing," he wrote on 21 October 1987. On 16 November he wrote, "As Rambo said in *First Blood*, once you accept a problem it's no longer there," and on 19 November, "A bullet in the right place often seems to do the trick." On 5 December, two days before his rampage, he wrote "I'm geared up . . . I'm a steam train coming through and everyone better get out of the way."

Vitkovic had had just one run-in with the law. On a summer afternoon in 1983, he was caught looking up a woman's skirt in a Preston shopping mall. Sexually naive and curious, rather like his hero King Kong, he was apparently goaded into the deed by some other boys, who disappeared as soon as the victim reciprocated his monkey antics with a Fay Wray impersonation. When the police arrived, it was agreed that no charges would be made against Vitkovic, provided he sought professional counselling.

A week after the incident, Mrs. Vitkovic took her boy to see a psychiatrist, who was of the opinion that Frank had suffered "a minor adjustment reaction of adolescence in the setting of a dysfunctional family." The mother and father—not a very close couple, the psychiatrist noted—expected their son to achieve very high standards, but while the mother was over-possessive of Frank, the father had a low opinion of him. The psychiatrist felt that Frank's problems were not sufficiently serious to warrant ongoing therapy and the Vitkovics made it clear that they were not interested in family counselling. There was nothing more to be done. Frank and his folks returned home, evidently relieved to put the whole shameful business behind them.

In the months leading up to his HSC examinations, Vitkovic studied harder than ever—ten, eleven, twelve hours a day. He played virtually no tennis and watched virtually no TV. His great dedication was rewarded when he passed his HSC with three A and two B grades. He was overjoyed, for the results would allow him entry to the Faculty of Law at Melbourne University.

In his first year at university, Vitkovic was his usual hard-working, perfectionist self. At weekends and during holidays, he played tennis and was a finalist in several club competitions. He seems to have made few friends at law school, though. His fellow students were, by and large, from wealthy and privileged families, and Vitkovic, not adept at socializing at the best of times, doubtless felt more intimidated than usual. He found law school a lot harder than high school in other ways, too. He passed his first-year examinations, but only with moderate grades.

In October 1984, while out jogging, Vitkovic injured his right knee. It was to prove a turning point in his life. Writing in his diary in 1987, he revealed that, "For 2 years when I was playing tennis regularly and winning trophies and getting better and better they were about the happiest years of my life . . . I'd never hurt either leg before in any way not even a sprain. Then all of a sudden my right felt like jelly. I knew the tennis was over. I felt a part of me died that night . . . I spent most of that summer brooding . . . By mid 1985 my studies had fallen away completely so I deferred the law course. I needed time off to get my head straight. I was still brooding about not being able to play tennis anymore and it had screwed up my studies." He later reflected on the fact that "after I stuffed my knee up I lost a lot of my determination and willpower." Over the next two and a half years, he would see countless doctors, receive numerous diagnoses and undergo two major operations to try to fix the knee, all to no avail.

In 1985, while trying to get himself straightened out, he apparently took up pool as an alternative to tennis, but the pain in his knee became so great that he could not stand up long enough to make his shots. In December 1985, having already seen a general surgeon and an orthopaedic surgeon, he was referred to a specialist who diagnosed stress in the joint from poor flexibility, and advised him how to exercise and care for his knee.

In March 1986, Vitkovic resumed his law degree at Melbourne University. In May, though, the pain in his leg was such that he went to see the specialist again. He was given an orthoscopy examination, which revealed that part of the cartilage was damaged. The knee was operated on, apparently to the satisfaction of the surgeon, but a few months later Vitkovic was seeing yet another specialist, complaining that the leg was still troubling him. The doctor concluded that the problem was not so much physical as mental and that Frank was suffering from post-surgical anxiety.

Meanwhile, his second year at law school had been a disaster. He had withdrawn from a large part of the course and failed the rest. He came to the attention of the university's Student Counselling Service after writing an essay which, while it might well have earned him full marks from *Dirty Harry*'s eponymous hero, was entirely inappropriate as a response to a property contracts examination question.

The reforms I would make to the present laws are to reintroduce capital punishment for all civil libertarians.

The present criminal laws are a farce. One person has lost all his civil rights (i.e. has been murdered) whilst the son of a bitch who killed him is entitled, according to the "civil libertarian philosophy" to have his future considered, his reform considered, his constitutional rights considered, his state of mind considered, the stress he was under, the "so called" provocation of the deceased (which by the way never occurred but is invented by the defendant and taken for granted by idiotic Judges), the fact that he only meant to scare the deceased the gun just "went off."

Finally the defendant is found not guilty of the murder of the man whom he shot through the head but guilty of manslaughter and given a minimum sentence of five years jail.

Warning—prophetic—St Paul.

Laws were created to ensure an order and coherent society. When laws are made impotent by groups in society who call themselves civil libertarians society regresses . . . It is an ever growing violent society

where no one feels safe. It is clear that violence
results from a chaotic society.

Vitkovic readily admitted to a psychologist from the Student Counselling Service that he was having problems. He
said that his life had become meaningless since he injured
his knee. He complained that friends had deserted him and
that his father was violent. He often thought of killing
himself, he said, by crashing his car into a tree. He also
thought about hurting other people. He felt that the whole
world deserved to perish in the nuclear holocaust that he
supposed was waiting just around the corner. A week later,
Vitkovic had a second session with the psychologist, during
which he retracted his earlier statement about his father.
He said that he respected and admired his father, and was
only sorry that, after all his family had done for him, he
could not be a better son. The counsellor suggested that he
might benefit from seeing a psychiatrist. Vitkovic agreed
to an appointment, but later cancelled it by telephone. The
counsellor was concerned but did not think Vitkovic was a
candidate for compulsory treatment.

It was now almost two years since he had last made an
entry in his diary. Other than the information recorded by
various official sources, little is known about Vitkovic's
activities in early 1987. On 24 February, he formally
withdrew from Melbourne University's Faculty of Law.
Between February and August, prior to undergoing a second operation on his knee, he saw a number of orthopaedic
surgeons and also several GPs, the latter about a variety
of evidently psychosomatic complaints. Later in the year,
suffering tremendous headaches, he would be given a brain
scan that would reveal no abnormalities. In September, a
month after the Hoddle Street massacre and his second knee
operation, Vitkovic went to the Firearms Registry office and
applied for a shooter's licence. He also resumed his diary.

All my friends have deserted me or treated me so
badly that I have deserted them . . . When I go out the

people don't seem real. I don't feel part of it. I never
have really. My life is such a failure. Since my HSC
success it's been all downhill . . . These damn knees
have destroyed me. *Diary: 16 September 1987*

At this rate I will be a cripple in two years or so . . .
My whole life is a shambles . . . Frustration, rejection,
humiliation are emotions I know very well. Happiness, friendship and a sense of belonging have never
been part of my life . . . I have always been a loner.
Diary: 21 September 1987

Death scares me but not so much as other people.
Diary: 26 September 1987

In early October, he went to the Firearms Registry office
to collect his shooter's licence. On 13 October, he put a
deposit down on an M-1 carbine and wrote in his diary,
"TODAY there is a change. The power I need is slowly but
surely coming together . . . I can't live in this world. There's
just no place for me." On 16 October, he paid the outstanding
balance on the gun. In his diary, he wrote, "I know the
end is near . . . Hate is the dominant emotion now . . . The
old Frank died years ago." From mid-October, Vitkovic's
mission of revenge and destruction gradually crystallized.
Having convinced himself that he no longer had it in
him to become the triumphant social misfit, achieving
success, wealth and happiness, against all the odds, like
Jerry Lewis, he slipped into the realm of his other great
hero, King Kong.

Nobody, not even those closest to him, realized there was
anything wrong. In the days leading up to the massacre,
Frank was, according to his sister, "completely normal and
we were proud of him and loved him." Everyone thought
of him as a perfectly normal young man. Nobody had even
the slightest idea that he was on the threshold of becoming
an armed mass killer. The logic that had brought him to this
abyss has probably inspired as many of history's heroes as

it has villains—certainly, it is easy enough to follow:

. . . the world is against me. *Diary: 23 March 1981*

This is the trap I'm in. I cannot escape. *Diary: 16 September 1987*

The world is full of vicious cruel people. *Diary: 21 October 1987*

There should not be people like that in this world. *Diary: 26 October 1987*

I will punish these evil vicious cruel scum people. *Diary: 26 October 1987*

Every dog has his day. *Diary: 26 October 1987*

God is on my side. *Diary: 26 October 1987*

I can see the path that's been laid out for me. *Diary: 6 December 1987*

There's no other way. *Diary: 7 December 1987*

At the same time as his mission was evolving, he also began focusing on a particular target group—people he felt were especially deserving of punishment.

I see those people in the city and I admire them and yet I hate them cos they've been the ones who've lumped shit on me all these years. *Diary: 11 October 1987*

. . . they have all the things I want and will never have. *Diary: 21 September 1987*

I'll never be part of that group even though deep
down I want to [be]. *Diary: 1 December 1987*

those greedy businessmen and women in the city . . .
They are all pigs. And pigs always end up in the
slaughterhouse. *Diary: 3 November 1987*

Finally, he zeroed in on the Australia Post building, in the
very heart of the city, where one of his former friends—
"My last so-called friend"—was working for the Telecom
Employees Credit Cooperative.

In the days immediately prior to the massacre, Vitkovic's
diary entries range from the pitiful—"I've got 'Elvis Love
Songs' . . . I cry a lot when I listen to the album"—to the
chilling: "I went out for a little trip around town . . . and
bought 2 spare magazines of the militia kind. I need them
for extra zap."

On 8 December, he sat in his bedroom, a *Rambo* poster
on his wardrobe door, his M-1 ready for action, and his last
words—a letter to his family—written.

To my Dear family. I'm sorry for all the trouble and
heartache I've caused you. I've been such a failure. I
went down the wrong path. I should have listened to
Pop and not played so much tennis . . . How I wish I
could change the last few years and make things right
and make you happy and proud of me.

To my dear Mum I love with all my heart. When I
think of how hard you worked for me and Diana and
the love you gave us it made me cry. It always makes
me cry . . . I've let you down very badly mama and
I'm so sorry . . . I knew I was not going to be successful and it hurt me a lot. Things looked so bright a
few years ago but it faded fast. I hope mum you can
remember me when I was a boy on your shoulders
and you carried me to kindergarten. Remember me

when I was a bright young boy of 12 who was so gentle and kind. Then I changed slowly but surely. I didn't want it to happen but it did . . . I just hope someday that you can forgive me and remember me once in a while because I'll never forget you mama. I'll love you always.

To Dear papa or pops. You deserved a better son than me. I was never good enough I admit that. I never pushed myself to the limit. I was lazy. I took the easy way out. I played too much tennis and wrecked my knee and eventually my whole life was wrecked. I know how disappointed you were. I saw the sadness in your eyes. You worked so hard to make a good life for me and I messed it all up because I thought I knew it all . . . We had some great times pop like our fishing trips . . . Or our trips to the espresso bar to play billiards . . . I always loved you too. You are just about the best father a boy could have. You gave me everything, you were so kind and loving. You're a great person there are not enough in the world like you pops. You were always good to me. I'll miss you so much I just can't describe it.

To my dear sister Diana what can I say. I wish I was never born might be the closest to the truth. But you could understand. You saw the stresses building up inside me . . . I was so frustrated. But you helped me through the bad times . . . I wish I could be a better brother but I can't change the way I am. We had so many fun times together it was just unreal. We had happy childhoods it was great. Things went sour for me but you kept me laughing . . . I hope you can forgive me for what I've done but even if you don't I'll understand it. It's hard to understand these things . . . I just can't go on. I just can't live in this world. I am ready to die. It's time for me to die. Life is just not worth living.

Mass Shootings in Europe

With remarkable synchronicity, Knight and Vitkovic appeared in Australia, Lortie and Nadeau appeared in Canada, Ryan, Fowler and Sartin appeared in England—and armed mass killers began rampaging through many other countries of Western Europe. In the city of Delft, in Holland, in April 1983, 27-year-old old Sevdet Yilmaz shot dead six people and wounded five others. At a school in the small town of Eppstein, near Frankfurt, West Germany, in June 1983, 34-year-old Karel Charva shot dead five people and wounded a further fourteen. In Lyons, France, in November 1983, 34-year-old Miloud Amrani shot dead five people and wounded three others. In the village of Zarza de Alange, in Spain, in August 1984, a 23-year-old bachelor shot nineteen people, two fatally, outside the town hall. In Brittany, in northern France, in June 1985, Guy Martell went on the rampage through a string of towns, shooting dead seven people and wounding five others. In 1987, as well as Michael Ryan's rampage in England, a gunman in Belgium massacred seven people. In 1988, a military policeman shot dead four people in Italy, and an army corporal shot sixteen people, four fatally, in Portugal. On Wednesday 12 July 1989, in a case that rivalled Michael Ryan's in its destructiveness, 31-year-old Christian Dornier shot dead fourteen people and wounded nine others in a rural area of France. It was the worst case of its kind on mainland Europe.

The Christian Dornier Case

In early July 1989, towns, cities and villages all across France were preparing to celebrate the anniversary of the violent and bloody French Revolution. The preparations were more extensive than usual because 14 July 1989 was not just any anniversary, but the bicentenary.

The village of Baumes-les-Dames, in the Doubs region of the country, was planning street dances and a fireworks display. Baumes-les-Dames was one of several closely grouped villages—Athose, Autechaux, Grosbois, Luxiol, Verne and Voillans—in what was a tightly knit rural community. In Luxiol, which had a population of just over 100, the Dorniers—Georges, his wife, Jeanne, and their three grown-up children, Christian, Corinne and Serge—were a long-established farming family. In the build-up to Bastille Day, they were in higher spirits than most, for they had just celebrated the marriage of 26-year-old Corinne and Monsieur Daniel Maillard, the previous Saturday. Only 31-year-old Christian, "a taciturn, depressed fellow," according to younger brother, Serge, did not share in the family's joy and excitement. He remained his usual, melancholy self.

On Wednesday 12 July, the Dorniers sat down for lunch with a visiting inseminator of cattle, Marcel Lechine. As Daniel Maillard would later remember it, "After drinking two or three *pastis*, Christian did not want to eat. We had finished lunch and I had gone to the bathroom when I heard shots being fired. I knew what they were right away and I fled through the bathroom window."

According to Serge Dornier, "There was no argument or quarrel of any kind . . . [Christian just] picked up his gun and fired it point-blank at Corinne, killing her instantly. Then . . . my mother, Jeanne, telephoned to the police . . . He fired and killed her, too." He shot his father, Georges, wounding him seriously, and he shot and killed Lechine.

There was no stopping Dornier now. He went outside and climbed into his car, a black Volkswagen Golf GTI and began driving around Luxiol, firing at everyone he came across. Pensioner Suzanne Lanoix was talking with a neighbour when they heard the shots. At first they thought it was firecrackers—"[the neighbour] said to me that this year the bangers for 14 July were going to be really loud"—but when they looked down the road, they saw neighbours falling and blood flowing. Within minutes, the streets would be littered with dead, dying and wounded people.

Pauline Faivre-Pierret, the 5-year-old niece of Roger Clausse, Mayor of Luxiol, was shot dead; two boys from the Masson family—14-year-old Johnny and 10-year-old Johann—were shot dead; 79-year-old Stanislas Périllard and his 81-year-old sister, Marie, were shot dead, as were two middle-aged men, Louis Cuenot and Louis Liard. As many people again were injured. Dornier himself was shot and wounded at one point.

Mayor's son Joël Clausse was at home at the family's *épicerie-tabac*, the only shop in the village, when he heard shooting and "went outside and saw a kid with an enormous hole in his side. I ran around to the garden to warn my mother away [Mme. Clausse had been out in her car and was just arriving home] and then I went back indoors to get a rifle. Our front door had been shattered by a gunshot and my father was crouched down, telephoning the police. I saw my mother's car coming back again and Dornier let off another round. I aimed through the window and fired, hitting him in the neck. He started to bleed and then he fled."

Dornier was injured but not disabled. His GTI sped out of the village on the road to Baumes-les-Dames. Along the way, he shot dead a man working in a field. Gendarme captain René Sarrazin (commander of the Baumes-les-Dames division) was heading for Luxiol when he saw Dornier's black VW speeding towards him. As the two cars crossed, Dornier opened fire, inflicting a serious wound to Sarrazin's arm, and then accelerated away. A kilometre farther along the road, the gunman's car approached a junction at the same time as two others. Again, he opened fire. Georges Pernin, a schoolteacher from Autechaux, and Marie-Alice Champroy, the wife of the Mayor of Voillans, were both shot dead. Dornier did a U-turn and headed back the way he had come. He shot again at gendarme René Sarrazin as he repassed him and then he turned onto the road to Verne, where he claimed his last victim, Pierre Boeuf.

The rampage finally came to an end when Dornier tried

to enter the village of Verne. He drove straight into a gen-
darmes ambush and was badly wounded in the shootout that
followed. Like Michael Ryan, though, he had already left
a quiet, rural community in ruins and his ignoble mark upon
the world. Celebrations of the Revolution were cancelled
throughout the region; instead 14 July saw fourteen funerals.

Christian Dornier had worked on his father's farm for most
of his life. His contemporaries had all married, settled down
and had children, but Dornier remained a solitary figure
who avoided other people and who was, in turn, avoided
by them. According to younger brother, Serge, "He had
no friends, hardly ever. talked to anyone." According to
Dominique Cuenot, a member of the Luxiol village council, "We knew he would create havoc one day and the
police should have dealt with him months ago. Unfortunately, our laws don't allow such preventive action." Mme.
Martine Fleury, the wife of another councillor, told reporters, "Everyone was frightened of him."
  Like Ryan, Dornier, before he went on the rampage,
was already intimately acquainted with the power of the
gun. About six weeks prior to 12 July, he fired shots at a
neighbour, Barrand Remy. Monsieur Remy was not hit on
that occasion, but would be among the injured on 12 July.
The incident was discussed at a meeting of the village council. According to Jacques Fleury, "We advised the family
to get [Christian] psychiatric treatment and they did." A
psychiatrist from Baumes-les-Dames apparently prescribed
him tranquillizers, but Serge Dornier said his brother did
not take them.
  There were rumours that Christian was bitter because
his elderly father would not turn the management of the
family farm over to him, and speculation that this may have
triggered the rampage. The Dorniers, however, believed that
Christian's problems began some years earlier. "We thought
something happened to him during his twelve months' military service about eight years ago," Serge revealed. "He was
never the same after that."

10

The Killer of Feminists

In the mid-1980s, Canada, the largest country in the Western hemisphere, spread across six time zones, maintained a low and stable murder rate. Its mass murder rate, in spite of Denis Lortie's 1984 rampage, was equally unspectacular—an abiding line of moderation, as straight and unambiguous as the border with the United States, or so it seemed. Just as the decade was drawing to a close, there was change.

Late in 1989, 25-year-old Marc Lépine loaded up a Ruger Mini-14 Rifle. He drove a rented car across town to the Université de Montréal and shot dead fourteen young women. As many people again were injured, several with wounds rated eight or nine on the one-to-ten trauma scale developed by the American College of Surgeons. It was far and away the worst massacre of its kind in Canadian history. It tarnished irrevocably Canada's image as one of the cleaner-lined, smoother-cornering models of pluralist democracy. *Hunting Humans* author, Elliott Leyton, was as stunned as his compatriots. "This thing has been a real kick in the teeth for sanctimonious types like me," he told the *New York Times*. "It shows we've fully entered the modern era and no longer have anything to be smug about."

The Montreal University Massacre

Marc Lépine sat in his apartment at 2175 rue de Bordeaux, in east-central Montreal, on the afternoon of 6 December, checking over his Ruger Mini-14 Rifle, a semi-automatic chambered for .223 Remington cartridges and able to be field-stripped to its basic subassemblies in seconds—a deadly piece of precision engineering. When he left his apartment, in the middle of the afternoon, he had the rifle concealed in a bin-liner, a hunting knife strapped to the belt of his jeans, an arsenal of five- and thirty-shot magazines in a carrier bag, and three boxes of .223 bullets stuffed in the pockets of his grey anorak. The light was already fading from the winter sky and the temperature had started to plunge. Lépine climbed into his rented car and joined the slow-moving traffic in the freezing drizzle on rue de Bordeaux. His destination was the École Polytechnique, the Université de Montréal's engineering school, five kilometres west across the city, on the slopes of Mont-Royal.

At the École Polytechnique, William Winegard, the federal Minister of State for Science and Technology, was in mid-visit, offering congratulations on the record 19 per cent enrolment of women in the first-year engineering programme, and discussing a federal scholarship plan aimed at bringing more women into engineering and science. In the ground floor cafeteria, bursting with "Bonne Année" decorations, streamers and balloons, there was a stronger than usual air of bonhomie. It was the last day of classes before the Christmas vacation. Barbara Klueznik, a first-year nursing student at the Université de Montréal, walked across the campus with her husband, Witold Widajewicz, a neurophysiologist. They had been high school sweethearts and had come to Canada from Poland in 1987. They headed for the École Polytechnique cafeteria.

Towards 5:10 P.M., in Room 230, on the second floor—
a room facing east, towards the Hôpital Général de
Montréal and the Cimetière de Notre-Dame-des-Neiges—
Luc Gauthier rose from his seat and quietly left the mechanical engineering class to pay a visit to the lavatory. As
he headed off down the corridor, he passed a man who
appeared to be in his early twenties, carrying a bin-liner
and wearing a "Montréal Tracteur" baseball cap. In Room
230, Professeurs Yvon Bouchard and Adrian Cernea sat
listening to an oral presentation by two of their students.
In the corridor, Lépine slid the Ruger out of the bin-liner.
Prof. Bouchard failed to see anyone enter the room but
became aware of the alien presence when Lépine demanded
that "everyone stop everything" and angled to within two
or three feet of the students giving the presentation. One
of the pair, Eric Chavarie, observed that Lépine "was
smiling . . . He was very calm." Many of the sixty-strong
class thought the gunman was an end-of-term prankster.
"It was our last hour of the term," student Pierre Robert
subsequently recalled. "We practically laughed." Even Eric
Chavarie, who could have considered himself to have been
in the most immediate danger, "thought it was a joke."

Lépine, still smiling, fired a shot into the ceiling and
addressed the class: "Separate yourselves. Girls to the left
and guys to the right." Nobody moved. Pierre Robert thought
the shot was a blank. Lépine repeated the order, managing to
inject sufficient authority into his voice for the class to start
separating. One or two of the more nervous students now
edged behind pillars and, in the confusion, males and females
became mixed in the two groups. What, in dreams, Lépine
had no doubt envisaged as a clockwork military operation,
was turning into a farce. He reiterated his demand that the
men assemble at the right-hand side of the room and that
the girls gather at the left. Eventually, the students were
divided as he wanted them. "OK," he said, "guys leave,
girls stay there." The male students, goaded by Lépine's
request to "move your asses," and still unsure what was

going on, began filing out into the corridor.

When the last man had left the room, Lépine turned to the nine female engineering majors who remained. He was positioned between them and the door and he asked them if they knew why he had come.

"No," replied one student, Nathalie Provost.

"I'm here to fight against feminism," said Lépine.

"Look, we are just women studying engineering," Provost tried to reason with him " . . . just students intent on leading a normal life."

"You're all a bunch of feminists!" Lépine yelled—and opened fire.

He sprayed the group of nine girls from left to right, emptying most, if not all, of the bullets of a thirty-shot magazine into their bodies. Nathalie Provost collapsed with wounds to her lower leg and a bullet graze above her left eye; she was one of the luckier ones. Six of her classmates fell dead. Their average age was 21 and the causes of death ranged from a single head wound, to massive haemorrhaging from nine bullets and four ricochets. Outside the room, the male students, hearing the shots, hightailed it to safety.

Lépine began stalking the second-floor corridors. He turned a corner and was faced, 30 metres away, with a group of people milling round a block of photocopiers. He raised the rifle and fired. Three people fell to the floor wounded. Eric Chavarie, who had lingered down at the far end of the corridor, now fled for the stairs. Other students in the vicinity did likewise. Lépine advanced past the photocopiers in classic military mode, back to the wall, wheeling and firing—in the circumstances (there was nobody shooting back at him), nothing more than an indulgent sequence of stylized gestures. Perhaps he thought it looked efficient, like a real soldier. Perhaps it helped him maintain the video-tape-thin illusion that he was something more than a man with a gun, taking easy potshots at defenceless young women—women who, like the one he hit and wounded slow-moving down an escalator in the second-floor foyer, were no more of a physical threat to him than tin ducks on a fairground rifle range.

"There is a hostage-taking, there is gunfire and there are lots of people wounded." The first 911 call from the École Polytechnique was logged at 5:12 P.M. Within minutes, the Montreal emergency communications system would be inundated with calls. Yet, for all its fibre optic cables, digital substations, computer-aided human operatives and VHF radio channels, its ability to get law enforcement officers on the scene was light years behind Lépine's ability to inflict death—armed as he was with a 1,000-metres-per-second muzzle velocity weapon. With impunity, he continued to roam the second-floor foyer, terrace café and corridors.

In the finance department, Maryse Laganière hurried to lock the office door. Lépine, stalking up the corridor turned and came trotting down, arriving in time to take aim through the window, which, unfortunately, squarely framed Laganière as she turned away into the interior of the office. He fired twice, one of the shots shattering her skull. Lépine returned to the now deserted second-floor foyer and stepped onto an escalator; heading down.

In the ground-floor cafeteria, Witold Widajewicz was trying to decide what he wanted to eat. His wife, Barbara Klueznik, had already filled her tray and paid the cashier. Suddenly, people came running, pushing Widajewicz into the cafeteria kitchen and slamming the door shut. He lay on the floor with the others and tried to work out what was happening. The chef was standing by the door with a knife. Meanwhile, a .223-calibre bullet entered Barbara Klueznik's lower back, lacerated her left kidney, pancreas, spleen, diaphragm, liver, heart and left lung, fractured her sixth and seventh ribs and exited from her left breast, the force of the shot skewing her so that a second bullet entered at the left breast, made an equally devastating reverse journey through her body, before exiting from her back—all prior to the brain of neurophysiologist Widajewicz registering the sound of gunshots and concluding there was a holdup:

"I believed it was only the cashier that was endangered." Barbara Maria Klueznik, needless to say, was already dead.

Lépine strolled the length of the cafeteria, firing off shots at will. Those who had not fled sought the desperately inadequate cover of moulded plastic chairs and laminated tables. By the time Lépine left the cafeteria by a door at the far end, two more young women lay dead and one other girl was wounded. He went in search of fresh prey on the third floor.

The first two police vehicles now arrived at the École Polytechnique, having, in the first instance, been directed to the Tour des Vierges (the student halls of residence). They were joined almost immediately by another from the same district. In the absence of a senior police official, the officers of one vehicle took charge, and proceeded to cordon off the college, positioning police cars to the southwest and northwest of the building. The district commander, his lieutenant, a tactical intervention unit, a scenes of crimes team and ambulances had all yet to arrive.

Suddenly, Lépine appeared in the third-floor foyer, shooting and wounding three students. Down the corridor, an engineering materials class was in progress. At the front of the class, Eric Forget, Maryse Leclair and Roger Thiffault were giving an oral presentation. They paused a moment, listening. To the ears of anyone unfamiliar with semi-automatic rifle fire, or conditioned only to its electronically enhanced representation on film soundtracks, the distant sound of gunshots could have been a dozen other things. "We thought it was something falling on the ground," Eric Forget would subsequently recall. "Everybody looked around, we wondered what it was, but we didn't realize it was gunshots," and they continued with their presentation.

A short while later, the door of the room burst open and Lépine entered, cradling the Ruger rifle. From Eric Forget's position, the example of high-specification mechanical engineering in Lépine's hands "could have been a toy"— an appraisal he would quickly revise as Lépine advanced, yelling, "Get out, get out," and shot and wounded Maryse Leclair. Forget and Thiffault, along with the two professors, scrambled for cover. Lépine shifted his stance to shoot into the front rows of the class, and swivelled again to target Maud Haviernick and Michèle Richard as they looped away, trying to reach the door. The two young women had worked all term on the same metals project and were also paired together in death.

Lépine began tracking up and down the aisle at the side of the room, firing between the rows of desks. Four students were hit. Roger Thiffault spotted a classmate, Annie Turcotte, between rows five and six, "moaning, crying out for help and bleeding and bleeding." Turcotte had been shot twice in the upper body. The blood was maple-leafed across her white blouse and she twitched under the desks like a nightmare Canadian flag. She would not survive.

There was a brief pause in the shooting, as Lépine came to the end of a magazine and swiftly reloaded. Two students took the opportunity to scurry to the door and escape to the safety of the corridor. Lépine stepped up on a chair, and began stomping across the desktops. Eric Forget kept his head down: "He was shooting all over the place. If you put your head out, he could take it off."

Maryse Leclair lay bleeding on the rostrum, a position she had been in ever since Lépine had entered the room and hit her with his initial shot. The bullet had shattered six of her ribs and bone splinters had lacerated her left lung. She gulped air as she moaned for help. Lépine leapt up on the rostrum next to her and drew his knife, the blade exposed with surgical candour in the flat, fluorescent light. The heaviest of three knife-blows found Maryse Leclair's heart and she moaned no more. She was the fourteenth fatality.

Lépine drew a deep breath and calmly put the knife down on the professor's desk, together with two boxes of cartridges and his baseball cap. He sat down and took off his anorak, revealing a "Skate Rags" sweater with a death's-head motif. He wrapped the anorak around the gun's barrel.

Those who were listening heard him mutter, "Oh shit"—those who were watching saw him squeeze the trigger, blowing the top off his own head. It was not yet 5:30 P.M. The rampage had lasted less than twenty minutes.

Outside in the freezing drizzle, the police cordon around the college had grown to seventeen vehicles and twenty-eight officers. At 5:35 P.M., just as news was coming through that the gunman had killed himself, the district commander arrived to take charge of the operation. One minute later, the first police officers entered the building.

Witold Widajewicz left the cafeteria kitchen by the fire escape, still under the impression that there had been a hold-up. In his laboratory, in the main building of the Université de Montréal, he heard the first radio reports of the massacre. He rushed back to the École Polytechnique. It was the middle of the night when police finally allowed him to re-enter the building: "I found Barbara in the cafeteria. She was still a little bit warm ... I opened the zipper and found a hole in the left breast, the breast I had kissed that day—one hole that finished everything, the American Dream in this country ... We believed that Canada was the safest place in the world. We could have gone to West Germany, or Switzerland."

Marc Lépine: né Gamil Rodrigue Gharbi

Monique Lépine, a Montreal nurse, was 26 years old when she met Algerian-born businessman Liesse Gharbi in 1962. Monique was from a middle-class, French-Canadian family—the daughter of a bank manager—and her professional devotion to the sick had superseded an earlier belief that she had a vocation in the Catholic Church. Liesse was 30 years old, a big, confident man—self-made and proud of it, like Charles Whitman's father—in the wheeler-dealer world of investment finance. "A very bright guy," according to his lawyer, Stanley Selinger. "He spoke a number of languages and was a fantastic salesman. A slick dresser. He could sell the Brooklyn Bridge to anyone." Monique fell for him and they married the following year, 1963, in New York State, USA.

The early years were a golden time for the Gharbis. Their first child, a son, was born on 26 October 1964, and christened Gamil Rodrigue; a daughter, Nadia, was born two years later. Liesse raked in the money through the booming mid-sixties and the family enjoyed smart homes, big cars and big parties. But the Gharbis' marriage soon began to sour. Monique found herself increasingly embarrassed and humiliated by her husband's incessant womanizing. There were rumours he had mistresses in Brossard and Longueuil. Closer to home, a neighbour, Francine Charron, said she was subjected to his attentions and his "fairly vulgar approach."

The glitzy social life of parties and dinners became an ordeal for Monique: "I feared those outings because . . . of the advances he made to women and his habit of rubbing himself against the women he danced with." She claimed he even indulged in frictional behaviour with total strangers on public transport. It was clear to many in the Gharbis' social circle, including Stanley Selinger, that "he never really respected women . . . His wife was not his equal, more like chattel." It was a philosophy that, as time went by, Liesse increasingly impressed upon his spouse with physical violence.

In 1972, Monique was granted custody of the two children and possession of the family apartment, on rue Prieur, in an affluent north-end neighbourhood. The separation from Liesse followed two particularly torrid years of marriage during which, she told a divorce hearing, she had been beaten by her husband in front of family and friends (slammed repeatedly into the stone wall of a cottage on one occasion), had liquor thrown in her face for returning home late from a social outing, cowered in a cellar for hours in fear of another beating, and witnessed the frequent thrashing of her children if they sang too loudly or failed to say good morning to their father.

Liesse was a violent man. Although he denied that he had ever physically abused his family to the extent Monique claimed—"It is certain that occasionally in life someone can receive a slap, but to hit someone and hurt them, no"— there was much corroborative testimony for his wife's allegations, and Quebec Superior Court Justice Jeanne Warren, particularly disturbed to learn of his refusals to allow Monique to console the children after he had beaten them, restricted his visits with Gamil and Nadia to once a month, and only under strict supervision. Liesse, however, took little subsequent interest in his offspring.

After the breakdown of the marriage, Monique returned to her nursing career. She worked long hours, studied hard and had little time to spare for the children. For a few years, until they were old enough to be left on their own, Gamil and Nadia were shuffled between the willing hands of relatives and friends. Gamil appears to have had a lot of affection for one uncle in particular, reportedly a former US Special Forces-trained paratrooper who taught him how to use a gun. During this period, Monique became so concerned by her and the children's "difficulties expressing our need to love and be loved" that she enrolled the family in psychotherapy. In the summer of 1976, with a year of psychotherapy behind them, she and the children also said goodbye to the bad memories of rue Prieur, and moved into a small house, on rue Perron, in Pierrefonds. There were woods and a river nearby and it seemed like a good place for wounds to heal.

When Gamil Gharbi started Grade 7 at École Secondaire St. Thomas, in Pointe Claire, he was a quiet, withdrawn young boy who habitually hid himself and his shock of black, curly hair under one of his many baseball caps. Jean Bélanger, also from the rue Perron neighbourhood, first came across him on the school bus: "So, here was this new guy on the bus and I'm the talkative type and he obviously wasn't. So I sat next to him." Gamil had found himself a friend. The two boys lived practically next door to each other, went to school together, spent the evenings and weekends together, and became great friends.

In Bélanger's opinion, "the guy was not nutso," although he clearly had some problems. When he first started visiting the Bélanger house, "he would get inside the front door, take off his boots, tug his hat down, and all but run past my parents . . . It was kind of as though he was afraid of something." However, it was never very easy for Jean to find out what was going on inside Gamil's head—"If he would have a problem, he would never ask for help. If something hurt him inside, he would keep it to himself"— and only once, after persistent probing, did Gamil refer to his violent father: "He told me they would be sitting at the dinner table and if his mother served Marc and Nadia before the father, the father would go nuts and start beating everybody."

At school, Gamil's academic record was good. Socially, he was a lot less competent. With the exception of Jean Bélanger, he avoided contact with other students as much as possible. He sat at the back of classes if he could manage it, and gave a wide berth to team sports, school clubs, even the cafeteria at lunchtimes. It was during a lunch hour, one day in Grade 8, sitting at a quiet spot in woods near the school, that Gamil told Jean he was going to take his mother's name: "He said he wanted my name, Jean, too. Jean Lépine. I said that would be too confusing—Jean and Jean—because we were together all the time. So he thought for a moment and said: 'OK, how about Marc? Marc Lépine?' " Thereafter, he went around calling himself Marc Lépine and signed his school work the same way.

Lépine's major interest was electronics and he wanted to be an electronics engineer or computer engineer. He spent much of his time with Jean in the basement of the Bélanger house, designing and assembling light sequencers, sound effects systems, mini-computers—anything they could construct from salvaged electronic junk. The boys were also interested in guns and warfare. They visited an army surplus store from time to time, but Bélanger observed no developing psychopathy in his friend's purchases: a gas mask here, a helmet there. It was the same when it came to shooting pigeons with their air guns: "He wasn't like, 'Yeah, I want to kill.' It was just fun. We were kids." Bélanger's recollection of their pigeon-shooting days is, nevertheless, somewhat chilling in the light of subsequent events: "We each had a pellet gun and when the pigeons would fly up from their perch, pow. He was better than me. He could shoot one while it was flying. He didn't miss a lot."

According to Bélanger, Lépine found little sister Nadia hard work: "She was the total opposite to Marc. He was the quiet intellectual. She used to taunt him all the time. She used to call him Gamil, Gamil, Gamil . . . if you wanted to really bug him, just call him Gamil." With Monique working and studying, Marc was given the task of looking after Nadia. He didn't get a summer job but he was paid by his mother to stay at home and do the chores.

In 1978, Monique enlisted the help of the Big Brothers Association to provide a surrogate father. The Big Brother was an easy-going man in his mid-forties, and Marc got along well with him; Jean too. He introduced them to photography and motorbikes, took them to the cinema, even bought them electronic equipment. The following year, 1979, the boys graduated from St. Thomas Junior High to Polyvalente des Sources, in Dollard des Ormeaux. Lépine maintained his reputation as a sound, if nondescript student. Robert Ouillette taught him maths: "He was very usual, average, plain and typical."

Lépine appears to have remained fairly happy through this period. The Big Brother was a lot of fun and although Jean Bélanger was now dating a girl, Gina Cousineau, Lépine had few fears of losing his buddy to Cupid. He was very shy around Gina at first but after getting to know her "he was fine. He said I was not just a typical girl . . . I was more like one of the guys . . . We were always together, the three of us . . . We became like the Three Musketeers." Bélanger encouraged Lépine to try dating for himself but "he had a lot of problems with that. It's not that he wasn't interested. Maybe the way that he approached women wasn't exactly the way women like." The Three Musketeers never got to be four.

In 1981, the Big Brother suddenly disappeared. Lépine told contradictory stories about what had happened. First he said that the man had simply taken off to Europe, then that he was gay, had assaulted a young boy, and been jailed. Bélanger was never sure which, if any, of the explanations was true. In the winter of 1981–2, in the wake of the Big Brother's disappearance, Lépine walked into the army recruiting office in downtown Montreal and filled out an application. The military rejected him—"interviewed, assessed and determined [him] to be unsuitable," according to the official statement. He was 17 years old.

Soon after the army rejection, Monique sold the house in Pierrefonds and moved the family into an apartment in Marlborough Court, on the western perimeter of the Aéroport de Cartierville, in St. Laurent. It was nearer to St. Jude de Laval Hospital, a long-term care facility, where she worked as a director of nursing. Of more relevance to Lépine, it was far enough away from Pierrefonds for him gradually to lose touch with his only close friend, Jean Bélanger. Bélanger thought that "Marc didn't seem very happy there. We had been together for so long, I guess maybe he was lonely."

In the autumn of 1982, Lépine enrolled at CEGEP St. Laurent (a community college), in a pure sciences course—a popular route to engineering school. At home, he was shutting himself away in his room with his books, piles of electronic components, and an old computer—the major input from the outside world being the sound of aircraft on the nearby flight path. On one of the last occasions Jean

Bélanger saw him, Lépine gave the impression that these days his best friend was the computer.

It was now that Lépine's plans for a career in engineering started to go awry. He failed two subjects in the first term of his course. His grades improved somewhat in term two but he decided, nevertheless, to make the first of what would develop into a bizarre geometry of career moves. In the autumn of 1983, he switched from pure sciences to a narrower programme in electronics. Then, strangely, in January 1986, with just a few months to go to graduation, he suddenly aborted the course. "He quit for reasons we don't know," Claude Boily, the director of CEGEP St. Laurent revealed. "He did not notify the college of his decision. He just stopped going to his classes." According to Boily's records, Lépine enrolled in a total of fifty-seven course components, passed in forty-one of them, leaving sixteen that he either failed or dropped. "[He] was never seen by any of our psychologists and there was not any report in his file noting that he had any behavioural problems." Boily's only clue to Lépine's motive for quitting came from a head of department who seemed to remember that he had talked about attending the École Polytechnique. Lépine's first verifiable visit to the engineering school was, in fact, on 11 September 1985—he made a purchase at the Students' Cooperative—and it was soon after this that his CEGEP tutor noticed an unexplained drop in his marks.

If Lépine quit CEGEP St. Laurent in the belief that the course components he had already completed were sufficient qualification for gaining admission to the École Polytechnique, then he was wrong. When he filed his application to the engineering school in 1986, he was deficient in two subjects. He was informed that his application could be reconsidered only after he had completed the two courses he was lacking. The rejection by the École Polytechnique appears to have outraged Lépine; certainly, it marked the end of his studies for a while. He got a job in the kitchens of St. Jude de Laval Hospital.

The work at St. Jude's failed to challenge his intellectual abilities, but the money he was earning did enable him to save for a new computer and to move out of his mother's house and rent a modern, one-bedroom apartment in Laval. In the eyes of landlord Luc Riopel, Lépine was a model tenant. He paid his rent on time, kept the place clean and was no bother to his neighbours: "He was a good guy. But he lived in isolation and did not appear very happy. He told me he didn't like working at the hospital. It was not what he wanted to do for a living. It was just a job for him. His real interest was in computers. And war books. He had a lot of war books."

At St. Jude's, Lépine's poor social skills made things difficult for him. He worked at a hundred miles an hour and tried to take on the persona of a wisecracking extrovert. Things got broken and nobody found him funny. Most people kept their distance. Dominique Leclair, a student who worked at the hospital on her summer vacation, was an exception: "I was kind to him because he was so hyperactive and nervous. Everyone else tried to avoid him because he was a bit strange because of his shyness." Lépine did a spell serving food out in the cafeteria but people complained about his acne. He was banished back to the kitchens and tried to grow a beard. When Dominique Leclair returned to college in the autumn, Lépine followed suit.

He enrolled in a short course at CEGEP Montmorency, studying mass communication, algebra and politics. He worked hard and completed the course, gaining marks of 75 per cent or higher in all three components. His enthusiasm for study rekindled, he took an entrance exam, and passed, for a $9,000 computer course at the private Control Data Institute in downtown Montreal. He began the course in March 1988. The setup at Control Data had a major attraction for him: students worked alone—no group work for him to try to avoid, no classes for him to try to find a back seat in. The only interaction necessary was with a computer and, true to form, he was known as the quiet guy who liked to wear baseball caps.

His studies, ostensibly, were leading him towards having another crack at getting a place at the École Polytechnique. Geographically, he was certainly gravitating towards the campus. He had started out in Pierrefonds, twenty kilometres from the Université de Montréal site; his final move, to 2175 rue de Bordeaux, took him to within five kilometres. He shared the second floor apartment there with an old high school acquaintance, Erik Cossette.

It was from around the time of this last change of address that some of the private turmoil going on inside Lépine's head began to manifest itself publicly. He was giving many people the impression that his sights were still set on gaining admission to the École Polytechnique; yet, other people were being fed a quite different story. Luc Riopel, the Laval landlord, said that when Lépine moved out, he had said that he was going off to join the army. Lépine also got in touch with his old buddy, Jean Bélanger, their first contact in about five years, and told him he was thinking of joining the military. He had gone to a high school reunion in the hope of seeing Bélanger, but Bélanger, in hospital after an accident, was unable to attend. Lépine did, however, see Bélanger's former sweetheart, Gina Cousineau, at the reunion. She was there with her fiancé. They talked at some length. Gina asked him how he came to finish working at St. Jude's: "He told me he had been fired by a woman and that another woman had taken his place."

Lépine's hostility towards women and his sexist views were becoming increasingly overt. His flatmate, Erik Cossette, found his views offensive but not unusual. He tended to put the bitter remarks down to Lépine's inability to establish intimate relationships with women and he felt that Lépine just needed to socialize more. As it was, he spent most of his free time with his computer and books, or watching videos from his large collection of mostly pirated

Pay-TV war movies, examining what Cossette called the "strategic aspect" of war.

As well as the programme at Control Data, Lépine had also enrolled in an evening update course in chemistry at CEGEP Vieux Montréal, a prerequisite for getting accepted by the École Polytechnique. Here, in February 1989, he met a young woman called Sylvie Drouin. Sylvie thought him quite a good-looking guy and asked him to be her lab partner. Their relationship got off to a poor start. Lépine called her "Fräulein" all the time and for the first few weeks "he was very severe with me. I was never correct. He was being a fascist." Sylvie finally gave him an ultimatum: leave off or get himself another partner. Lépine began treating her with a bit more respect.

Sylvie was also taking a course in computers and asked Lépine if he could help her. She suggested maybe she could come over to his place. "In the beginning, he was a lot of fun. I remember the first time I walked in and he told me to sit on the chair and he showed me all these things he could do with his computer—colours, three-dimensional stuff, that kind of thing." But Lépine was not a very good teacher and when it came to Sylvie's homework, he simply wanted to solve the problems himself and hand the finished result over to her. Sylvie, nevertheless, continued her visits. They spent about a dozen evenings together in the spring and early summer of 1989, but the relationship remained platonic and Lépine became increasingly uncommunicative and withdrawn.

Although the world inside Lépine's head spilled into the public domain less frequently now, on the occasions when it did, it showed itself to be a more sinister world than had previously been seen. One day he turned up at the chemistry class with a newspaper clipping about a police-woman, bitterly complaining that women should not be allowed on the police force. In the ensuing discussion, the lab assistant, André Tremblay, submitted that the Montreal police had a large number of female officers, a suggestion with which Lépine took fierce issue: "He said 'to date, I have only found the names of six of them in newspaper stories.' " Erik Cossette also received lectures from Lépine on women in "male" occupations, as did the employees in a neighbourhood grocery store.

The one place where an altogether happier Lépine could be found, was Checkmate Sports, a gunshop, on rue St. Hubert. An assistant at Checkmate would later recall, "He used to come in like many young punks, browsing around . . . [He] didn't appear crazier than anybody else . . . he seemed like a happy guy. I guess he felt good here . . . It isn't a place where you see a lot of women. It is like a boys' club—toys for boys."

Sylvie Drouin saw Lépine one final time, about a week after the chemistry class finished in May 1989. She was still unaware that as long ago as March he had quit the Control Data computer course. "The reason he gave," said Jean Cloutier, the director of Control Data, "was that he was going to change his career. He did not say what his plans were." Sylvie told Lépine she had been accepted for an engineering programme at the Université du Québec a Trois Rivières. He told her he would be going to the École Polytechnique in the autumn.

Lépine, in fact, was going nowhere. All his ambitions had come to nothing. The weeks passed. Sylvie had said she might phone him through the summer, but never did. At the end of the summer, Erik Cossette deserted him to go back-packing in South America. On 5 September, Lépine applied for, and subsequently received, a Firearms Acquisition Permit. On 21 November, he purchased the Ruger Mini-14 Rifle and a hundred rounds of ammunition from Checkmate Sports. The next day, he was seen wandering the second floor of the École Polytechnique. He was seen again at the engineering school on 1 December (twice), 4 December, and 5 December. On the afternoon of 5 December, he also rented a car. The following day, Wednesday 6 December, he drove the car through a freezing drizzle to the

École Polytechnique. It was the last day of classes before the Christmas vacation; and it was the last hour of life for Marc Lépine. He parked the car in a tow-away area.

The Aftermath

In the course of the police investigation of the massacre, various theories for Lépine's motives were formulated and tested. Did he, perhaps, set out to kill one particular woman, and then get carried away? It was, in fact, soon established that his last victim, Maryse Leclair, was a cousin of Dominique Leclair, the girl who had befriended him when he was working in the kitchens of St. Jude de Laval Hospital. There were possibilities in this. Had he intended to kill Dominique but mistaken Maryse for her? Did he know Maryse herself, through Dominique? Had he intended to kill Maryse? The possibilities along these lines seemed promising because of the particular circumstances of Maryse's murder; she was the only victim who had been stabbed to death and Lépine had committed suicide immediately after killing her.

It took little further investigation, however, to dismiss these theories. First, Dominique and Maryse looked nothing like each other. It seemed impossible that Lépine could have mistaken one for the other. Secondly, no evidence emerged to suggest that he had ever met Maryse. Finally, even if he had known Maryse (unbeknown to any of her friends or acquaintances), had known which classroom she would be in on the afternoon of 6 December, and had set out to kill her, it would have been unlikely that he would have found her because the room the class was held in was changed at the last minute. All the evidence suggested that the Lépine-Leclair connection was a coincidence, and there was no evidence linking him to any of his other victims. Ultimately, the police team investigating the murders "could not find one single event to explain what triggered the assault. Only one person could tell us what went on . . . but regrettably he is dead."

Lépine did, as it happens, leave an explanation for his actions, in a three-page, handwritten letter, found on his body. The letter was dated 6 December 1989.

Please note that if I am committing suicide today . . . it is not for economic reasons . . . but for political reasons. For I have decided to send Ad Patres the feminists who have always ruined my life. For seven years my life has been joyless . . . and I have decided to put an end to those viragos.

I had already tried in my youth to enlist in the Forces as an officer cadet, which would have allowed me to enter the arsenal and precede Lortie in a rampage. They refused me because asocial. So I waited until this day to execute all my projects. In between, I continued my studies in a haphazard way for they never really interested me, knowing in advance my fate. Which did not prevent me from obtaining very good marks despite not handing in my theory works and the lack of studying before exams.

Even if the Mad Killer epithet will be attributed to me by the media, I consider myself a rational erudite [person] that only the arrival of the Grim Reaper has forced to take extreme acts.

. . . feminists always have a talent to enrage me. They want to keep the advantages of women (e.g. cheaper insurance, extended maternity leave . . .) while trying to grab those of the men. Thus, it is an obvious truth that if the Olympic Games removed the Men-Women distinction, there would be women only in the graceful events. So the feminists are not fighting to remove that barrier. They are so opportunistic they neglect to profit from the knowledge accumulated by men through the ages. They always try to misrepresent them every time they can. Thus, the other day. I heard they were honouring the Canadian men and women who fought at the frontline during the world wars. How can you explain then that women were not authorized to go to the frontline??? Will we hear of Caesar's female legions and female galley slaves who of course took up 50 per cent of the ranks of history, though they never existed. A real Causus Belli.

The letter was followed by the names of nineteen female public figures, with an added note: "Nearly died today. The lack of time (because I started too late) has allowed those radical feminists to survive. Alea Jacta Est."

Lépine's letter raises many more questions than it answers. It does not tell us, for instance, why he chose to take the action he did when countless other men feel a well-placed fist is sufficient contribution to the misogynist cause. Neither does it tell us why he waited so long to "execute all my projects," or why, in fact, he did not attempt to execute *all* of them. Why did he not pursue the nineteen prominent women on his hate list? He cites "the lack of time," but this is a man who, by his own claims, had been pondering the murder of feminists for seven years. Why, we may wonder, did he have no apparent urge to target his mother, as some of our other killers have? Was not Monique, the director of nursing, who had paid him to stay at home and do the household chores as a teenager, the epitome of the career women he so hated? Was he really motivated by "political reasons"? Or are, perhaps, the bloody heiroglyphics, written across the three floors of the École Polytechnique, more revealing of his motives than the pretentious prattle of revolutionary martyrdom scrawled in the three pages of his suicide letter?

The Killer's Life and Crimes

Examining the biography of Marc Lépine, it is hard not to conclude that early in life he was primed, like a virus-loaded computer, to explode—in one way or another—at some future date. Furthermore, this explosion had the potential to take a mass murderous form, for he possessed many of the key traits of the pseudo-commando killer. In particular, he had much in common with University of Texas sniper, and struggling engineering junior, Charles Whitman.

Like Whitman, Lépine developed a preoccupation with status, which grew from his relationship with his father. For Lépine, the idea of himself as a white Canadian Francophile was particularly potent because he so badly wanted to reject his paternal heritage: he detested his Algerian-born father, could not ditch the Muslim name he had been given fast enough, and remained ever self-conscious about his black, curly hair. Although he doubtless found the material trappings of success, in which he was swaddled through early childhood, desirable, his father's wheeler-dealer status he certainly did not, and as a teenager he developed a grand, but conspicuously conventional, male Francophile ambition; he set his heart on studying to become an engineer at the Université de Montréal, the largest French-speaking university outside of France, and one of the most highly respected. Similarly, Charles Whitman despised the "semi-literate" entrepreneur Charles Sen., and badly wanted to succeed at the prestigious University of Texas.

Lépine and Whitman were both introduced to guns and violence at an early age; and both their fathers were wife-beaters. While Whitman grew up detesting his father for beating his mother but went on to beat his own wife—and kill her—Lépine vehemently hated Liesse but, nevertheless, developed the same philosophy of women as inferior beings, designed to do the bidding of men and to be violently punished if they stepped out of line. Just as the infant Gamil hugged his father's legs while he was being thrashed, so the adult Marc embraced his father's ideas about women. Some strands of his paternal heritage he was never able to discard.

If Charles Whitman functioned reasonably well socially, Lépine was a more obvious loner, although in his teenage years, with his great friend, Jean Bélanger, most people (including Lépine himself, one suspects) were lulled into seeing little more to him than healthy normality. He did, however, have problems, as Bélanger noticed. Liesse's violence, coupled with the fact that he forbade Monique to console the children after he beat them, had a damaging effect on the family, manifesting itself most conspicuously in the difficulties they had in showing their love for one another. Despite the year of counselling, acute emotional inhibitions would plague Lépine all his life, making it extremely difficult for him to establish close relationships. As late as 1989, according to his flatmate, Erik Cossette, his inability to communicate feelings of warmth towards people was still a millstone around his neck: "Doing favours was his way of expressing his affection."

Like Charles Whitman, the first thing Lépine did on entering adulthood was apply to join the military. While Whitman succeeded, though, and was able to gain direct entry to the University of Texas, sponsored by the navy, Lépine failed and had to embark upon a pre-engineering school programme at CEGEP St. Laurent. In his suicide letter, Lépine claimed that he had tried to enlist in the army in order to gain access to weapons "and precede Lortie in a rampage." This claim is nonsense; nothing more than retrospective oneupmanship. At the time he filed his application, he was looking forward to a bright and successful future. There was no reason for him to commit wholesale slaughter.

His disclosure that "for seven years my life has been joyless," is more credible, for it was in 1982 that the potentially dangerous components in his character first began to be wired into what would become a mass murderous personality. The pivotal event of the period was the move from Pierrefonds to St. Laurent. Lépine lost the only close friend he had ever had, Jean Bélanger, the cover that had for so long protected him from the need to socialize on any wider scale.

Alone in adulthood, Lépine's poor social skills were painfully exposed—recall his occasional and ludicrous attempts to play the wisecracking extrovert—and he struggled in vain to establish any close and lasting relationships. His emotional inhibitions, harnessed to his sexist views made intimate friendships with women particularly problematic. While the handsome and socially competent Charles Whitman was able to get himself a wife, Lépine was forever retreating to his room with his tail between his legs; back to the safe, impersonal—but lonely—world of his books, videos and computers. As time went by, he projected his own inadequacies onto the women who were rejecting him— women who tended to be, because of his engineering student aspirations and limited social life, fellow students, including, like Sylvie Drouin, aspiring engineers.

Socially inept and isolated, Lépine invested his hopes for happiness in achieving his career ambitions. Gaining admission to the École Polytechnique was now extremely important to him. Not only would he gain public confirmation of his status as a Canadian Francophile male— the status he so coveted—but it would also validate the quiet, intellectual social identity he was constructing for himself, and provide compensation for the joyless nature of his personal life—thus killing, with one stone, all the birds that were forever pecking away at his self-esteem, and allowing him to take what he believed was his *rightful* place in society.

Although Canada's murder rate changed little during Lépine's lifetime, elsewhere in Canadian society there were vast and widespread transformations—evolutionary strands as disparate as the decline of the railways, the rise of the car as king, and the emergence of the Women's Movement. Canada's particularly strong feminist lobby achieved more success in raising women's consciousness and getting progressive ideas enshrined in legislation than the feminist lobbies in many other nations—in part, perhaps, because the Canadian political system makes it easier to pass radical legislation than, say, the American congressional system. Between 1967 and 1987, the number of women in the workforce rose from less than 33 per cent to approaching 45 per cent. Canadian women also made great strides in education. While the number of men (under 24 years old) with university degrees barely changed between 1976 and 1986 (around 74,000) the number of women leapt from 73,000 to almost 91,000.

Lépine was applying for admission to the École Polytechnique at a time when competition from women was unprecedentedly strong, and he felt deeply humiliated and angered when he was rejected. Already intensely insecure about his social identity, he refused to accept that he, the techno-intellectual, could have been rejected on any legitimate, academic grounds, and the rise of the female student provided him with an extremely convenient scapegoat. Indeed, were these not also the very same women responsible for the misery in his personal life?

His hostility towards female students, particularly female engineering students, was now two-pronged. Not only were they unwilling to be seduced by him, but they had also now denied him the successful career and social status that he so badly wanted. His conviction that they were the cause of all his problems grew.

After being rejected by the École Polytechnique, and after overcoming his initial outrage, Lépine returned to his studies, at first with enthusiasm, then half-heartedly and with increasing disillusionment. With similarly unsatisfactory results he persisted in trying to establish relationships with women. Although publicly he was still insisting that he was either going to engineering school or going to join the army, in reality, these were no longer goals he was working towards but past failures with which he was becoming increasingly obsessed. It was a sign of his desperation that he sought out, after five contactless years, his old friend,

Jean Bélanger. However, the high school reunion held no joy for him. Any hopes he harboured that the golden years of Pierrefonds might somehow be recreated—if only for a night—were quickly dashed. The hospitalized Bélanger was not even able to attend, while the third "Musketeer," Gina Cousineau, was engaged to be married.

In the summer of 1989, the last of Lépine's all too common cycles of underachievement came to an end. It seems to have been at this point that the gaping chasm between his high ambitions and low achievements—and the impossibility of his ever rectifying the situation—became clear in his own mind. To rub salt into his wounds, Sylvie Drouin was accepted for an engineering programme at the Université du Québec a Trois Rivières, and deserted him. Soon after, he lost his flatmate, Erik Cossette. More isolated than ever, the future stretching ahead as an interminable hell of impotence and frustration, he brooded on his broken dreams.

Lépine had been reduced, in his own mind, as all our killers are, to a nobody, a nothing man—the mere shell of everything he had hoped and expected to be. It was a situation that the acutely status-conscious man found intolerable. With the Ruger Mini-14 Rifle, he set out to take the active, aggressive role in society, which had been denied him, and to make his mark forcibly upon the world. That his "achievements" would only be a warped reflection of the achievements that had eluded him in twenty-five years as a regular, law-abiding citizen, was unimportant to him. As we have seen before, for the nouveau nobody, revenge is sweet and status, at any cost, a mesmeric reward.

In killing female engineering students at the École Polytechnique in quasi-military fashion, Lépine was gaining three-fold revenge: on the social group and the two institutions that had rejected him. His targets, his weapon, and his chosen battlefield were all heavily charged with personal meaning for him, but what the case demonstrates with particular clarity is the influence of social dynamics and cultural tensions on the incidence of mass murder.

11

GUNWOMEN

At the same time that Marc Lépine was developing the urge to murder female engineering students in Canada, a disturbing new phenomenon—related to the same cultural dynamics that were helping shape him—appeared in the United States; rampaging gunwomen. In comparison to men, their number was small but it was, nevertheless, a significant development for there was no precedent.

Historically, the female mass murderer, although not unknown, is rare. Women have been the perpetrators in some family, suicide-by-proxy cases, and have also killed for profit. There are women who have been seduced by aggressive ideologies and become mass killers—on behalf of the state, or on behalf of violent anti-government organizations. From time to time, women have appeared— usually in a subordinate role—alongside mass-murdering men; Caril Ann Fugate, for example, accompanied Charles Starkweather on a rampage through Nebraska in 1958. If such women are rare, though, then the female mass killer who kills outside of the family, for no financial gain and with no sponsorship from any other party, is rarer still— an occasional anomaly in most cultures.

On Monday 29 January 1979, the day newspaper heiress turned armed robber Patricia Hearst had her prison sentence commuted by President Jimmy Carter, 16-year-old Brenda Spencer opened fire with a .22-calibre rifle on the Cleveland Elementary School, opposite her home in the San Carlos area of San Diego. She shot dead the principal, Burton Wragg, and another employee, Michael Suchar, and she wounded a policeman and eight children. Her grandfather was a former Chula Vista mayor; her father, Wallace, was a supervisor at the San Diego State University and her mother, Dorothy, was a bookkeeper for the Andy Williams San Diego Open Golf Tournament. Brenda was a great fan of a TV series, *SWAT*, and was obsessed with guns. The .22 she used in the shootings—which she had apparently been planning for days or even weeks—was a Christmas present from her father.

At the time, Spencer's actions were generally regarded as an extreme and freak manifestation of juvenile delinquency and seemed so superlatively nihilistic that the then punk rocker Bob Geldof was inspired to pen the lyrics for the Boomtown Rats' chart smash "I Don't Like Mondays." When other rampaging gunwomen appeared, though, hard on Spencer's heels, they could not be so easily dismissed. Indeed, if this recent development—like the Lépine killings—owes more to particular cultural dynamics than it does to bizarre, individual psychopathology, then rampaging gunwomen—women like 25-year-old Sylvia Seegrist, who shot dead three people and wounded seven others in a Philadelphia shopping mall in 1985, and 30-year-old Laurie Dann, who shot seven people, one fatally, and attempted to kill literally dozens of others, in Illinois in 1988—may not be so rare in the future.

Women today, particularly those from families wealthy enough to invest in good education for their daughters, face new and onerous pressures. If they are ever to regard themselves as anything like successful, they must meet the extremely testing demands of influential cultural legislators, such as magazines and advertising images, on what the modern woman should be: she must have a successful career and still be able to get her man and run an efficient and happy home. To succeed, she must develop a strong sense of personal sovereignty, and kindle the aggressive self-interest demanded by the environment of competitive individualism in which she finds herself. Significantly, rampaging gunwomen have tended to come from ambitious, well-to-do families—exactly the kind of women who feel these pressures most acutely—and there is no better example than Laurie Wasserman Dann.

The Killer's Life

Norman Wasserman and Edith Lewis grew up together between the wars in the South Shore area of Chicago. Norman was a conscientious student and a talented tennis player. Edith was a year younger than he and the daughter of a gifted attorney. They were not long out of high school when they married in 1950 and, in 1952, when their first child, a son, Mark, was born, Norman had only just qualified as a public accountant. Five years later, on 18 October 1957, they had a second child, a girl, Laurie.

By the early 1960s, many professional people were abandoning the city's inner suburbs. Norman's accountancy practice was booming and the Wassermans were able to ride the migratory wave all the way out to the exclusive villages of the North Shore. Their first North Shore home was in the less desirable southwest section of Highland Park, and they made few friends in the neighbourhood. People got the impression Edith was a snob and that she thought Mark and Laurie were too good for the other kids on the street. Mark was not around much, anyway—he was invariably off somewhere with his high school friends—but Laurie, five years younger and attending the nearby West Ridge Elementary School, naturally looked to the local children for friendship and company.

Now and again, Edith would allow Laurie to invite a select group of neighbourhood girls into the Wasserman home, a three-storey brick house with big bay windows, where they would play with Laurie's huge collection of beautiful dolls and ugly trolls. If Laurie ventured out into the street, though, it would never be very long before her mother was yelling at her to get back indoors. The other kids would not see her again for the rest of the day; sometimes not for several days. In the neighbourhood and at school, she was known as a shy and somewhat morose little girl who always seemed to be on the periphery of things.

According to many people who knew the Wassermans, Norman and Edith were a very formal and mannerly couple, and not given to overt displays of emotion or affection. A high school sweetheart of Laurie's got the impression that Norman was too busy with work to give his daughter much attention and that Edith was concerned only with appearances—whether Laurie was nicely turned out and whether she would be able to get into a respectable college. Laurie herself often complained that her parents gave her little real love or support. They gave her a wealth of toys, treats and other expensive gifts, including plastic surgery. Laurie, as a child, had Mickey Mouse ears and an outsize nose. By the time she graduated from high school, though, she looked rather less like her trolls and more like Barbie.

Norman and Edith may have been able to buy their daughter a cute face, but they could not buy her academic and social success. According to one schoolfellow, at Red Oak Junior High, "She was very, very quiet and she was very strange because you'd walk down the hall and say 'Hi' and she wouldn't say anything . . . It didn't seem she had many friends." The *Red Oak Leaves* yearbook of 1971 included a prophecy for each student. Bernie Hirsch was one of the co-authors. "It's really weird because everyone else gets, like 20 words," he would tell reporters many years later. "She gets one . . . Laurie Wasserman 'grows.'"

It referred to the fact that she was the only girl in the class who had still to show any physical signs of maturity.

From 1971 to 1973, Laurie attended Highland Park High School, where social and academic success continued to elude her. Her closest relationship was with a senior from Maine North High, whom she met in the summer of 1972 (their families were holidaying at the same Hawaii resort), but the romance faded when he graduated the following summer. That same summer, the Wassermans moved to Glencoe—to a ranch-style house on a half-acre plot. It cost $100,000, but by Glencoe standards was a modest home. The move—and a nose job at around the same time—gave Laurie, who had suffered two miserable years at Highland Park High, the chance of a fresh start.

With her refined looks and expensive clothes, she was quite the centre of attention when she first walked into New Trier East High School in Winnetka in September 1973. The spotlight did not stay on her for long, though. She lacked the social skills and confidence to make her presence felt and loitered uneasily on the periphery of the cliques she admired. She tried out for the cheerleaders but failed to impress. It was a similar story with boys. There were plenty who gave her more than a passing glance, thanks to the plastic surgeon, but those who got close to her tended to discover that she lacked personality and that she was possessive and dependent. Still, for every boy who ditched her, there was always another ready to take his place. According to one classmate, "She always had a boyfriend and was really clingy, draped around him." One of them would later tell reporters that she was "real cute and had a great figure," but "I can't remember that she had any friends of her own." Laurie graduated from New Trier East High, in 1975, a mediocre student, a social dud and a big disappointment to her parents.

Her college career was equally unimpressive. She started out at Drake University, a small private school in Des

Moines, popular with the parents of North Shore under-
achievers, and then transferred the following year to the
more glamorous University of Arizona, in Tucson. She
studied education in preparation for a career as an elementary school teacher. She also studied men. She was apparently
looking for a husband and arranged dates with dozens of
potential candidates. Her longest relationship was with a
pre-med student, but her possessiveness was so intense
and her devotion to him so slavish that he finally deserted
her. Laurie was devastated. She withdrew from UA-Tucson
and returned home to Illinois. Her plan was to live with
her parents and finish her studies at nearby Northwestern
University.

In the autumn of 1980, she enrolled in a psychology
course, but it bored her and she quit. Other unfinished
courses followed. Perhaps to commit herself more resolutely to the university, she took a suite at the Lake Shore Club,
a Northwestern dormitory, and, as if to convince herself that
she really could make it at Northwestern, she constantly
wore purple, one of the school's colours. According to
Joel Kaplan, George Papajohn and Eric Zorn, in *Murder
of Innocence*, "It was such a memorable fixation that when
the residents played the Galaxian video game they referred
to the purple-colored aliens as Wassermans."

To help support herself, Laurie worked as a waitress at
the Green Acres Country Club in Northbrook. It was there,
in the spring of 1981, that she first met Russell Dann,
a young and dynamic sales executive who had followed
both his father, Armand, and older brother, Scott, into the
family business—Dann Brothers Insurance Company—one
of the biggest independent commercial insurance operators
in Chicago. According to Charles Dann, an uncle, "You
could characterize Russell as an all-American boy. Very
outgoing, a great number of friends, well-liked."

Their first dates went well and Laurie set about winning Russell's love with careful determination. She avoided making most of the mistakes that had turned her past

relationships sour and she came across as an unassuming, intelligent (she exaggerated her academic achievements no end), and beautiful young woman. What quirky and inappropriate behaviour she did exhibit was overlooked by the love-struck Russell, and what vague reservations his family and friends had about her they kept largely to themselves. On 11 September 1982, Russell and Laurie were married. It was a small wedding. Other than her family, there were only a few people Laurie knew well enough to invite, and Russell was obliged to prune his guest list drastically to bring it into line.

On their honeymoon in the Virgin Islands, Laurie's lack of self-confidence and social adroitness seemed to Russell to be more conspicuous than usual, and on their return to Chicago, when Laurie moved in with him, he gradually began to notice other things about her that during their courtship he either had not seen or had paid no heed to. Her life was governed by childish little superstitions—she would not step on pavement cracks, for example—but as time went by these became more numerous and debilitating, badly interfering with her life. She developed an aversion for putting tops and lids back on containers and many other irrational fears that reduced the house to a shambles. Her academic failings, her inability to hold down a job (she was hired and fired by countless North Shore employers) and her lack of aptitude for country club sports were also soon exposed.

According to Kaplan, Papajohn and Zorn, "All Laurie Wasserman Dann ever wanted, really, was to be someone else—a girl from a happy family, popular, a good student, a college graduate and a presentable housewife. She had no idea what to do with the person she was." On numerous occasions, she confided in people that she felt terribly intimidated and outclassed by the other women in her husband's life. Russell's mother was a commodities broker and a red-hot tennis player. His sister, Susie, was outgoing and popular, a former teacher and a mother of three children.

The wives of all Russell's friends were super-successful modern women and Laurie felt she simply could not compete. "She . . . killed her days by shopping, going to lunch with her mom, sleeping, watching TV and worrying that her own failings would destroy the marriage she had wanted so badly," say Kaplan, Papajohn and Zorn. The superstitions and rituals—which, psychiatrists say, often spring from feelings of helplessness and a desperate need to feel some measure of control—only made things worse.

Less than two years into the marriage, and seeing Russell's support and patience beginning to wear thin, Laurie told him she would seek professional help. She started seeing Dr. Robert Greendale, a Highland Park psychiatrist but, after just a few sessions, telephoned to say she would not be returning. In a follow-up letter, the doctor told her:

> I am genuinely concerned about your ability to cope with the problems that you have been struggling with. I think it is important for you to realize, if you don't already, that the nature of your problems goes back long before you married your husband and it relates very much to your childhood upbringing . . . Furthermore, the use of medication can only result in a symptomatic improvement and not in a definitive cure for the kinds of difficulties that you are experiencing . . . I feel that it is of extreme importance that you reconsider some kind of professional help.

Russell showed the letter to Norman Wasserman. Norman thought psychiatry was a load of hogwash and Laurie took the same line. She would not go back into therapy.

In early 1985, Russell and Laurie moved from their small town house in Northbrook to a five-bedroom house in Highland Park. If Russell harboured any hopes that the move would bring about an improvement in Laurie, then they were quickly dashed. Nothing changed. Laurie began using the wealth of appliances in her new kitchen in accordance with some private logic of her own. She stored money in the oven, make-up in the microwave, and tinned food in the dishwasher.

It was unfathomable to Russell, and as embarrassing as the day she had served frozen vegetables at one of their dinner parties. Serving guests frozen vegetables is a serious crime on the North Shore and it demonstrates both how out of touch Laurie was, and also, with suitably beguiling nicety, how efficient and ruthless the élite social groups are at exposing, belittling and excluding not only unsuitable aspirants from the lower orders but also the runts, misfits and underachievers that the élite itself occasionally produces. Laurie had never learnt basic social skills, never mind the finer points of North Shore etiquette, and Russell left her before the year was out. He could not help her and she did not seem willing to help herself.

The separation was messy and, for a while, ambiguous. Laurie lived with her parents in Glencoe for some of the time, but at other times she stayed with Russell. Russell continued to give her financial support, including a cheque to cover tuition fees at the National College of Education in Evanston, so that she could finish her studies and become a teacher, which, she said, was what she had always wanted to be.

According to Russell, Laurie still entertained hopes of saving the marriage. "I can be a normal person in the right situation," she told him on one occasion. "I think I've learned a lot. This whole experience has been good for me, and now I think I'm ready," but Russell would have none of it.

On 2 January 1986, Laurie filed for dissolution of the marriage. A month later, Russell filed a counterpetition. The divorce would become a bitter and protracted business; an almost endless series of petitions and counterpetitions. Outside the court, though, the feud was uglier still. On 8 April, Laurie called the Highland Park police, claiming Russell had verbally and physically assaulted her. She declined to sign a complaint form. Later the same month, she called the Glencoe police, claiming there had been a burglary at her parents' home and that Russell was responsible. The evidence was wholly inconclusive and the detective assigned to the case, Floyd Mohr, had his doubts not just about Russell's alleged involvement but about whether there had been a burglary at all.

Then Russell started to receive mysterious hang-up phone calls. He was not the only one. There were many targets in the campaign of harassment and intimidation that Laurie had embarked upon. Russell's family and friends were pestered by calls—dozens of them, often late at night—and the telephone also started to take on sinister connotations for many of Laurie's old flames and others whose paths had crossed hers in high school or college. Her covert campaign, which on 20 May 1988 would finally become an open declaration of war, was more than just an attack on certain individuals, though; it was an assault on the whole North Shore community whose values, she believed, had condemned her to her miserable existence. North Shore children may have been quietly taking their own lives at a rate three times higher than the national average, but Laurie would seek revenge before she sought oblivion.

On 5 May she walked into a gunshop in Glenview, picked out a Smith & Wesson .357-calibre Magnum and filled out an application for an Illinois Firearm Owner's Identification Card. According to John Morgan, the proprietor, "There was absolutely nothing unusual about her." On 10 May, after her application for a firearms licence had been accepted (it was more or less a formality as she had answered the undemanding questions truthfully), Laurie returned to the shop to collect the Magnum—and 100 rounds of ammunition. A friend of the Dann family happened to be there, too. He was so concerned to see her buying a gun that he telephoned Russell's father, Armand. When he couldn't get hold of Armand, he called Russell's uncle, Charles, and when Russell heard the news he called the police.

Floyd Mohr, the Glencoe detective who had investigated the alleged burglary at the home of Laurie's parents, was very worried by this new development. He had no legal grounds for confiscating the gun, but went to considerable lengths to try to persuade Laurie to relinquish it voluntarily. He spoke to Laurie herself and to her father. Finally, after a lot of badgering, Norman appeared to capitulate. He promised Mohr that the gun would be stored in a safe-deposit box at a Glencoe bank. Mohr asked if he could inspect the box, but Norman and Laurie both said no.

Laurie lived with her parents for most of 1986. In the late summer, she struck up a friendship with a neighbour, John Childs, who was a couple of years older than she, and also living at home with his folks. Laurie told him she was an instructor at the National College of Education. They started dating but the relationship was rather antiseptic—in more ways than one, according to John's mother, Alexandra: Laurie washed her hands all the time, picked up cutlery with her sleeves and did not like being touched. "I sure pick winners," John told his mother.

In the early hours of the morning of 30 September, Russell Dann telephoned the Highland Park police. He claimed an intruder had stabbed him in the chest with an ice pick while he slept, and that the intruder was Laurie. The police were not convinced, Russell failed a lie detector test and the Lake County prosecutors decided there was insufficient evidence to charge anyone with the stabbing. Meanwhile, all across the North Shore—and beyond—the hang-up phone calls continued unabated. In December, Laurie was arrested by the Highland Park police on telephone harassment charges. Two hang-up calls to Russell's sister, Susie Taylor, had been successfully traced. Three months later, the Lake County prosecutors dropped the charges, citing insufficient evidence.

On the evening of 20 April 1987, Norman and Edith Wasserman were out of town and Laurie invited John Childs over to watch a video. Then John headed home and Laurie headed for the bath. In the early hours of the morning of 21 April, Glencoe police got a call from Laurie, claiming she had just been threatened and sexually assaulted by Russell. She told the responding officers:

> It was about one in the morning when I got out of the tub, and I heard noises in the other room. So I put on a sweatshirt, underwear and a dress and went into my father's office. Russell was standing there, wearing surgical gloves . . . he grabbed me by the arm, dragged me into my parents' bedroom . . . pulled off my dress and my panties with one yank, and started saying how much he hated me and how he wanted to see me dead or at least a paraplegic so I would suffer. He pulled out a little steak knife and put it up against my neck . . . he told me I'd better sign the divorce papers by Friday or else. He . . . stuck [the knife] into my vagina. He said, "You sign the papers or I cut you all the way up, bitch."

On 27 April 1987, the marriage of Russell and Laurie Dann was dissolved in the Cook County Court. Two weeks later Laurie called the Glencoe police claiming Russell had thrown a Molotov cocktail into her parents' home. As with the sexual assault allegation, the physical evidence was inconclusive and in no way implicated Russell. No charges were filed.

The divorce was another public censure for Laurie. She needed little reminding that in every department of North Shore womanhood she was an abject failure: she was husbandless, childless, careerless and just about friendless. Like so many mass killers, she looked upon those who were succeeding where she had failed with a mixture of admiration and loathing. She was obsessed with university life, and a campus was ever her preferred habitat. In the summer of 1987, she leased an apartment in the Kellogg Living Learning Center, a student dormitory in Evanston.

Once again, she was back in the college environment that had exposed her academic limitations. She had also started to take on babysitting jobs around the North Shore, giving her access to the homes of successful people, and allowing her to examine their lives at her leisure, looking, perhaps, for clues to where her own had gone wrong.

Laurie lied to her employers about her background and experience. Often she said she was a nursery school teacher at the National College of Education. She also told her first clients, Marian and Padraig Rushe of Winnetka, that her name was Laurie Porter, and it was as if, by giving herself a new name, she became, in one sphere of her life at least, a new and more successful person. She had some talent for childcare and Marian and Padraig certainly had no qualms about recommending her to their friends. "Our daughter loved her," Craig Bayless, one of the Rushes' Winnetka neighbours would later tell reporters. "She was great with kids." Other North Shore families agreed. "She had an almost childlike quality about her," said Bruce Benton, of Glencoe. "But she had a great uneasiness with adults."

At the Kellogg Living Learning Center, Laurie spent a lot of her time taking lifts up and down the building or sitting in the downstairs lounge, watching television. She often wore rubber gloves, and she occasionally dated a student whom she met in the TV lounge. One evening they had a video-viewing session in his apartment. Laurie's favourite was *Black Widow*, described by *Daily Variety* as "A moderately interesting tale of one woman's obsession for another's glamorous and criminal lifestyle."

From time to time, Laurie was seen by Kellogg personnel in parts of the complex that students had no access to. Petty crime—pilfering and vandalism—plagued the dormitory that summer and Laurie was the number one suspect. Finally, in early September, she was caught red-handed with a stolen passkey by two Kellogg managers. They told her they would not prosecute her provided she vacated the building. She told them, "You can't do this to me. I want both your

names, I want your titles, I want your phone numbers."
When Norman Wasserman heard that his daughter could
face criminal charges, he had her out of the building and
back home to Glencoe at double-quick speed.

At home again with her parents, Laurie put her heart
and soul into the one thing she seemed to have an aptitude
for; babysitting. She expanded her clientele and became
a more or less full-time sitter. However, there were soon
indications that her new career was heading the same way
as every other career she had ever embarked upon. Pam and
Kenneth Beckman hired Laurie on two consecutive nights
in September. On the second night, after Laurie had gone
home, the Beckmans discovered that a pile of gourmet food
was missing from the freezer and that a pair of shoes had
disappeared, along with various toiletries. They called the
police. "The items she stole from us were so weird that I felt
very disturbed about her, and I did not want her sitting for
anyone else," Pam would later reveal. Her husband told the
police that they intended to put an advertisement in the local
paper, warning other parents, but the police told them that
they could end up facing a libel action and they reluctantly
dropped the idea.

A week after the incident at the Beckmans' home, police
received another complaint from another Glencoe couple,
Bruce and Dolores Benton. They had discovered hundreds
of dollars worth of prime steak and seafood missing from
their freezer, and a neighbour had seen Laurie struggling
to haul a bursting bin-liner out to her car. Detective Floyd
Mohr handled the case and saw the theft merely as a mis-
demeanour. Laurie's father agreed to pay compensation and
wrote Bruce a cheque for $400. Soon after, the Bentons
started getting hang-up phone calls.

Finally, after four separate complaints to police by
Laurie's clients, Floyd Mohr and Norman Wasserman
struck a deal: Laurie would take on no new babysitting
jobs but could keep working for the families who were
happy with her. Her final stab at a career—even if it was,

by North Shore standards, an unmentionably inferior one—had ended in failure.

On 7 November, Laurie paid another visit to the gunshop. She bought a .32-calibre Smith & Wesson revolver.

She had seen several doctors and psychiatrists in the three and a half years since her first visit to Dr. Robert Greendale. In 1987, though, she was diagnosed as a probable sufferer of Obsessive Compulsive Disorder (OCD), a mental ailment that received enormous media coverage that year, in part because new research had revealed that it was a lot more prevalent than doctors had previously thought, in part because an experimental drug called clomipramine seemed to be proving highly successful in its treatment and in part because OCD sufferers were not known to be violent but did indulge in bizarre ritual behaviour, such as obsessive hand-washing and vacuuming family pets. In other words, events conspired, in 1987, to make OCD a prime subject for prime time TV: OCD was both funny and sad, without being too harrowing or upsetting for viewers, and the story had that most important ingredient of all, a happy ending—the wonder drug clomipramine.

In November 1987, Norman Wasserman wrote to Dr. John Greist at the University of Wisconsin Hospital in Madison, one of the twenty or so clinics in the country participating in the clomipramine trials, asking if he would be willing to treat Laurie. Dr. Greist agreed and Laurie was enthusiastic about returning once again to a college environment. In late November, she drove up to Madison, rented a room near the University Hospital, and began her treatment.

She told Dr. Greist she was already taking clomipramine (it was being prescribed her by a Chicago psychiatrist, Dr. Phillip Epstein, through a Montreal pharmacy, in technical violation of guidelines issued by the US Food and Drug Administration). Dr. Greist increased the dosage and had her attend behaviour therapy sessions three days a week. Laurie apparently made some progress in modifying her ritualistic behaviour before she returned home to Glencoe for the Christmas vacation.

Over the holidays, the telephone harassment on the North Shore was so bad that a group of the worst-affected victims arranged a meeting with Floyd Mohr's boss, Glencoe Police Chief Robert Bonneville. The delegation did not include Russell Dann, whose relationship with the authorities had long since soured. Chief Bonneville could only assure the delegation that the police department was doing its best.

On 29 December 1987, Laurie paid yet another visit to the gunshop. She bought her third weapon, a .22-calibre Beretta semi-automatic pistol.

When she returned to Madison after the Christmas holidays, she moved into a luxury suite in the private Towers of Madison student dormitory. She lied that she was a graduate student. She took to the lifts and the TV lounge— and the pay phones in the lobby. Her telephone terror tactics changed. As well as the hang-up calls she started to make death threats. According to Russell's sister, Susie, Laurie "would say things like, 'Susie, Susie, Susie, you are going to die. Goodbye.' She would say, 'I'm a psychopath,' and she would laugh." Russell's brother, Scott, and other members of the Dann family received similar threats. Friends of Russell's were threatened, as were a number of Laurie's former babysitting clients. One mother who had complained to police about her, was told "Your children are going to die." Ex-boyfriends of Laurie's received death threats. John Childs's mother, Alexandra, was threatened. It was a ferocious escalation of the hate campaign.

Meanwhile, Laurie continued her treatment under Dr. Greist. He increased her dosage of clomipramine and also added lithium carbonate. It can never be known for sure how many different drugs Laurie may have taken, but it is known that, aside from antibiotics, aspirin and birth control pills (which she seems to have consumed in enormous quantities), she was prescribed seven other drugs, most of them within the space of a few months and the majority to treat depression.

There are several points to note about Laurie's association with drugs. First, the assortment of drugs was prescribed by several different doctors, most of whom were unaware of the treatment Laurie received at the hands of their colleagues. Secondly, several of the drugs, according to recognized medical opinion, should not normally be taken in conjunction with one another. And thirdly, judging by the range of drugs she was prescribed, there appears to have been little inter-rater agreement about what mental ailment or ailments Laurie was suffering; while several of the drugs have proved very useful in the treatment of one particular problem, they have proved equally damaging in the treatment of others. The manufacturer of clomipramine (trade name Anafranil), for example, warns specifically of the danger of using the drug on pre-schizophrenic or schizophrenic patients and on patients with manic depressive tendencies.

Although it would appear that Laurie had been on a collision course with death and destruction for quite some time, the fact remains that during her most intensive period of medical care she went downhill very rapidly—either because of, or in spite of, the treatment she received.

In March, she stole bottles of lead and arsenic solution from a laboratory near Dr. Greist's office and books about poisons and poisoning from the Madison City Library. That same month, she was caught shoplifting various items, including four wigs, at a Madison shopping mall. She was charged with the thefts and released on bail.

Meanwhile, her telephone death threat campaign continued. She tracked down the pre-med student she had dated at the University of Arizona and threatened to kill him. His was one more name on a long list.

At the Towers dormitory, students noticed changes in Laurie since her first arrival. She had put on weight, about three stone, and her face had become bloated and bovine.

She walked around in a daze and her speech was often wild and fragmented. Her behaviour was becoming increasingly irrational. She stopped seeing Dr. Greist. Greist had come to feel that she had deteriorated so badly that she needed to be treated as a hospital inpatient. Laurie added his name to her hit list.

According to Kaplan, Papajohn and Zorn, "Her only known sexual partner during her stay at the Towers was . . . a sophomore with whom she fell into a pattern of loveless intercourse . . . [He] favored combat fatigues and left copies of *Soldier of Fortune* lying around his dorm room."[1] Laurie's own reading material at the time included the books on poisoning; another with the title *Famous Feats of Detection and Deduction*; a large collection of *Penthouse* and *Penthouse Letters* magazines, to which her statements to police, alleging sexual assaults by her former husband, owed a certain stylistic debt; and various newspaper clippings, including a *Wisconsin State Journal* story, with the headline "Police Trace Threats, Attacks to Victim" and a *Chicago Tribune* story, with the headline "Failed Suicide Provides Patient with a Cure," which described how a man suffering from OCD was cured after shooting himself in the mouth.

In early May, Susie Taylor picked up the telephone. Laurie was on the other end: "Susie, Mother's Day, are you all getting together? You shall die." In Arizona, meanwhile, Laurie's former boyfriend had managed to get the FBI involved and on 9 May they successfully recorded a death-threat call. "It sounded like the voice of the Wicked Witch of the West," according to Lou Spivack, an assistant county prosecutor.

The recorded death threat, in conjunction with information provided by Illinois police departments, persuaded the FBI to seek an indictment against Laurie at a federal grand jury session scheduled for 18 May.

Revenge

On 16 May Laurie caught an early morning Greyhound bus out of Madison, back home to Chicago. All the FBI found when they went to the Towers, the following day, were abandoned fragments of her twisted life: books, magazines and newspaper clippings; names, addresses and photographs, sheets of scrawled numbers, which may have been lift-riding schedules; and pages of fractured vitriol—"hate pain . . . abuse . . . hurt . . . why gun . . . scum paraplegic . . . suffer forever . . . Harm children to pay a bill."

The day after arriving home in Glencoe, Laurie apparently telephoned two schools in Highland Park—Kennedy School and Ravinia Elementary—and asked what time the children arrived in the mornings. She had connections with the parents of several pupils. Susie Taylor, for instance, had kids at both facilities. On Thursday, in the guise of a representative of a modelling agency, Laurie phoned a former New Trier East High School cheerleader, and invited her and her children to a get-together for prospective models, at the Hubbard Woods Elementary School, in Winnetka, the following morning. The previous Saturday, according to a Highland Park couple, Laurie had wandered into their back garden saying she was looking for a short cut she used to take when she lived in the area and went to West Ridge Elementary School.

On Wednesday 18 May, Laurie drove out to see Marian Rushe, in Winnetka, one of her oldest babysitting clients. Marian greeted her warmly but was shocked to see her looking in such poor shape. Laurie said there had been a death in the family and that her allergies were troubling her. She also lied that she was working as a nurse at Evanston Hospital and that the hospital was having a carnival on Friday morning. She asked if she could take Marian's two youngest children. "It's especially for younger kids," she said. "I'm sure they'd enjoy it." Later that same day, Laurie sent a parcel, containing Rice Krispies treats spiked with arsenic, to a woman in Los Angeles; they had both lived at the Lake Shore Club student dormitory back in 1980–81. On the Thursday evening, she baked more batches of Krispies treats.

In the early hours of the morning of Friday 20 May, she injected arsenic and lead into the Krispies and into foil pouches of fruit juice and cartons of popcorn. She put some of the fruit juice packets into envelopes, on which she had handwritten "Free Sample" and addressed them to various people on her hit list, including Russell Dann, Dr. Greist and Peter Smith, a former babysitting client in Wilmette.

At about 6:30 A.M. she loaded the doctored goodies, her three handguns, ammunition and a cocktail of incendiary chemicals into her father's immaculate white Toyota Cressida. For the next two hours or so she toured the North Shore, leaving a trail of poisoned food at addresses throughout the community. It was attempted mass murder on a scale not seen in the north Chicago villages since the mysterious Tylenol poisoner claimed seven lives in 1982.

The Wassermans' next-door neighbours found a poisoned juice pouch in their mailbox, as did members and friends of the Dann family, numerous former babysitting clients of Laurie's, and many other people whose lives, at one time or another, had crossed hers. In some cases the link was tenuous, but in all cases there was one. Scott Freidheim, for example, had once given Laurie a lift when her car broke down. It was the only contact he ever had with her but it earned him a delivery of poisoned goodies. "My mom picked it up from the front step," he later told reporters. "She said 'Too bad, it looks as though the birds ate it.' "

At the Psi Upsilon fraternity house at Northwestern University, Laurie left more poisoned food: Rice Krispies treats, popcorn and juice, together with a note reading "Enjoy, from your little sisters." She made a similar delivery next door, at the Alpha Tau Omega fraternity house, and left another, similar note. She made further deliveries to the Kappa

Sigma fraternity and to the J L Kellogg Graduate School of Management. Finally, she headed for Marian Rushe's house in Winnetka.

She arrived a little before 8:45 A.M., carrying a plate of Rice Krispies treats and a plastic Mickey Mouse cup with feet at the bottom and ears on the no-spill lid. She set the poisoned Krispies down on the table and surreptitiously slipped a few drops of arsenic solution into Marian's big jug of milk, from which she then filled the Mickey Mouse cup. "Okay, I guess we can leave now," she said with a careful look at the clock. Marian followed them outside and helped strap 6-year-old Patrick and 4-year-old Carl into the back seat of the car. She waved goodbye as Laurie pulled out of the drive and accelerated away.

Having spent the early morning furtively implementing a massive clandestine operation to murder all the individuals who had ever—whether they realized it or not—personally offended her, Laurie embarked upon the second phase of her campaign; a spectacular and explosive public assault. She planned to steal the one thing that could really hurt the families of the North Shore: their children's lives.

Laurie headed for the schools. Schools and childhood had deep personal resonance for her and her failure to realize her ambition to teach was a failure to achieve one of the most important goals—a professional career—by which a modern woman, from a well-to-do family, is judged a success. Furthermore, all her problems, as psychiatrists had been telling her for years, were rooted in her childhood. As she drove north into Highland Park, she evidently found the prospect of the heinous assault she was about to commit so comprehensively gratifying that any moral inhibitions she may have had left intact after her earlier crimes were completely overridden.

She pulled up outside the Ravinia Elementary School, where close to 300 pupils were enrolled, just before 9:00 A.M. She told the two Rushe boys to stay put in the back of the car. Then she got out, took a bag from the boot and walked, unchallenged, into the school. The bag she carried contained bottles of highly flammable liquids, acids and toxic chemicals. She hid the bag in a playhouse, set the drawstring alight and ran back out to the car. Fortunately, an eagle-eyed pupil spotted the burning bomb just moments later and a teacher was able to extinguish the flames before it blew.

Laurie, meanwhile, had jumped back in the car and was heading for the nearby Kennedy School, which at the time was being operated as a day-care centre for over 150 children. She passed the Mickey Mouse cup, full of poisoned milk, to Patrick and Carl but they took no more than a sip or two each because it tasted so bad. When they got to the school, Laurie got out of the car and told the boys to come with her. She pulled on a blue, plastic bin-liner, with holes cut for the arms and head, which made her look like a demented, comic-book superhero. Patrick and Carl found the costume funny and she took it off again. She took a can of petrol from the car boot and led the boys towards the main entrance of the school. Staff would not allow her to enter with the can. Laurie said something about having run out of gas and a staff member kindly accompanied her back to her car and helped pour the petrol into the Toyota's tank. Laurie strapped the children back into their seats and drove away, seething.

Shortly after 10:00 A.M., they arrived back at the Rushe house in Winnetka. Laurie told Marian she had got the wrong date for the kiddies' carnival and that they had gone to a park instead. The two women and the two children went down to the basement, where Marian was doing the laundry. A short while later, Laurie said she had to get something from the car. She went back upstairs, and halfway up took a bottle of petrol from her shopping bag and doused the carpet. She threw down a lighted match, rushed to the back door, locked it, and locked the front door on her way out of the house. By the time the smoke detector went off, the stairwell was ablaze—and Marian and the two children were trapped in the basement, which was rapidly filling with dense, black fumes. Eventually, with a great deal of difficulty, and suffering some nasty cuts, they were able to escape through a window, high up near the ceiling, which, aside from the stairs, was the only exit from the basement.

Laurie, meanwhile, had driven to the nearby Hubbard Woods Elementary School, where over 300 pupils were enrolled. Shortly before 10:30 A.M., she entered the building by a side door. Her three guns were tucked in the waistband of her Bermuda shorts, concealed by her baggy T-shirt, which bore a skeleton motif. She wandered the corridors, finally entering a classroom. Substitute teacher Amy Moses was teaching twenty-four children. "May I help you?" asked Amy. It was not unusual for students from the National College of Education in Evanston to come to observe teachers at work and a student was what Amy presumed she was. Laurie said nothing, but took a seat at the front of the class, near the computer terminal, and Amy continued with the lesson. She grew rather disconcerted by the stranger's apparent lack of interest and fixed expression—"She was so lifeless; her face was so hard"—and she was startled when, after a few minutes, Laurie suddenly got up and left the room.

Out in the corridor again, Laurie dragged 6-year-old Robert Trossman away from a drinking fountain and into the boys' washroom. She pulled the .22-calibre Beretta pistol from her shorts and shot him in the chest at almost point-blank range. He slumped to the floor. Two boys who entered the washroom just as he was shot, turned and raced back to their classroom. Laurie headed back to Amy Moses's class. "I'm shot. Am I going to die?" Robert Trossman said to the teacher who came to his aid, while Laurie told Amy "Put the children in a corner."

"What are you talking about?" Amy replied. She was more confused than alarmed. "I heard what she said, but I didn't understand." Laurie brought the Beretta into view. "She said, 'I have a gun . . . It's real, and I have another one.' " Amy grabbed at her wrist. "I just acted instinctually. I just wanted to protect . . . I really just went on automatic pilot." She managed to wrestle Laurie several feet towards the classroom door and yell, "There's a woman in here with a gun. Get help," but then Laurie broke free, pulled out the .32-calibre Smith & Wesson, and shot one of the children, 8-year-old Mark Teborek, in the neck.

"I can't explain how unreal the whole situation was," Amy would later tell newsmen. "When the first child went down, my first thought was, 'They're filming a movie and they forgot to tell me.' " It was a measure of how badly she wanted some kind of sane explanation for what was otherwise a terrifying and inexplicable madness that had descended on the classroom.

Laurie had a gun in each hand and was firing coolly and deliberately. "She went up to each child she shot and shot point-blank," all the while making her way towards the playground door: 8-year-old Nicholas Corwin was shot in the upper left side of the back, the bullet travelling through the left lung and pulmonary artery and exiting from the right side of his chest; 8-year-old Lindsay Fisher took a bullet in the chest, which ricocheted around inside her, puncturing her right lung, liver and stomach; 7-year-old Kathryn Miller was shot in the left side of the chest; and 8-year-old Peter Munro was shot in the abdomen.

Then, suddenly, the gunwoman was gone. She left a classroom full of blood, one child dead and five others who had to be rushed to hospital; she left a school full of traumatized children and teachers, who had to be interviewed by police and counselled by therapists. And she left a whole community devastated. Winnetka had not known so much as a single murder since a police officer was killed in 1957—the year Laurie Wasserman was born.

The white Toyota sped away from Hubbard Woods, heading towards Tower Road, a main east-west artery that runs through the village. After taking a right turn, though, just half a block from the school, Laurie was confronted by a police squad car stationed across the road. The officer was on a routine traffic assignment, clearing the street for a funeral cortege, but Laurie panicked, evidently thinking the cops were onto her. She pulled a squealing U-turn and accelerated away down a dead-end street. She barely reduced her speed when she entered the driveway of a Tudor mansion at the end of the road and failed to negotiate the loop at the end, which would have taken her back out again. The car skidded and was impaled on a large rock. Laurie got out, took off her shorts and tied the plastic bin-liner around her. She could hear sirens over towards Hubbard Woods and she sprinted in the opposite direction, through the trees on the west side of the mansion, with her shiny, plastic cape flowing behind her.

She found herself, finally, in the driveway of another mansion, number 2 Kent Road. She ran up through the garden and entered the house by the back door, a gun in each hand. "She just came running in, out of breath," Ruth Ann Andrew, who was in the kitchen with her 20-year-old son Philip, later told reporters. "You are my hostages," Laurie said. She claimed she had been raped, had shot her assailant and was afraid of the police. The story seemed plausible enough to begin with, less so the more details Phil Andrew coaxed out of her. "Isn't there someone you could call?" he asked her. "I could call my mother," Laurie said. "She lives in Glencoe." Laurie would phone Edith no fewer than three times during the course of the siege, babbling a miserable and monotonous lament: "Mom, I've done something terrible. People won't understand. I'm going to have to kill myself . . . I shot someone . . . Tell Dad I'm sorry . . . I'm sorry to both of you, Mom and Dad . . . I'm sorry . . ."

Several times Phil Andrew and his father, Raymond, who returned home from an errand to become another hostage in the siege, took the phone from Laurie to explain the situation to Edith and to beg her to come over and help.

"I don't have a car," Edith said. "My husband has the car."

"Can't you take a cab? Borrow a neighbour's car?" Phil said. "You've got to come here and help us."

"No, I just can't," Edith said. "I can't."

Phil had better luck with Laurie. He managed to persuade her to release first his mother and later his father. He also managed to take one of her guns off her; the Beretta. In a show of goodwill, he unclipped the magazine. He put the pistol in one pocket of his shorts and the magazine in the other. Ruth Ann and Raymond, meanwhile, had been able to inform the police, who were swarming over the Kent Road neighbourhood, of the precise location of the gunwoman and of the situation inside the house.

Shortly before midday, Phil Andrew was reflecting on the fact that his parents were safe, that Laurie was amenable to persuasion and that she seemed reasonably calm. She was looking idly out of the kitchen window and although she still had her finger on the trigger of the .32, she no longer had the gun doggedly trained on him. He tried to figure out his next move. Laurie turned back from the window to look at him. Her expression did not change and neither did she speak. As Phil later recalled it, "I was leaning up near the microwave. I had made no move, and she shot me point-blank . . . I dove around the corner into the pantry and put the magazine back into the Beretta."

Laurie had disappeared. The bullet she had fired had torn through one of Phil's lungs and lodged near his heart. He was having difficulty breathing. He gritted his teeth and edged cautiously towards the back door—unaware that Laurie was making her way upstairs—expecting her to spring out and shoot him again at any moment. He staggered out into the garden and around to the front of the house. "We almost shot him because he was waving a gun," a patrolman would later reveal. "I can't believe she shot me," Phil cried, before collapsing in the driveway.

Norman and Edith Wasserman arrived in Kent Road in the early afternoon. Both were crying as they were led to the police command post. "If this is true," Norman said, "if this

is Laurie and she did these things, my life is over." Edith
would later tell a county prosecutor, "This sounds terrible
for a mother to say . . . [but] she's in so much trouble I think
it would be better if she didn't come out of this alive."

Meanwhile, police tried to make contact with Laurie by
telephone and by bullhorn—but with no success. Finally, at
7:00 P.M., Floyd Mohr led Norman Wasserman out to plead
with his daughter through the bullhorn. Norman's mournful
voice echoed around the neighbourhood: "Please come out
of there if you can hear me, please. Laurie, please come
out. Laurie, pick up the phone. Laurie pick up the phone.
Please . . . please."

At the same time, unbeknown to Norman, an assault team
was entering the twenty-two-room mansion. They finally
found Laurie in a top floor bedroom, lying face down in
a pool of blood. She had shot herself in the mouth with
the Smith & Wesson and the bullet had torn clean through
her brain. It was an ugly wound but a painless one. The
wounds she had inflicted on the North Shore community
were altogether more appalling.

If Laurie Wasserman Dann had fatally poisoned everyone
she had hoped to with the doctored treats she either personally delivered or whose delivery she entrusted to the United
States Postal Service, then in excess of fifty people would
have died from circulatory failure and shock brought on by
massive dehydration and electrolyte imbalance. If her attack
on Marian Rushe's house and the three schools, with around
750 students in total, had been more successful, then who
knows how many more people would have perished. And
where had she planned to go after Hubbard Woods? How
long would the list of victims have grown?

As it was, the arsenic solution she had stolen was highly
diluted, containing just one-tenth of one per cent arsenic;
she was hindered by the courage and will-to-live of those
she wished to destroy; she was handicapped by her own
ineptitude; and she was looked upon unfavourably by Lady

Luck. Laurie had hoped to murder perhaps hundreds, but she murdered only one.

It was, of course, no consolation to the parents of 8-year-old Nicholas Corwin, who died where he fell at the Hubbard Woods Elementary School. Joel Corwin, a corporate lawyer, and Linda, a member of the local school board, were overwhelmed with grief. "He brightened our lives with such a brilliant light that we cannot believe he is gone," Linda wrote in a statement released to the press.

Nicholas Corwin was, by all accounts, a remarkable young boy. He was a talented student and a fine sports player; a "sweet and loving child," who was, in turn, much-loved. He was, in fact, just the kind of big-hearted youngster who would doubtless have helped and encouraged, had he been around, a shy little girl with Mickey Mouse ears who found it hard to make friends.

12

The End Zone

The 1980s were years of unprecedented violence on the part of armed mass killers. Not only did they strike more frequently than ever they had before, but they struck with greater ferocity. In the United States, the mass-murder rate, which had begun to climb dramatically in the late 1960s and early 1970s, continued its meteoric rise; James Huberty launched a more destructive attack than any previously seen; and Laurie Dann announced, in no uncertain terms, the arrival of the rampaging gunwoman. Elsewhere in the world, young pseudo-commandos exploded into violence. It was a decade of terrible slaughter. Moreover, Marc Lépine's massacre in Montreal at Christmas 1989 was not so much a bloody, bullet-riddled and castrato note to end the decade as it was a portent for the new one.

In the terminal years of the century, the armed mass killer continues to wreak havoc. Already Huberty's record number of victims has been "beaten," when George Hennard went on the rampage in Killeen, Texas, and, on the other side of the world, New Zealand, "the last paradise," has succumbed to the phenomenon, when David Gray, a 33-year-old loner, decimated a small, seaside hamlet called Aramoana, killing thirteen people and wounding three others.

The slaughter in Aramoana began just before dusk, on the evening of 13 November 1990. Gray gunned down a neighbour, Garry Holden, and torched his home. He also killed Holden's 11-year-old daughter, Jasmine, and shot and wounded 9-year-old Chiquita. The flames from the Holdens' burning house brought many of Aramoana's residents out into the street, and Gray, dressed in combat gear, with his face blacked out, fired on them indiscriminately. As darkness fell, the death toll mounted. The village, sitting on a spit at the entrance to Otago Harbour, was sealed off by the police, but the gunman remained at large for twenty-two hours. He was finally shot dead by anti-terrorist squad officers after bursting out of a vacant property with his gun blazing. "Kill me, kill me," he yelled.

Last Rites

There seems to be no way of preventing tragedies like the massacre in Aramoana, and no way of halting the rise of the pseudo-commando. Like Sylvester Stallone's Rambo character, who "No man, no law, no war can stop," the David Grays of the world seem impossible to contain. Very little deters such a killer.

The death penalty is no deterrent, as the US experience has graphically demonstrated, for the killer's own death is a central element of his mission, and he typically orchestrates it long before the state has a chance to take control. Even if he does survive his rampage, he generally begs the authorities to put him to death, as Wagner and Unruh did. Indeed, the death penalty could well be, for the pseudo-commando, more than just a complete non-deterrent; quite possibly, as part of an ideology that insists that killing is justified in some circumstances, it positively encourages him in his abominable deeds, for his destiny, as he sees it, is not to commit gratuitous murder, but to punish evil, exact retribution and see justice done.

Gun-toting police officers are no deterrent to him either, for he not only plans his operation so meticulously that most of his principal targets are dead long before anyone has had a chance to respond, let alone the nearest cop, but, frequently, a final shootout with the police—pitting his marksmanship against the experts—is an integral part of his mission. As such, SWAT, SOG, and other tactical firearms units are, again, for the pseudo-commando, not just a complete non-deterrent but a positive incentive.

His potential victims—the general public—are as impotent as the authorities. While thieves may be deterred with window locks, video surveillance, magic eyes, ferocious dogs, high walls crowned with barbed wire or broken glass; while muggers and rapists may be deterred with shrieking alarms, martial arts skills, steel combs or CS gas; while there is a growing number of goods, gadgets, skills and pets to reduce the chances of becoming victims of most types of crime, there is nothing to prevent anyone falling foul of the berserk gunman.

Explanations for why he commits his terrible deeds are equally thin on the ground. Those who believe a lifetime of crushing poverty and deprivation to be the cause of most social ills are confounded by him, for there are many poorer men than he and many who have suffered worse deprivation. Those who believe that the "permissive society" is the root of all evil are equally bewildered, for our killer makes nonsense of the theory: he is not a revolutionary, junkie, dissident, alternative lifestyler, nor even liberal, but a deeply conservative individual who himself vehemently condemns permissiveness and liberalism in the modern world. Frank Vitkovic, for example, wrote a vitriolic attack on the "civil libertarian philosophy" in his law school exams, while David Gray, George Hennard and, most notably, Marc Lépine, all railed against "modern women." Calls for a return to Victorian values and traditional family life are only relevant to, say, James Huberty, because his murderous mission grew from the depth of his yearning for

just such an elusive world—a world that was never the
nirvana nostalgia has rendered it, and that today exists, in
unadulterated perfection, only in the popular imagination
and in the elaborate fantasies of Disney, McDonald's and
other corporate dream-spinners.

It is hard to get away from the fact that most of these
killers are, up until the day they commit their deeds, "extraordinarily ordinary,"[1] as criminologists Levin and Fox have
put it.

If they are invariably preoccupied with status—whether it
be on a grand scale, like Wagner and Whitman, or in a small
community, like Howard Unruh—then their preoccupation
is shared by the rest of us, for the modern social system
demands we be socially ambitious. If they invariably fail
to find the success and level of social standing they believe
they deserve, then there are thousands of others who suffer
the same ignominy—without reaching for a Remington or a
Luger. If they are, without exception, far from fully rational
and rounded human beings, then the same can be said of
most of us. Many thousands have lived lives of conspicuous social isolation, like David Gray, without picking up
a Norinco rifle. Many thousands more have lived among
friends, but with well-concealed feelings of social inadequacy and isolation, like Frank Vitkovic, without picking
up an M-1 carbine.

If invariably these killers have a preoccupation with firearms, and are often former soldiers, then the world contains
many gun freaks and ex-military men who do not open fire
on innocent civilians with an M-14. If the killer is often the
only or eldest child of a doting mother, not every mother's
boy reaches for a Kalashnikov, as Michael Ryan did, and
if the killer often has a hostile or absent father, not all such
individuals reach, as Marc Lépine did, for a Ruger.

While there are undoubtedly many traits—ranging from
gender, race and social class, to family structure, parent-
sibling relationships and individual preoccupations—which
render those who possess them more susceptible than others

to becoming pseudo-commando killers, such an outcome remains far from inevitable. If the killer's sense of personal sovereignty is *unusually* profound, if his obsession with status is *particularly* strong, and if he feels *especially* isolated from his fellows, then these are not factors that can be easily measured in advance of his crime, but only become apparent in his committing of the deed. Killers are, for most of their lives, law-abiding and aspiring model citizens. If some do, occasionally and publicly, show a capacity for violence, it tends to be in minor confrontations—Huberty's petty disputes with his neighbours, for example—giving few clues to the enormity of the assault to come. Are there any signs at all, then, that a man or woman is on the threshold of unleashing a mass murderous assault?

Invariably, in the aftermath of a rampage, investigators are searching for clues to explain what "triggered" the violence. Although it is rare for anything other than a most spurious trigger to be found—Unruh returning home to find that his yard gate had been removed from its hinges, for instance—the idea that some significant event, immediately prior to the massacre, was the catalyst for violence that would otherwise never have erupted, seems to have retained its validity in the public imagination.

The evidence of many cases, however, points clearly to the fact that the killer plans his murderous mission, certainly for days, and often for weeks, months or even years, in advance. He gradually succumbs to the idea. Wagner von Degerloch, for example, first conceptualized his campaign six years before he executed it. During the incubation period he "retrained" and "indoctrinated" himself, and deceived and deluded himself until finally he had conditioned himself to such an extent that the killings went "like clockwork, quite mechanically." Whether by this stage such a killer's internal reality is so out of sync with the external world that he can be described as "mad," remains debatable, and is, in any case, only of critical importance to the courts, which must decide his fate on the basis of such considerations.

The significant point is that during the incubation period between conceptualizing the massacre and perpetrating it, there is at least a possibility of the killer betraying his *intentions*.

The Negotiation of the Identity of the Avenging Commando Killer

From the writings of those killers who have documented their self-indoctrination (notably Frank Vitkovic), from the statements of those who have survived their rampages and who have been willing to discuss their lives and crimes (Wagner, Unruh and Knight), and from examples of other pseudo-commando killers from around the world, it is shown to be inevitable that certain clues to the killer's plan become publicly visible.

Doubtless, before the process begins in earnest, the killer-to-be experiences the kind of idle daydreams we all indulge from time to time—fantasies of great success for ourselves and of doom and failure for our rivals and competitors. What aspiring writer, numbed by the rhythm of the typewriter or the repetitive strokes of the pen, has not drifted off into daydreams of great literary success and fame, as Wagner did? What young army officer cadet, standing a lonely watch under a drowsy moon, has not fantasized about performing heroic deeds on the battlefield, as Julian Knight did? There may be negative fantasies, too. The man who is fired from his job may find himself daydreaming about disaster striking the company that dismissed him. The man who has been overlooked for promotion may find himself fantasizing about all sorts of misfortunes befalling his boss or his rivals. By and large, though, such fantasies are idle and fleeting. The out-of-work man may suddenly find himself in a new and more rewarding job; the unpromoted man may take a holiday and return to work revitalized; and there are many other things that can keep us from sliding into terminal disillusionment and bitterness.

The killer, however, extremely prone to overestimating his talents and abilities, is vulnerable to ongoing dissatisfaction with his lot. In addition, his lack of social adroitness and his feelings of isolation, limit his opportunities for compensatory success and joy in other areas of his life. His daydreams grow more persistent, particularly if he finds himself with time on his hands. Frank Vitkovic was sufficiently aware of this to note in his diary: "Being unemployed does not help because it gives you too much time to brood. Brooding leads to sick fantasies." true

Still, though, there are thousands of people who indulge vague dreams of revenge on a cruel and unjust world, who idly long for a day, as Vitkovic did, when "everyone will pay for their sins," and who construct for themselves, as the criminologist Bolitho noted in *Murder for Profit*, "a life-romance, a personal myth in which they are the maltreated hero." Indeed, "in such comforting day-dreams many an honest man has drugged himself against despair." For most men, however, fantasies of revenge end almost before they have begun, for want of the means to pursue them further. Such a man simply snaps out of the daydream—and this happens whenever he indulges it.

For an individual who happens to live in a culture in which violent death by firearms is a principal motif and in which sophisticated weapons of mass destruction are widely available, the daydream may develop a little further, but still, unless he goes to the trouble of thoroughly familiarizing himself with guns, will tend to peter out harmlessly. If, on the other hand, he does familiarize himself with guns, or if he already owns firearms and is intimately acquainted with their specifications, capabilities and use, his daydreams are free to develop a whole lot further. In fact, with no real effort on his part, an idle fantasy of revenge on the world can be pursued to a point where it actually becomes viable, in practical terms. As an aspiring,

ex-, or quasi-military man, he may already be well practised, as Julian Knight was, in indulging broadly correlative
combat fantasies.

The realization that there is nothing to stop him, logisti-
cally, from taking revenge on the world, is a key difference
between the killer-to-be and thousands of other idle day-
dreamers. However, even our future killer, at this early
stage, is liable to find himself, to a greater or lesser degree,
"too weak," as Wagner was, to transform his fantasy into
reality—even if the idea of doing so has enormous appeal
for him. First, he must be able to justify such a course
of action in his own mind, and it is at this point that the
self-indoctrination process begins in earnest.

James Huberty, who, according to his wife, was "extremely fond of children, and . . . always talked vehemently about
what should happen to people who hurt children," must
retrain himself so that he is able to cold-bloodedly kill them.
Julian Knight, who had always "wanted to kill someone in
combat," must retrain himself so that he sees an assault on
an urban clearway as something altogether different from
the murder of innocent civilians in a singularly cowardly
fashion. All killers must reach a point, as Vitkovic did,
where "Hate is the dominant emotion . . . The old Frank
died years ago." For some the process takes longer than
others, but for all the process clearly takes place.

The killer must persuade himself that other people—
particularly those who will come to constitute his target
group—are evil and deserve to be destroyed. During the
incubation period, he invariably becomes more isolated and
withdrawn, shutting himself off from other people; alienat-
ing himself. The more sociable he is at the outset, the more
obvious is the withdrawal. Knight and Vitkovic, for example, both became hostile to friends for no obvious reason,
breaking ties with them and driving them away. Even in
individuals who are socially isolated to begin with, a change
is noticeable. David Gray had a cordial seven-year acquain-
tanceship with the owner of a bookstore where he purchased

Soldier of Fortune magazines, but became overtly hostile in the months leading up to the massacre. Howard Unruh's neighbours had always considered him quiet and shy, but during the incubation period came to see him as quiet and *moody*.

The future killer is, then, unable to contain the self-indoctrination process entirely within his head, and an unprovoked, resolute social withdrawal is one of the visible clues to the fact that the process is taking place.

Having isolated himself from other people, it is easier for him to see them as enemies—and, like a dogged detective, he builds his case against them. He may even, as Howard Unruh did, document all the offences committed against him—the slights, insults, innuendos, pointed comments and put-downs. His growing conviction that he is an object of public scorn and the butt of public jokes may manifest itself in curious ways: Gray, Ryan and Sherrill, for example, were all hypersensitive about their developing baldness; Frank Vitkovic about his limp and his ballooning weight.

Rather perversely, given the atrociousness of the deeds he will later commit, the killer often worries constantly about crime and violence, about people harming him, his family, or his property. Wagner and Unruh were both scared stiff of being attacked in the street by their neighbours; Huberty was so concerned about the safety of his two young daughters that he insisted they learn judo, and was so concerned about the safety of his property that he raised dogs to protect it; Cruse and Gray were both extraordinarily anxious about people trespassing on their land; while Frank Vitkovic fretted endlessly about "an ever growing violent society where no one feels safe." PARNOIA

For the killer, the world is a hostile place, populated by those who, in one way or another, are out to get him. The alienated killer-to-be begins rationalizing a grotesque fantasy of mass murder as a shining mission of punishment and justice: "Time to pay," "redress the balance," "He'll get what he so richly deserves," "Harm children to pay a bill"—these themes become obsessive. As a deeply conservative individual, he mercilessly plunders the dominant ideology of his culture for the appropriate doctrine: death is a just punishment for evil people, the killing of innocents is not taboo but an option to be weighed against potential rewards, the end justifies the means, confrontation is the best way of solving disputes and problems, massive retaliation is a legitimate response for a man or a nation under threat or attack, the waging of war is a glorious and noble pastime—any or all of these and other principles he can readily commandeer for his own purposes.

Frank Vitkovic drew encouragement for his mission from sources as diverse as King Kong and Rambo. Other killers may well gain momentum from the many "dirty cops" who have shot their way through cinemas in recent years. One thing is certain, though: in his desperation to justify a ferocious assault on innocent people, any plank of common doctrine or conventional wisdom he can ally himself to, he will. If he is especially desperate, he may turn to the prospect of imminent biblical apocalypse, nuclear Armageddon, or ecological catastrophe—ideas that have special resonance in the twilight years of the millenium—and cast himself as a herald of divine justice, and his deeds as an expression of God's will. "God's on my side," Vitkovic wrote in his diary. "Don't worry God I will punish these evil vicious cruel scum people. I will destroy the evil . . . I know I'm ready for the mission."

If the mind mutates itself in order to construct and hold in place the elaborate and fragile matrix of diverse, fractured and often contradictory ideas that is the rationale for mass murder, then there are often side-effects. One of the most common and visible seems to be the onset of psychosomatic illnesses. Certainly Wagner, Whitman, Ryan and Vitkovic all suffered these kinds of complaints for they visited doctors with them on numerous occasions during the incubation period.

Another visible clue, and a more concrete one, to the impending massacre, is in the killer's relationship with firearms. If he does not already own or have access to a gun, he will purchase one (or several), and almost certainly it will be a rapid-fire weapon, typically one of the less sophisticated types, compatible with his inexperience. The Ruger rifle purchased by Marc Lépine would be a good example. More frequently, though, the killer-to-be is already an owner and purchaser of firearms, but during the incubation period shows quantitative and qualitative change in his weapons purchases. He becomes less interested in revolvers, shotguns and hunting rifles, preferring, instead, sophisticated semi-automatic weapons, capable of taking large capacity magazines. The pattern of gun-buying by Joseph Wesbecker—his SIG-Sauer, MAC-11 and AK-47 purchases in the months leading up to the massacre—is a good illustration; likewise, the changing face of Michael Ryan's arsenal in the first half of 1987, before his August rampage. What is also sometimes visible during this period is a marked intensification in his shooting practice. Unruh and Sherrill, for example, both set up firing ranges in their homes, while Ryan trained virtually every other day at his gun club for two months solid.

Clearly, by this stage, scenarios of revenge on the world are no longer idle daydreams, but controlled fantasies, mental preparations for a reality that he is moving ever closer to implementing. Doubtless, he experiments with different locations, days of the week, times of day and weapons, honing his plans, exploring possible eventualities, refining his timetable and the list of equipment he needs, running the fantasies again and again and again, until, finally, he is satisfied, in his own mind, that he is as fully prepared as he can ever be, that, as Vitkovic stated in his diary, "Fate has taken its turn," and "Today I must do it there's no other way out."

Almost certainly, those who reach the end of the process, and become avenging commando killers, are but a small percentage of the men who embark upon it. We can guess that there must be many who fail to make one of the numerous leaps in thinking necessary to progress, many who simply cannot bring themselves to cross certain thresholds, many whose rationale—an unstable house of cards—collapses before completion, and many more who voluntarily abandon the process after rediscovering hope and optimism—finding a new job, perhaps, or becoming lucky in love.

The journey, even for those few who do finally emerge as mass murderers, is far from straightforward, and anything but a simple progression of sustained momentum from A to B. Rather it is full of contradictions and detours; stops and starts; raised and dashed hopes. His yearning to be a part of society—to belong—vies with his hatred for the world and his desire to destroy it. His narcissism battles with his self-loathing; his belief that he deserves to be a "somebody" with his lowly station of a nobody. At times he may move rapidly towards his grand, final gesture. At other times he may make plans for a return to the fold, and regular citizenship—applying for jobs or plotting a new career.

Often, at some point during the incubation period, he will seek professional help. Charles Whitman visited a university doctor who referred him to a psychiatrist; Laurie Dann saw several psychiatrists; James Huberty turned himself in to police as a "war criminal" and certainly considered, and possibly sought, psychiatric assistance; Wagner and Ryan took their psychosomatic illnesses to doctors; Vitkovic went to his GP with similar complaints and underwent a brain scan. Whether these are genuine attempts to get help, though, or merely part of the process of self-indoctrination, is debatable. Laurie Dann apparently revealed very little to her psychiatrists; Vitkovic terminated his sessions with a student counsellor after just two, and cancelled his first appointment with a psychiatrist; Charles Whitman failed to keep a second appointment with his, and James Huberty may never even have made one. Whatever the meaning of these superficial and often brief brushes with social welfare agents, they subsequently enhance the killer's conviction that, as Huberty put it, "Society had their chance."

The whole self-indoctrination process can probably never be fully understood. It is extremely complex and fragile, and to some extent haphazard—and this, no doubt, is why so few are able to complete it. Wagner von Degerloch has made perhaps the most succinct and illuminating comment on its mechanics. "I have played around with death," he wrote in his autobiography, "the way I always play around, until I become deadly serious."

The Final Reckoning

With hindsight, those studying the mass killer can probably say of most: here is a man who possessed the key characteristics of the pseudo-commando killer, in terms of gender, race, social class, family dynamics and personal preoccupations; here is a man who also, in the months leading up to the massacre, left many of the clues that pseudo-commando killers tend to leave; here is a man, finally, who had considerable potential for unleashing a mass murderous campaign.

Unfortunately, though, such an analysis is only possible after he has committed his deeds, when a wealth of information about him and his life suddenly comes into the public domain. Prior to his crime, the various pieces of the jigsaw are held in numerous hands and, while some may hold several pieces, nobody has the complete picture. For all practical purposes, the information does not exist.

The only thing gunshop owner Jack Tilford knew, when he sold Joseph Wesbecker a pair of MAC-11 pistols, was that his client possessed a valid shooter's licence and seemed "normal in every way." All PC Trevor Wainwright knew, when he visited Michael Ryan, in connection with Ryan's application to have his firearms certificate amended to cover a Kalashnikov AK-47 rifle, was that "he was not a yob or mixed with yobs. He was not a villain and I knew he did not have a criminal record. He was a loner but you could not hold that against him." Even in the case of Laurie Dann, who gave numerous people enormous cause for concern, no meaningful preventive action could be taken. The unfortunate fact is that preventive action, in the case of the pseudo-commando killer, would require a regime so repressive and intolerant of individual rights that very few people would find it acceptable.

Damage limitation is one area in which practical measures can be taken: a tightening of gun laws and improvements and refinements in the responses of the emergency services, for example. Many nations have made some progress along these lines in recent years. However, it seems reasonable to assume that the killer will merely adapt, and circumvent new obstacles placed in his path. If there is a reduction in the number of guns he can own, in the types of ammunition he can purchase, in the capacity of his magazine, in the rate of his fire and in the police response time to his crime, then he will doubtless train harder, improve his marksmanship, choose his location more carefully and generally modify his methods. While preventive action is wholly unrealistic, damage limitation is probably of only minimal benefit.

There is, perhaps, one area in which a major positive step can be taken to eliminate at least one of the killer's principal *incentives*: the reward of status. While I am all too aware that I could be charged with complicity in affording him exactly this, I am convinced that it is the particular nature of the status we bestow on killers that is important. The *Sunday Times* put it in a nutshell after Michael Ryan's rampage through Hungerford: "Ryan died as he lived, an enigma." This, beyond the short-lived gratification of revenge, is the reward a killer prizes most highly—for it is as an enigma, as a man of mystery, that he is guaranteed a special and lasting place in the public imagination. Ultimately, this is his victory, his great triumph.

Even as the first news bulletins flash onto television screens and the first newspapers roll off the presses, the enigma is created—in the announcement of the search for the ever-elusive event that "triggered" the violence, in the plethora of irresponsibly hasty psychiatric diagnoses, and most of all in the obstinate insistence that the killer is a breed apart. In our eagerness to absolve humanity's collective conscience, we present him with the dazzling reward of our failure to recognize him for what he is: a terrible manifestation of some of our own most narcissistic, infantile, mean and mercenary urges, and a terrible manifestation of some of the principal tensions and themes of our modern social system and culture.

"I like being the mystery man," Frank Vitkovic revealed in his diary. Perhaps he and his fellow killers are a little less of a mystery now.

NOTES

Introduction
Sources of information on the George Hennard case were: the *Daily Mirror* (London); the *National Enquirer*; the *New York Times*; *The Times* (London).

CHAPTER 1
The source of information on the Wagner von Degerloch case was Hilde Bruch, "Mass Murder: The Wagner Case," *American Journal of Psychiatry*, Vol 124:5, Nov. 1967, the American Psychiatric Association.

CHAPTER 2
Sources of information on the Howard Unruh case were: the *Courier-Post* (Camden); the *New York Times*; Georgina Lloyd, *One Was Not Enough*; David Redstone, "Fantasy of Death," in Art Crockett ed., *Spree Killers*; the State of New Jersey Department of Human Services; Ronald Tobias, *They Shoot to Kill: A Psycho–survey of Criminal Sniping*.
1 Conversation abstracted from *Courier-Post*, 6 September 1949.
2 Milgram, *Obedience to Authority*, cited in Colin Wilson, *A Criminal History of Mankind*, London, Grafton, 1986, p. 61.

CHAPTER 3
Sources of information on the Charles Whitman case were: Associated Press; the *New York Times*; Zarko Franks, "Massacre at the University of Texas," in Crockett ed., *Spree Killers*; Tobias, *They Shoot to Kill*; *Time*; United Press International.

CHAPTER 4

Sources of information on the James Huberty case were: Associated Press; Elliott Leyton, *Hunting Humans*; the *Los Angeles Times*; the *New York Times*; Tom Basinski, "I'm Going Hunting Humans!" in Crockett ed., *Spree Killers*; *The Times* (London); United Press International; *USA Today*.

CHAPTER 5

Sources of information on the William Cruse case were: Associated Press; the *Chicago Tribune*; the *New York Times*; Don Unatin, "The Man with a Rage to Kill!" in Crockett ed., *Spree Killers*.
Sources of information on the Patrick Sherrill case were: Associated Press; the *New York Times*; Bill Ryder, "A Maniac's Rage Claimed 15 Lives!" in Crockett ed., *Spree Killers*; *USA Today*.
Sources of information on the Joseph Wesbecker case were: Associated Press; the *Chicago Tribune*; the *New York Times*; *USA Today*.

CHAPTER 6

1 "It appears that . . ." P. Wilson and S. Nugent, "Sexually Explicit and Violent Media Material: Research and Policy Implications," in Paul Wilson ed., *Trends and Issues in Criminal Justice* (1987), cited in Andreas Kapardis, *They Wrought Mayhem: An Insight into Mass Murder*, Melbourne, River Seine, 1989, p. 52.

CHAPTER 7

Sources of information on the Michael Ryan case were: the *Wiltshire Gazette & Herald*; the *Newbury Weekly News*; a BBC Wales Television documentary, *A Place Like Hungerford*; the *Sunday Times*; *The Times* (London).
1 Anthony Beevor, *Inside the British Army*, London, Chatto & Windus, 1990, p. xxi.

CHAPTER 8

Sources of information on the Julian Knight case were: the *Age* (Melbourne); the *Australasian Post*; the *Canberra Times*; an ABC Melbourne Television documentary, *Hoddle Street*; Andreas Kapardis, *They Wrought Mayhem: An Insight into Mass Murder*; *The Times* (London).

CHAPTER 9

Sources of information on the Denis Lortie case were: the *Gazette* (Montreal); the *New York Times*; *The Times* (London).
Sources of information on the Frank Vitkovic case were: the

Age (Melbourne); the *Canberra Times*; Kapardis, *They Wrought Mayhem*; *The Times* (London); Vitkovic's diaries.
Sources of information on the Christian Dornier case were: Associated Press; *Le Monde* (Paris); *The Times* (London).

CHAPTER 10
Sources of information on the Marc Lépine case were: Associated Press; Noah Richler, *"The Sex War Killings"* in *Esquire* (November 1991); the *Gazette* (Montreal); the *Globe & Mail* (Toronto); the *New York Times*; Teresa Sourour, *Rapport d'Investigation du Coroner* (Montreal: Bureau du Coroner, 10 May 1990); the *Toronto Star*.

CHAPTER 11
Sources of information on the Laurie Dann case were: Associated Press; the *Chicago Tribune*; Joyce Egginton, *Day of Fury*; Joel Kaplan, George Papajohn and Eric Zorn, *Murder of Innocence*; the *New York Times*; an ABC News *Nightline* television broadcast.
1 Kaplan, Papajohn and Zorn, *Murder of Innocence*, p. 199.

CHAPTER 12
1 Levin and Fox, *Mass Murder: America's Growing Menace*, p. 42.

Select Bibliography

Beevor, Anthony, *Inside the British Army*, London, Chatto & Windus, 1990

Bolitho, William, *Murder for Profit*, London, Jonathan Cape, 1926

Bowen-Jones, Carys, "Children Who Carry Guns," *Marie Claire* (UK edition), April 1992

Bruch, Hilde, "Mass Murder: The Wagner Case," *American Journal of Psychiatry*, vol. 124, 5 November 1967

Crockett, Art (ed.), *Spree Killers*, New York, Pinnacle Books, 1991

Dicks, Henry V., *Licensed Mass Murder: A Socio-psychological Study of Some SS Killers*, New York, Basic Books, 1972

Egginton, Joyce, *Day of Fury*, New York, William Morrow, 1991

Friedland, Martin L., *A Century of Criminal Justice*, Toronto, Carswell Legal Publications, 1984

Hernon, Peter, *A Terrible Thunder: The Story of the New Orleans Sniper*, New York, Doubleday, 1978

Kapardis, Andreas, *They Wrought Mayhem: An Insight into Mass Murder*, Melbourne, River Seine Press, 1989

Kaplan, Joel, Papajohn, George and Zorn, Eric, *Murder of Innocence*, New York, Warner Books, 1990

Levin, Jack and Fox, James Alan, *Mass Murder: America's Growing Menace*, New York, Berkley Books, 1991

Leyton, Elliott, *Hunting Humans*, New York, Pocket Books, 1988

Lloyd, Georgina, *One Was Not Enough*, London, Bantam Books, 1989

Richler, Noah, "The Sex War Killings," *Esquire*, November 1991

Sourour, Teresa Z., *Rapport d'Investigation du Coroner*, Montreal, Bureau du Coroner, 10 May 1990

Tobias, Ronald, *They Shoot to Kill: A Psycho-survey of Criminal Sniping*, Boulder, Paladin Press, 1981

Wilson, Colin, *A Criminal History of Mankind*, London, Grafton Books, 1986

Wilson, Colin and Pitman, Patricia, *Encyclopaedia of Murder*, London, Pan Books, 1984

Wilson, Colin and Seaman, Donald, *Encyclopaedia of Modern Murder*, London, Pan Books, 1989

Index